WESTWOOD

Great Moments in Black History

Wade in the Water

Lerone Bennett, Jr.

Johnson Publishing Company, Inc. — Chicago, Illinois, USA

Previously copyrighted material in slightly altered form appeared in EBONY Magazine: 2/4/6/10—1975; 1/2/5/9/10/11—1976 and 2/5/9—1977. Ch. 15, *The Day They Marched*, introduction to book by same name, pub. by Johnson Publishing Co., © 1963, ed. by D. E. Saunders.

Line drawings by Orville A. Hurt
Photographs from collection of EBONY Magazine

Library of Congress Cataloging in Publication Data
Bennett, Lerone, 1928-
    Wade in the water.
Bibliography: p.
1. Afro-American-History-Addresses, essays, lectures.
2. United States-Race relations-Addresses, essays, lectures.
I. Title
E185.B44   973'.04'96073   79-14771
ISBN 0-87485-079-1

Designed by Norman L. Hunter
Production Coordinator: Carmel E. Tinkchell

PRINTED IN THE UNITED STATES OF AMERICA

For
Ola Mae Sylvester,
Elnor Hickman,
Thelma Blackmon and
Mildred Moore

Preface

Certain landmark experiences in the history of black and white Americans—the passage of the Thirteenth Amendment, the Supreme Court decision on school segregation, the first day of the Montgomery Bus Boycott—have become such an integral part of our consciousness that they are taken for granted by almost everyone. But if you question almost any American on the details of these events, it becomes immediately apparent that very little is known about them. Take, for example, the Supreme Court decision on school segregation. Most Americans know that this decision was handed down on a fateful Monday in 1954. But what was the concrete story behind this story? How did the individual justices approach their date with history? What was the atmosphere in the courtroom? And what was the immediate reaction? Did black people dance in the streets? Did white people pour into the streets with outrage? How, in other words, was a fundamental turning point in American history experienced by the people who lived through it?

Another example of more recent memory is the Montgomery Bus Boycott. It is by now a matter of public knowledge that the boycott started when Rosa Parks refused to give her bus seat to a white man. But what were the events leading up to this dramatic turning point in race relations? More importantly, what happened in Montgomery in the crucial minutes that followed the arrest?

This book is an attempt to answer these and other questions about central events in the shaping of black-white America. It is an attempt to view history from the inside, and it is based, wherever possible, on the reports of participants and contemporary observers. The book explores fifteen dramatic turning points, from the first black national convention to the March on Washington; and it is based on the idea that in history, as in art, there is a dialectical connection between the inner detail and the whole, neither of which can be understood or explained without reference to the other.

Although I alone am responsible for whatever shortcomings this book may have, I am indebted to many people, including my wife, Gloria; my publisher, John H. Johnson; Herbert Nipson, executive editor of *Ebony* Magazine; Doris E. Saunders, Norman L. Hunter and Basil Phillips of the Johnson Publishing Company Book Division; Pamela J. Cash, Kathleen Bethel and Alice Denton of the Johnson Publishing Company Special Library; Donald Joyce and Kathleen McKnight of the Harsh Collection of the Woodson Regional Library; and the staff of the Newberry Library.

Portions of this book appeared in abridged form in *Ebony* Magazine and *Redbook* Magazine.

Lerone Bennett, Jr., January, 1979.

Preface
To Second Edition

This book grew out of a series of articles called "Great Moments in Black History." In this revision, we are returning to the original title with the original subtitle, "Wade In The Water." But whether the emphasis is placed on the great moments or the wading in historical waters, with the connotation of confronting or grappling with historical reality, the book focuses primarily on the human drama implicit in the major events that defined African-Americans and white Americans. The language has been changed in a few sections to improve readability, but the message hasn't changed; and we continue to believe that no man or woman born here can understand himself or herself without a deeper understanding of this neglected history. In preparing this revision, I have been helped enormously by book designer Norman L. Hunter, Basil Phillips and production coordinator Carmel Tinkchell.

Lerone Bennett, Jr.
February, 1992

Contents

Wade in the water, children,
Wade in the water, children,
Wade in the water, children,
God's gonna trouble the water.

—Spiritual

Great
Moments
in Black
History
Wade in the Water

A Home in That Rock

First Black Convention

SINCE the first light of dawn, he had been besieged by tumultuous emotions. And now, as the steamboat chugged into the Philadelphia harbor, he was beside himself with anticipation. Something was going to happen that had never happened before; and it seemed to him, as he surveyed the approaching scene, that every animate and inanimate thing was awaiting the events of this day. To his rear, on the opposite shore, was the state of New Jersey. Before him, on the west bank of the Delaware River, the two- and three-story red brick houses of Philadelphia marched in serried phalanxes to the eminence of the State House, where certain men, all of them white, some of them slaveholders, most of them foes of black freedom, had drafted the United States Constitution. A lot of water had flowed out of the Delaware River into the Atlantic Ocean since then; and now, forty-three years later, on Wednesday, September 15, 1830, certain men, all of them black, most of them former slaves, all of them friends of black freedom, were going to hold the first national black convention.

Richard Allen, first bishop of AME Church, was president and leading force in America's first black national convention.

A national black convention—the very idea made Hezekiah Grice's heart beat faster, and he bounded from the steamboat with the first passengers and made his way down the cobblestone streets to the Philadelphia ghetto—a tall man, "six feet high, well-proportioned, of a dark bronze complexion, broad brow," and that telltale demeanor of the true believer who knows why the flags are flying and men are marching. The sounds of the city, the cries of the hawkers, the rumble and rattle of the drays: none of this reached him, for every fiber of his being was attuned to the great project ahead. The thing was so unprecedented, so audacious, so *right*, that it seemed to him, in his innocence, that the whole city was consumed by it. And so he stopped every black man he met and asked about it.

Delegates from nine states debated racial strategy in sessions at Philadelphia's Bethel AME Church.

What were they saying about the convention?

What did they think of this bold new venture of the blacks of America?

The response was something less than encouraging. The first man he asked didn't know the meaning of the word *convention*. The second man was indignant. "Who ever heard," he asked, "of colored people holding a convention—convention indeed!"

Undaunted by the ridicule of this doubting Thomas, Grice quickened his pace, lamenting, no doubt, the low level of consciousness of some of his brothers and thinking of the chain of events that had brought him and other blacks to Philadelphia on this day. Grice himself was a major link in that chain, and to understand him and the approaching event, we must pause for a moment and sketch in the background and motivating shadows. Grice was only twenty-nine years old on this pivotal day. He had been born in Baltimore in 1801 and had been apprenticed at the age of sixteen to a white man who lived some two hundred miles from the

7

city. One day while he was working around the house, "the mistress," according to a later account, "came out and gave him a furious scolding, so furious, indeed, that her husband mildly interfered; she drove the latter away, and threatened to take the Baltimore out of the lad with cow-hide, &c., &c." At that precise moment, Grice was, he said later, "converted"—that is to say, he decided at that precise moment that he was going to be his own master for as long as he lived. Acting upon the letter and spirit of that decision, he ran away that night and made his way to Baltimore, where he soon mastered the craft of butchering. But his real vocation, then and later, was freedom. In obedience to that vocation, he spent his spare moments working with antislavery agitators like Benjamin Lundy and William Lloyd Garrison, the publisher and editor of the Baltimore paper, the *Genius of Universal Emancipation*. By 1828, Grice was the Baltimore agent of the first black newspaper, *Freedom's Journal*, and a leader of the radical black activists of the city. By that time, too, he was gravely concerned about the worsening conditions of the black population of America.

There was a great deal to be concerned about. Slavery and the spirit of slavery were triumphant everywhere, and there was a burgeoning national movement to force free blacks to leave America. This campaign was pursued on one level by the American Colonization Society, which denounced free blacks as "a useless and dangerous element" and urged them to move to Liberia. On another and more ominous level, white labor and other anti-black elements were pushing an increasingly successful campaign that bordered on genocide. This effort reached a peak in Ohio, where the anti-black riots of 1829 drove more than a thousand blacks from the state.

Hezekiah Grice looked on these auguries with alarm. He had an eye, Hezekiah Grice, and he saw with the insight of a seer that if blacks were not going to emigrate, they had better get ready for a fight. In his heart of hearts, he believed the struggle was useless and that it was better for blacks to emigrate to Canada or Haiti or Africa. But he was a modest young man, willing to consider the views of his elders. The problem, however, was that there was no collective mechanism for determining the views of the 319,599 free blacks. There had been local conventions and exchanges of views in *Freedom's Journal*, but there had never been a national convention of representative black leaders. Grice decided that there should be such a convention "in some place north of the Potomac, for the purpose of comparing views and of adopting a harmonious movement either of emigration, or of determination to remain in the United States. . . ."

On Friday, April 2, 1830, he sat down and addressed a circular "to prominent colored men in the free States, requesting their opinions on the necessity and propriety of holding such convention. . . ." The response was silence. May passed and June and July, and there was not a single reply. Then, on August 11, he received "a sudden and peremptory order . . . to come instantly to Philadelphia, about the emigration matter." The order came from Richard Allen, bishop of the African Methodist Episcopal Church (AME) and a man generally considered the leading black of his generation. Since Bishop Allen was clearly not a man to whom many people said no, Grice immediately complied with the order, arriving in Philadelphia in the midst of a general meeting called to consider conflicting reports on the prospects for black settlers in Canada. Grice undoubtedly expected an immediate explanation of the letter and the summons. But this was not the way the crafty old bishop worked. For almost two days, he said nothing about the convention or his urgent letter. Then, on the second night "and near the adjournment" of the meeting, he called Grice aside and showed him a printed circular issued by New York City black leaders, strongly approving Grice's call for a convention. Fixing Grice with a penetrating eye, the bishop said: "My dear child, we must take some action immediately, *or else these New Yorkers will get ahead of us! . . .*" Having made his point and having prepared the ground for a favorable decision, Bishop Allen left the meeting to attend a lecture on chemistry by a brilliant young black doctor named Wells. In his absence, and in compliance with his wishes, Grice introduced the subject to the gathering. The idea was approved, and a committee of five (Bishop Allen, Benjamin Paschall, Cyrus Black, James Cornish and Junius C. Morel) was appointed "to lay the matter before the colored people of Philadelphia." Without losing any time, this committee, no doubt led by Bishop Allen, issued a call "for a convention of the colored men of the United States," to be held in the city of Philadelphia at Bethel AME Church.

The call came at a favorable moment. New York had just emancipated its slaves. In Boston, a used clothes dealer, a man named David Walker, had just published a fiery appeal for insurrection.* In Southampton County, Virginia, a prophet and a slave, a man named Nat Turner, was

_____
* *Walker's Appeal.*

brooding over violent visions that commanded him to rise up and slay whites with their own weapons. In Southampton, in Boston, in Baltimore, in cities and counties all over America, a new and nameless thing was stirring in the breasts of blacks. Looking back twenty-nine years later, an anonymous writer in the *Anglo-African* magazine said that this black awakening coincided with the birth of a new spirit of freedom in the world. "Great Britain," he wrote, "was in the midst of that bloodless revolution which, two years afterwards, culminated in the passage of the Reform Bill, and thus prepared the joyous and generous state of the British heart which dictated the West India Emancipation Act. France was rejoicing in the not bloodless *trois jours de Juliet.* Indeed, the whole world seemed stirred up with a universal excitement. . . ."

Heartened by these general developments and by the new spirit he found in Philadelphia, Grice returned to Baltimore to prepare for the convention. On the boat that carried him down the Chesapeake, he was "accosted" by one Mr. Zollickoffer, a Philadelphia Quaker who was known as "a warm and true friend of the blacks." Zollickoffer spoke heatedly and forcefully against the idea of a black convention, "pointing out the dangers and difficulties of the same should it succeed, and the deep injury it would do to the cause in case of failure." Zollickoffer was hardly alone. The idea of a black national convention alarmed many whites, who believed generally that it was a dangerous and provocative act.

Because of this and other warnings, and the generally hostile climate of Philadelphia, the organizers decided to hold secret sessions. And when Grice returned to Philadelphia in September, he found the five men who called the convention "in solemn conclave" behind closed doors in Bethel AME Church on the east side of Sixth Street, near Lombard. The central figure in this group was Bishop Allen.

Allen had been born in slavery in Philadelphia in 1760 and had come to maturity on a farm in Delaware. Always industrious, always thrifty, he had managed by economies to accumulate enough money to buy his own freedom. Returning to Philadelphia in 1786 as a strolling preacher, he had organized, with Absalsom Jones, one of the first black organizations, the Free African Society. Twenty-nine years later, in 1816, he became the first bishop and the founding father of the African Methodist Episcopal Church, the first black interstate organization. Now seventy and on the edge of the grave, he was still a man of considerable presence and force. He was, according to contemporary reports, "thoroughly antislavery" and his home, it was said, was a haven "for the refugees from American oppression." One of his AME colleagues, the Reverend Walter Proctor, said Allen was "a man of mixed blood, his mother being a mulatto and his father a pure African; this gave his complexion a soft chestnut tint. . . . The expansive forehead and the fullness of the lower eyelids [indicated] expansiveness of intellect and a ready command of language."

Such was the man who had almost singlehandedly created the convention structure and who now presided over the "solemn conclave" of five. The other delegates (Benjamin Paschall, Cyrus Black, James Cornish, and James Morel) were veteran Philadelphia activists. Grice, who came with credentials from the free blacks of Baltimore, was warmly greeted by the bishop and admitted as a delegate. Soon afterwards, he recalled later, "Dr. [Belfast] Burton, of Philadelphia, dropped in, and demanded by what right the six gentlemen held their seats as members of the Convention. On a hint from Bishop Allen, Mr. Paschall moved that Dr. Burton be elected an honorary member of the Convention, which softened the Doctor. In half an hour, five or six tall, grave, stern-looking men, members of the Zion Methodist body in Philadelphia, entered, and also demanded by what right the members present held their seats and undertook to represent the colored people. Another hint from the Bishop, and it was moved that these gentlemen be elected honorary members. But the gentlemen would submit to no such thing, and would accept nothing short of full membership, which was granted them."

While all this was going on, other delegates were approaching Philadelphia by land and water. Travel was difficult and uncertain in these days for all Americans. But for black Americans it was a hazardous undertaking, which oftentimes led to violence, kidnapping, and death. Nothing more clearly shows the difficulties encountered by the delegates than the odyssey of Austin Steward, the delegate from Rochester, New York. Steward had reserved a seat on "Mr. Coe's stage coach" and was permitted to ride in comfort from Rochester to Auburn. At this point, a white passenger objected to his presence, and he was seated on the outside of the coach. Steward, a former slave and a prominent Rochester grocer, protested and was told that he could either ride on the outside or get off. Steward continued the journey under protest and later filed an unsuccessful suit against the company.

This little incident is illuminating, for it illustrates perfectly one of the problems blacks faced in organizing and attending a national convention. Another problem, recognized by most delegates, was the lack of publicity or, as one delegate put it, the "want of extensive notice in time."

In addition to these problems, the number of blacks in attendance was limited by rivalries between members of different religious denominations and citizens of different cities. There was a superficial but bitter chasm between black New Yorkers and black Philadelphians, and it is well worth noting that none of the major New York City leaders attended. Finally, there were the spoken and unspoken apprehensions of some black leaders who were scared away by the warnings of whites and/or the terror of taking a hazardous and uncharted step into the white unknown.

Despite these and other problems, at least forty delegates from nine states had assembled at Bethel by the end of the week. The minutes of the convention listed the following official delegates: *Pennsylvania* [37,930 free blacks and 403 slaves]—Rev. Richard Allen, Dr. Belfast Burton, Cyrus Black, Junius C. Morel, Benjamin Paschall, Jr., James Cornish, William S. Whipper, Peter Gardiner, John Allen, James Newman, Charles H. Leveck, Frederick A. Hinton; *New York* [44,870 free blacks and 75 slaves]—Austin Steward, Joseph Adams, George L. Brown; *Connecticut* [8,047 free blacks and 25 slaves]—Scipio C. Augustus; *Rhode Island* [3,561 free blacks and 17 slaves]—George C. Willis, Alfred Niger; *Maryland* [52,938 free blacks and 102,994 slaves]—James Deaver, Hezekiah Grice, Aaron Wilson, Robert Cowley; *Delaware* [15,855 free blacks and 3,292 slaves]—Abraham D. Shadd; *Virginia* [47,348 free blacks and 469,757 slaves]—Arthur M. Waring, William Duncan, James West, Jr. The minutes also listed the following honorary delegates: *Pennsylvania*—Robert Brown, William Rogers, John Bowers, Richard Howell, Daniel Peterson, Charles Shorts; *New York*—Leven Williams; *Maryland*—James P. Walker; *New Jersey*—[18,303 free blacks and 2,254 slaves]—John Arnold, Sampson Peters; *Delaware*—Anthony Campbell, Don Carlos Hall. John W. Cromwell* listed two additional delegates: Rev. Samuel Todd of Maryland and John Robinson of Ohio.

In years to come, these delegates would be called by historian Cromwell "the forty immortals in our Valhalla"—a fine and somewhat ironic

* *The Negro in American History.*

phrase in view of the fact that none of the immortals, Richard Allen excepted, is honored or even remembered today.

Who were these forgotten immortals?

They were pioneers, way-showers, men of large visions and even larger hopes. All were legally free. Some, like Allen, were former slaves who had purchased their freedom. Others, like Steward, had escaped from slavery. Still others, like John C. Bowers and Whipper, had never known the shackles of slavery. But all, the former slaves and the free men alike, lived in a twilight world between slavery and freedom, a world in which black men, even free black men, had few rights white people were bound to respect. The important point here is that slavery was no mere theory to the delegates. Slavery had shaped their lives and was a constant threat to their freedom. Slavery, in fact, was only one or two generations away for practically all of the delegates to this prototypal convention.

Slavery and color apart, there was nothing to distinguish this group from similar gatherings of white doers and thinkers. Bishop Allen and most of the delegates were dressed in the frock coats fashionable at that date. Some of the delegates, notably the twenty-five-year-old Whipper and the twenty-nine-year-old Grice, seemed to be somewhat young for this setting; but most were seasoned veterans of decades of struggle and organizing. As in most gatherings of this sort, the leading men were professionals, independent artisans, and businessmen. One delegate, Belfast Burton, was a physician; another delegate, Peter Gardiner, also of Philadelphia, was a botanic physician.

The artisan and business classes were generously represented. Richard Allen was, among other things, one of the richest black businessmen of the day, and he had only recently retired from active management of a lucrative boot and shoe store. John C. Bowers owned and managed "a fashionable merchant tailor house" and was, according to a later account by Martin Delaney,* "one of the best, if not the very best, mercer in the city" of Philadelphia. His style of cutting and fitting, Delaney added, was "preferred by the first businessmen and other gentlemen of Philadelphia...." Equally renowned in the Philadelphia business world were Frederick A. Hinton, a hairdresser and owner of a fashionable "gentle-

---

*The Condition, Elevation, Emigration, and Destiny of the Colored People of the United States.

men's dressing room," and William S. Whipper, a wealthy businessman who had inherited a large Columbia, Pennsylvania, lumber company from his white father. Other delegates, like clothier Daniel Peterson and hotel owner Daniel Shorts, operated on a somewhat smaller scale but were nevertheless independent businessmen of vision and considerable resources. It is perhaps worth noting, at least in passing, that Short's Union Hotel accommodated "people of colour, strangers, and citizens."

There were, additionally, several artisans and laborers in the convention. John Allen, according to the 1839 city directory, was either a bricklayer or a waiter or both; Charles H. Leveck was a porter; James Newman was a whitewasher; and, as we have already noted, Hezekiah Grice was a butcher.

Rather surprisingly, there were only four ministers: Allen, Anthony Campbell, Samuel Todd, and Sampson Peters.* Almost all of the delegates, however, were organizers and members of the independent Black Church movement. In addition to the large delegations from the AME and AME Zion churches, there were representatives of the First African Episcopal Church of St. Thomas (vestrymen John Allen, John C. Bowers and Frederick Hinton), and the African Ecclesiastical Society, Congregationalist, of New Haven, Connecticut (Scipio Augustus).

Whatever their background, whatever their vocation, whatever their faith, the "black immortals" were "race men." Most were involved in one way or another with the Underground Railroad, and most had played leading roles in the organization of independent black organizations. Hezekiah Grice and Robert Cowley of Baltimore and George C. Willis of Providence, Rhode Island, had served as authorized agents of *Freedom's Journal.* John C. Bowers and Charles Leveck were eloquent organizers of black educational and literary societies in Philadelphia. James Cornish was an organizer and leading spokesman of the Philadelphia Free Produce movement, which was boycotting slave-produced products. His Philadelphia colleague, Junius Morel, was virtually a professional parliamentarian and spent practically all his spare time organizing and agitating. The same thing was said of William Whipper, who was not much of a speaker but was a consummate committeeman and a major angel of black and abolitionist causes. One of his contemporaries, William Still, said later that "in the more important conventions which have

---

* Only two ministers—Allen and Campbell—are listed in the minutes. We know from other sources that Peters and Todd were ministers in 1830 or became ministers shortly afterwards.

been held among the colored people for the last thirty years, perhaps no other colored man has been so often called on to draft resolutions and prepare addresses, as the modest and earnest William Whipper."*

Although all delegates defined themselves as "race men," the problem—then and now—was that different delegates had different ideas about what that meant. And so, as a matter of course, the delegations consisted of militants and moderates, nationalists and integrationists. Grice, for example, was a protonationalist, while Whipper was an extreme integrationist who opposed all "complexional institutions." Interestingly enough, most of the delegates rejected the views of both Whipper and Grice and opted for a course that can be defined broadly as pluralism. Stated somewhat differently, most of the delegates came out in favor of a policy of American citizenship *and* continued support of independent black institutions.

There were divergent views on other issues, including the issue of nonviolence. Some of the men held advanced views on the right of self-defense. Others—again Whipper is the best example—were for nonviolence on practical if not moral grounds. In this case, as in others, Whipper dared to face the full logic of his ideas. In fact, he was perhaps the first American, and one of the first men in the world, to offer a systematic explication of the nonviolent philosophy. Seven years later, he published an "Address on Non-Resistance to Offensive Aggression." In this essay, which antedated Thoreau's celebrated essay by twelve years, Whipper said that "the practice of non-resistance to physical aggression is not only consistent with reason, but the surest method of obtaining a speedy triumph of the principles of universal peace."

Whipper pressed his views and was heard. Grice pressed his views and was heard. But this was not Whipper's convention or Grice's convention. This was, above all else, Richard Allen's convention, and the delegates generally followed the militant/moderate, nationalist/integrationist line the old bishop believed a majority of free blacks would support.

These were the men—militants, moderates, nationalists, integrationists— who joined now in creating the first national structure of black protest and affirmation. By all accounts, they approached the tasks with seriousness, spending the first few days organizing and settling disputes over

---

* *The Underground Railroad.*

credentials. Then, throwing caution to the wind, they decided to hold open sessions. The first open session was apparently held at 10:00 A.M. on Monday, September 20. After "a chaste and appropriate" prayer, the convention was organized by the election of the following officers: Richard Allen, president; Belfast Burton and Austin Steward, vice-presidents; Junius C. Morel, secretary; Robert Cowley, assistant secretary.

With the formalities out of the way, the convention got down to the hard task of assessing the condition of blacks and recommending solutions. The main topic of discussion was the plight of black refugees from Ohio and other states and the issue of emigration to Canada. Looking back many years later, Grice recalled that "Junius C. Morel, Chairman of a committee [on emigration to Canada] presented a report, on which there was a two days' discussion; the point discussed was, that the report stated that 'the lands in Canada were *synonymous* with those of the Northern States.' The word *synonymous* was objected to, and the word *similar* was proposed in its stead. Mr. Morel, with great vigor and ingenuity, defended the report, but was finally voted down, and the word *similar* adopted."

From the vantage point of the twentieth century, this debate seems to have been not only asinine but pointless. How could grown men spend two days debating the question of whether the lands of Canada were synonymous with or similar to the lands of the United States? What difference did it make? The answer is that it made all the difference in the world. For behind the somewhat acrimonious debate over the meaning of words was a deeper and more dangerous question: Should blacks emigrate to Africa or stay in America and fight? That was the question. And flowing with and out of that question were other questions: Who were they and where was their home? The American Colonization Society said they were strangers and aliens who should be returned to their home in Africa. With near-unanimity, the delegates rejected this argument, saying in so many words that they were already at home and that nothing and no one would drive them from land watered by the blood and sweat of their fathers.

Who were they? The assembled representatives of the black people of America said in their founding convention that they were Americans or, to be more precise, African-Americans. So saying, they closed one of the mighty doors of history. For it was still possible at that point to "solve" some racial issues by emigration. As a matter of fact, this was probably the last chance for a solution by mass flight. The delegates rejected that solution in a decision that would echo and re-echo down the corridors of American time. And it seems from available evidence that they accurately reflected the views of most free blacks, who had adopted strong anti-colonization platforms in a number of local conventions. "This is our home," the report of the New York convention said, "and this is our country. Beneath its sod lies the bones of our fathers; for it, some of them fought, bled, and died. Here we were born and here we will die."

It was one thing to say this; it was another and quite different thing to live it. The delegates and their real or potential constituencies lived in a world of white power which treated them like strangers and outcasts. And they knew, deep in their hearts, that this situation was not going to change for a long, long time, no matter what they said, and no matter what they believed about the ultimate outcome of the struggle. Hence, their dilemma. Hence, the desperation and, yes, the grandeur—some called it the madness—of their task.

It was in this context, and against this background, that the delegates wrestled with the words *similar* and *synonymous*. Having decided to affirm the right of blacks to remain in America, they were forced, by the pressure of circumstances, to speak to the needs of hard-pressed black refugees who were being driven from American cities and had to go somewhere. To meet the needs of these refugees and to counter the propaganda of the American Colonization Society, the delegates urged black refugees to settle in Canada, which was close enough, in its similarity, if not in its synonymity, to maintain their original point that they were native sons. Pursuing this point, the delegates criticized the American Colonization Society and created the foundations—fateful move— for the first black protest and defense organization.

In the incomplete reports that have come down to us, no mention is made of the extracurricular life of the delegates. But one can readily imagine the earnest and sober delegates touring the black community and gathering in the well-appointed parlors of community leaders. Some doubtlessly observed, as a later visitor observed, that "the parlors [of black community leaders] were carpeted and furnished with sofas, side-boards, card-tables, mirrors, &c. &c. with, in many instances, the addition of the piano forte." It would have been observed also that the overwhelming majority of the fifteen thousand free blacks of Philadelphia lived in squalid cellars and shanties along narrow streets and alleys. Since most of the delegates were ardent temperance men, there was apparently little or no opportunity to sample Philadelphia's fiery liquor, which sold for one cent a glass.

Before adjourning on Friday, September 24, the delegates visited the Lombard Street Free School for Colored Children (190 boys, 251 girls). They were, according to the minutes, "highly gratified at the order, regularity and improvement discoverable in the various departments. . . . Their specimens in writing, needle-work, &c. &c. made a deep impression on the Convention. . . ."

Two months after adjournment, convention leaders created the permanent organization mandated by the delegates. The organization was called the American Society of Free Persons of Colour, and its purpose was to improve the conditions of blacks in the United States and to establish a settlement in Upper Canada. Membership was limited to "such persons of colour as shall pay not less than twenty-five cents on entering and thereafter quarterly, eighteen and three-quarter cents." The first meeting of the new organization was held on Monday, November 30, in Philadelphia. Richard Allen was elected president, and William Whipper was named secretary. In an address "to the free people of colour," issued in the name of the convention, the organizers criticized the American Colonization Society and declared that "our forlorn and deplorable situation earnestly and loudly demands of us to devise and pursue all legal means for the speedy elevation of ourselves and our brethren to the scale and standing of men." The address endorsed settlements in Canada, where "the language, climate, soil and productions are similar to those in this country." Then, looking beyond the immediate struggle, the address called for unity, renewal, and reaffirmation.

"Before we close," the document said, "we would just remark, that it has been a subject of deep regret to this convention, that we as a people have not availingly appreciated every opportunity placed within our power by the benevolent efforts of the friends of humanity in elevating our condition to the rank of freemen. That our mental and physical qualities have not been more actively engaged in pursuits more lasting, is attributable in a great measure to a want of unity among ourselves; whilst our only stimulus to action has been to become domestics, which at best is but a precarious and degraded situation.

"It is to obviate these evils, that we have recommended our views to our fellow-citizens in the foregoing instrument, with a desire of raising the moral and political standing of ourselves; and we cannot devise any plan more likely to accomplish this end, than by encouraging agriculture and mechanical arts: for by the first, we shall be enabled to act with a degree of independence, which as yet has fallen to the lot of but few among us; and the faithful pursuit of the latter, in connection with the sciences, which expand and ennoble the mind, will eventually give us the standing and condition we desire."

Thus, the first stone was laid. And on this stone rose a superstructure of local and national organizations, including the National Negro Convention movement, which met intermittently throughout the antebellum period.

Although the deliberations of the pioneer black convention did not lead immediately to emancipation, it was nevertheless a watershed, with streams running in one direction backward to the communal meetings of Africa, and in another direction forward to the national black conventions of today. In sum, the pioneer black convention was a seed experience. It brought new forces to the surface, expanded the channels of communication and gave blacks a new conception of themselves and their possibilities. At the same time, and in the same way, the convention deepened the consciousness and changed the direction of the pioneer white abolitionists.

Many of the delegates to the first convention assumed leading roles in later conventions. But others, most notably Richard Allen and Hezekiah Grice, made, in different ways, a separate peace. Five months after the Philadelphia meeting, Richard Allen died and was borne to his grave by "an immense concourse of coloured people." By the time of Allen's funeral, Grice was having second thoughts about the direction of the movement he helped to initiate. At any rate, he did not attend the 1831 convention and was denied a seat at the 1832 convention, presumably because he lacked credentials. In 1832, "chagrined at the colored people of the United States," he migrated to Haiti, where, in 1843, he was appointed director of public works in Port-au-Prince. But he never forgot his day in the American sun. And until his death, he loved to tell the story of the day in 1830 when a twenty-nine-year-old butcher and a seventy-year-old patriarch laid the first stone of a new order in the city of Philadelphia in the United States of America.

No Hidin' Place

Nat Turner's Bloody Sermon

IT was Sunday, and there was an air of torpor and slumbering, shimmering ease in Southampton. It had always been like this on Sundays in late August in Southampton County, which was in the southeastern corner of Virginia, just across the border from North Carolina. Most of the 6,461 whites and the 6,625 slaves who lived in the county were idle on this Sunday. The crops were in, and there was little or no movement in the cornfields and cotton fields. The slaves, who did most of the work, were out of sight and out of mind. The white people, who owned the land and the slaves, sat on porches and under shade trees, sipped the famous Southampton apple brandy, and talked of the camp meeting in nearby Gates County, North Carolina, and the big fox hunt scheduled for Monday.

Under the circumstances, it is scarcely surprising that no one perceived the magnitude of the disaster that lay ahead. Joseph Travis, a luckless slaveowner who was about to die a horrible death, followed the same routine on this Sunday that he always followed. He went to church in the morning and visited friends in the afternoon before returning to his home near the Cross Keys neighborhood. Several miles to the north-east, the socially prominent Catherine Whitehead was resting in her comfortable home, surrounded by doting children and grandchildren and passels of slaves. Rebecca Vaughan, another well-to-do matron and another slaveowner, was entertaining her niece, Ann Eliza Vaughan, who was said to be "the beauty of the county." Mrs. Vaughan had promised to entertain the fox hunters on Monday, and the two women were preoc-cupied with the myriad details such an occasion demands.

So it went, from house to house, in Southampton County on Sunday, August 21, 1831. If the Travises and the Whiteheads and the Vaughans could have seen into the mind of a certain Southampton slave, they doubtlessly would have arranged their day differently. But nothing in the face or the gestures of this slave betrayed the secret in his heart. The slave's name was Nat Turner. And to grasp the full dimensions of the nightmare that would envelop Southampton, one must have some picture of him.

It would be said later that Nat Turner "made an impact upon the people of his section as great as that of John C. Calhoun or Jefferson Davis." But in Southampton in August, 1831, he was just another slave, and a rather ordinary-looking slave at that. According to an official proclamation issued later, Turner was, "between 30 & 35 years old, 5 feet 6 or 8 inches high . . . between 150 and 160 lbs., rather bright com-plexion, but not a mulatto—broad shouldered—large flat nose—large eyes—broad flat feet—rather knock-kneed—walks brisk and active—hair on the top of the head very thin—no beard except on the upper lip, and the tip of the chin—a scar on one of his temples—also one on the back of his neck—a large knob on one of the bones of his right arm near the wrist produced by a blow."*

The description was accurate enough, but, like most official descrip-tions, it omitted the salient features. There was no mention of the pres-ence and the bearing of the man. Nor, incredibly, was there a mention of the eyes. All who knew Nat and who afterwards looked back on him

---

*This reconstruction of the Nat Turner insurrection is based on *The Confessions of Nat Turner*, Thomas R. Gray, editor, and contemporary news accounts and documents. See also Henry Irving Tragle, *The Southampton Slave Revolt of 1831: A Compilation of Source Material*; William Sidney Drewry, *Slave Insurrections in Virginia, 1830-1865*; Herbert Aptheker, *Nat Turner's Slave Rebellion*; William Wells Brown, *The Negro in the Rebellion*; Thomas Wentworth Higginson, *Travellers and Outlaws*.

through a haze of blood commented on the eyes. The eyes, it was said, were the eyes of a saint or a revolutionary or a mad man. They were the eyes of Single Purpose. They were the eyes of a man who had seen other worlds. A hostile white man who saw him later said he answered "exactly the description annexed to the Governor's Proclamation, except that he is of a darker hue, and his eyes, though large, are not prominent—they are very long, deeply seated in his head, and have rather a sinister expression."

Later, when the blood and terror were behind him, Nat said he had

Route of Nat Turner raid is indicated by **bold** line. Some sixty whites were killed.

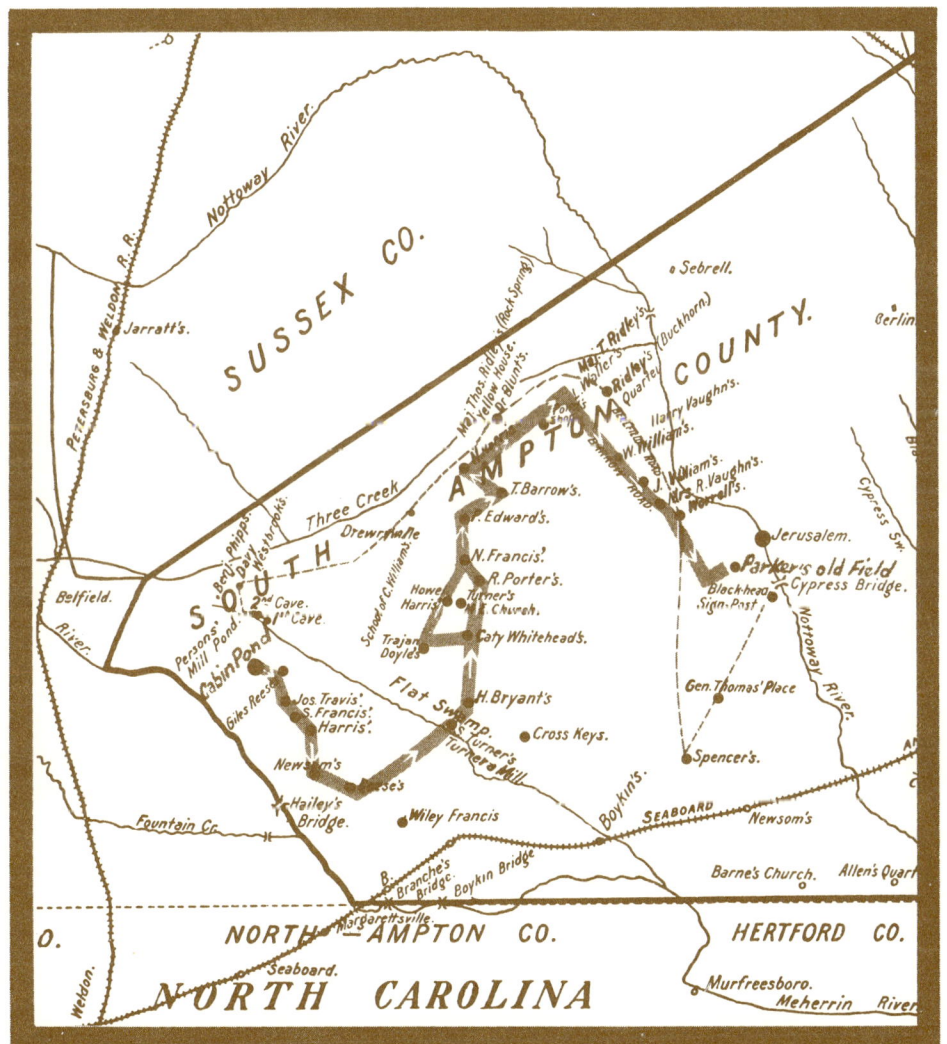

believed since his birth that he was destined for some great act. He had been born on October 2, 1800, in Southampton to two African-born slaves; he was thus thirty when he burst upon the guilty consciousness of the slave South. His mother, it is said, was a spirited woman who did not want to bring another slave child into the world. According to historian William Sidney Drewry, she was "so wild at Nat's birth that she had to be tied to prevent her from murdering him."

Nat Turner survived, the mother relented, and Nat and his mother and father entered into a conspiracy with a reality on the other side of slavery. Young Nat, who had, he said, "a restless, inquisitive, observant" mind and who was capable, a white witness said, "of attaining anything,"

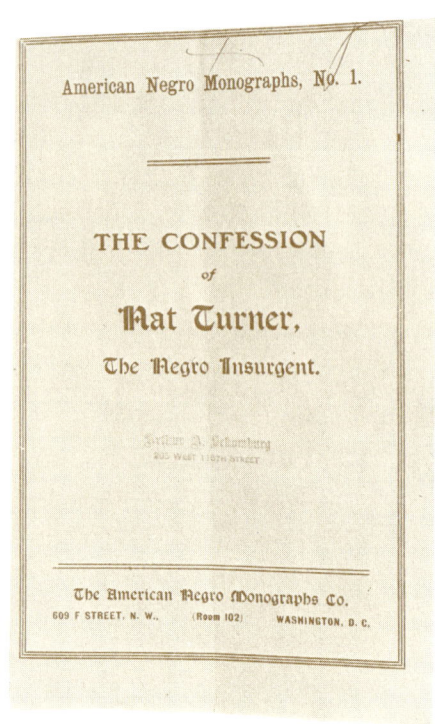

The Confessions of Nat Turner was dictated to local white lawyer.

seems to have learned how to read and write almost overnight; and he was always astounding—and frightening—people with his prophecies. A typical instance of this took place when he was three or four. "Being at play with other children . . . ," he said, "I was telling them something, which my mother, overhearing, said it had happened before I was born— I stuck to my story, however, and related some things which went, in her opinion, to confirm it—others being called on were greatly astonished, knowing that these things had happened, and caused them to say in my hearing, I surely would be a prophet, as the Lord had shewn me things that had happened before my birth. And my father and mother strengthened me in this, my first impression, saying in my presence, I was intended for some great purpose. . . . My grand mother, who was very religious, and to whom I was very much attached—my master, who belonged to the church, and other religious persons who visited the house, and whom I often saw at prayers, noticing the singularity of my manners, I suppose, and my uncommon intelligence for a child, remarked that I had too much sense to be raised, and if I was, I would never be of any service to anyone as a slave. . . ."

The details of the early life of this remarkable slave are necessarily incomplete, but the few glimpses we get from the *Confessions* and other sources are memorable and instructive. Nat seems, for instance, to have lived a dual life. He worked in the fields, married a comely slave and followed the routines of the slave quarters. But he also lived a secret life, fasting and praying and "making experiments in casting different things in molds made of earth, in attempting to make paper, gun-powder, and many other experiments. . . ."

Captured after six-week search, Nat was taken to Jerusalem and hanged.

By the 1820s, Nat was something of a local celebrity in Southampton, and he shrewdly and brilliantly exploited his reputation "by the austerity of [his] life and manners, which became the subject of remark by white and black." Like all great leaders, and perhaps like all great prophets, Nat was something of an actor. Having discovered that "to be great, [one] must appear so," he avoided mixing in society and wrapped himself in mystery. It was said afterwards, in all seriousness, that no one had ever seen him smile. Thomas R. Gray, the Southampton lawyer who recorded and edited the *Confessions*, said "it is notorious that he was never known to have a dollar in his life, to swear an oath, or drink a drop of spirits."

It was perhaps inevitable that this strange and brilliant slave should turn to religion, which was, in a manner of speaking, the only politics open to slaves. Indeed, there is no more remarkable chapter in the history of slavery than the story of how Nat Turner seized the weapon of Christianity and turned its sharp edge against slaveholding Christians. No one knows how or when he was called to the ministry. He simply materialized one day as a preacher of the Gospel—a preacher who claimed divine inspiration. He tells us in the *Confessions* that God appeared to him in visions and spoke to him, revealing "the knowledge of the elements, the revolution of the planets, the operation of tides, and changes of the seasons." One day while he was praying at the plough, the Spirit, he said, spoke to him, saying, "Seek ye the kingdom of Heaven and all things shall be added unto you." This "greatly astonished" him and for two years he "prayed continually, whenever my duty would permit—and then again I had the same revelation, which fully confirmed me in the impression that I was ordained for some great purpose in the hands of the Almighty."

From this time forward, Nat began "to direct [his] attention to this great object, to fulfill the purpose for which, by this time, I felt assured I was intended." By this time, he had obtained considerable influence over the minds of his fellow slaves, who believed he was a prophet and that his wisdom came from God. And it was no doubt at this moment that he began to prepare the slaves by telling them that "something was about to happen that would terminate in fulfilling the great promises that had been made to me."

Not only slaves but free men—black and white—heard and heeded

Turner's message. He converted at least one white man—Etheldred T. Brantley, who was, according to Drewry, "a respectable overseer." Nat said that his message had a "wonderful effect" on Brantley and that "he ceased from his wickedness, and was attacked immediately with a cutaneous eruption, and blood oozed from the pores of his skin, and after praying and fasting nine days, he was healed, and the Spirit appeared to me again, and said, as the Savior had been baptised so should we be also—and when the white people would not let us be baptised by the church, we went down into the water together, in the sight of many who reviled us, and were baptised by the Spirit. . . ."

There are indications in the record that Nat saw where all this would end. He believed, apparently, that he was a Jesus-like figure, and he apparently had a premonition that the road he was travelling would lead to a cross of some kind. It is interesting, therefore, to note that his road to judgment was marked by curious moments of indecision in which he struggled against the destiny that beckoned him. On one occasion, he tells us, he ran away "and after remaining in the woods thirty days, I returned, to the astonishment of the Negroes on the plantation, who thought I had made my escape to some other part of the country, as my father had done before me. But the reason for my return was, that the Spirit appeared to me and said I had my wishes directed to the things of this world, and not to the kingdom of Heaven, and that I should return to the service of my earthly master—'For he who knoweth his Master's will, and doeth it not, shall be beaten with many stripes, and thus have I chastened you.'" (A well-informed Southampton white man said later that around 1828 "Nat received a whipping from his master, for saying that the blacks ought to be free, and that they would be free one day or other.") This is a remarkable passage. In it, Nat makes, on one level, a brilliant distinction between the personal freedom that was within his grasp, i.e., an individual flight to the North, and the struggle for the collective freedom of his people. And then, playing with words, he makes a firm and final distinction between his "earthly master" and his Master.

Throughout all this—and on into the thirties—the mind of Nat Turner was assaulted and overwhelmed by visions and voices. He saw "white spirits and black spirits engaged in battle, and the sun was darkened—the thunder rolled in the Heavens, and blood flowed in streams. . . ." Blood—there was blood everywhere. While working in the fields, he discovered "drops of blood on the corn as though it were dew from heaven." While walking in the woods, he discovered on the leaves "hieroglyphic characters, and numbers, with the forms of men in different attitudes portrayed in blood. . . ."

Blood, blood on the leaves, blood on the corn—what was the meaning of all this blood?

The meaning, according to the messages Nat said he received from the Holy Ghost, was that "the great day of judgment was at hand" and that "the time was fast approaching when the first should be last and the last should be first." On May 12, 1828, the Spirit appeared and told him, he said, that "the Serpent was loosened" and on the appearance of the sign he was to rise up and slay his enemies with their own weapons.

The sign—the eclipse of the sun on February 12, 1831—removed the seal from Nat's lips, and he selected four disciples—Henry Porter, Hark Travis, Sam Francis, and Nelson Williams—and a date, July 4, 1831. But Nat fell ill at the last moment and Southampton celebrated Independence Day without incident. Then, on Saturday, August 13, another sign appeared. There was a greenish tint to the sun on that day and a big black spot passed over its surface. There could be no doubt about the portent of this, and Nat called a war council for Sunday, August 21, telling his disciples that "as the black spot had passed over the sun, so would the blacks pass over the earth."

From Saturday, August 13, to Sunday, August 21, Nat worked behind the scenes. We don't know, we will never know, the details of his itinerary, but there are tantalizing hints in the record. There was, for example, a disturbance at Barnes's Church on the Sunday after the appearance of the sign. The nature of the disturbance is not clear, but John Hampden Pleasants, a Richmond editor who later served with the militia in Southampton, said in a dispatch of August 25 that "the Negroes . . . were observed to be disorderly, took offence at something; (it is not known what). . . ." There is another reference to the same incident in the Ph.D. dissertation of William Sidney Drewry, who interviewed the living survivors of the Southampton insurrection some sixty years later. "The whites," he wrote, "were conducting a revival service at Barnes' on the 14th of August, and many Negroes were present who had the privilege of worshiping with the whites and also of attending services conducted by preachers of their own color. Nat preached on this day, and seemed to have gained many sympathizers, who signified their willingness to cooperate with him by wearing around their necks red bandana handkerchiefs, and who in many ways showed their rebellious spirit." What precisely did the rebellious slaves do? Drewry said "they tried to ride over white people."

After the Barnes's Church incident, Nat retreated into the shadows. There are indications that he or his disciples made discreet overtures to some slaves. At any rate, a list of some twenty names was found later in his papers, which contained other items of interest, including a map of Southampton County, drawn in poke-berry juice, and documents filled with hieroglyphical characters. A Southampton white man who inspected the papers after the insurrection said "the characters on the oldest paper, apparently appear to have been traced with blood; and on each paper, a crucifix and the sun, is distinctly visible; with the figures, 6,000, 30,000, 80,000 &c...." Were these estimates of forces? We don't know, but it should be noted for the record that the white population of Southampton was about six thousand in 1830.

It was one thing to plan an insurrection; it was another and quite different matter to prevent premature disclosure of a planned insurrection. Having learned from some source the details of previous slave insurrections, Nat told his disciples that the greatest danger they faced just then was loose talk. But some of the initiates could not resist the temptation of dropping veiled hints. On the Thursday before the uprising, Nelson told a *white overseer* that "they [white people] might look out and take care of themselves—that something would happen before long —that anybody of his practice could tell these things."

During the same critical time period, there was a great deal of apparently unauthorized recruiting. On Saturday a slave named Isham, who was not one of the four initiates, told a slave named Henry, according to later court testimony, "that Genl. Nat was going to rise and murder all the whites and that the witness [Henry] must join them or that if he did not they would kill him if they caught him." Interestingly enough, Henry did not pass this information on to his master until after the event; and so Sunday, August 21, came, with no one the wiser. Before midday on this Sunday, Turner's disciples slipped away from their cabins and gathered on the banks of Cabin Pond, a densely wooded area near the home of Joseph Travis, who had married the widow of Turner's last master and who had thus inherited Nat and death.

The gathering of the disciples was deceptively festive. Hark brought a pig, which was roasted and washed down with brandy. There were six men at the feast, including two newcomers, Jack and Will. Will was, according to a later account by William Wells Brown, a bitter slave who "scorned the idea of taking his master's name." His wife, Brown said, without citing his source, had been sold to the "Negro-trader, and taken away, never to be beheld by him again in this life." Will's back, Brown said, "was covered with scars, from his shoulders to his feet, and a large scar, running from his right eye to his chin, showed that he had lived with a cruel master." Nearly six feet tall, strong and graceful, Will would soon avenge his ordeal by wielding a big broad ax with slashing impartiality.

Will was one individualist; a very different one was Hark, a handsome fearless man who was identified in some contemporary reports as General Moore and Turner's second-in-command. Hark was, like Nat, a slave of Joseph Travis. A local white man who saw him later said he was "the most perfectly framed man he ever saw—a regular black Apollo."

These were the men who partied and plotted on the banks of Cabin Pond while Southampton slumbered in the late August sun. Nat, who knew the value of a delayed and dramatic entrance, didn't join the group until three in the afternoon. And the first thing he noticed was the presence of the two newcomers.

"I saluted them on coming up," he said, "and asked Will how came he there, he answered, his life was worth no more than others, and his liberty as dear to him. I asked him if he thought to obtain it? He said he would, or lose his life. This was enough to put him in full confidence."

Nat was a man of few words, and he didn't waste any time with Jack Reese, the other newcomer. He knew Jack; he knew that Jack was weak; and he knew that Jack was "only a tool in the hands of Hark," who was married to Jack's sister. So, without further discussion, he tackled the first item on the agenda—insurrection. And he did this in a curious way, taking the men aside, one by one, and developing his plans to each man privately. Having searched and appraised each man, Nat returned to the group and opened a general war council. Jack immediately raised objections, saying that the idea was impractical and doomed to failure. Nat, unflustered, assured Jack and the group of the "practicality" of his idea, "saying that their numbers would increase as they went along; and stated, that his reasons for not telling of it before, was, that the Negroes had frequently attempted similar things, confided their purpose to several, and that it had always leaked out; but his resolve was that their march of destruction and murder, should be the first news of the insurrection."

This silenced all doubters, and it was "quickly agreed," Nat said, "we should commence at home [at the home of Joseph Travis] on that night, and until we had armed and equipped ourselves, and gathered sufficient force, neither age nor sex was to be spared." Nat told the men that "indiscriminate slaughter was not their intention" and was to be "resorted to in the first instance to strike terror and alarm." After obtaining a foothold, he added, women and children would be spared, "and men too who ceased to resist."

Before leaving Cabin Pond, Nat, according to Willaim Wells Brown, addressed his disciples. The words reported by Brown were apparently written after the event, but they do not depart from the facts as we know them; and they give an eloquent, though perhaps fanciful, picture of General Nat as he stood on the edge of immortality.

"Friends and Brothers!" Nat reportedly said. "We are to commence a great work to-night. Our race is to be delivered from slavery, and God has appointed us as the men to do his bidding; and let us be worthy of our calling. I am told to slay all the whites we encounter, without regard to age or sex. We have no arms or ammunition, but we will find these in the houses of our oppressors; and, as we go on, others can join us. Remember that we do not go forth for the sake of blood and carnage; but it is necessary, that, in the commencement of this revolution, all the whites we meet should die, until we have an army strong enough to carry on the war upon a Christian basis. Remember that ours is not a war for robbery, or to satisfy our passions; it is a struggle for freedom. Ours must be deeds, and not words. Then let's away to the scene of action."

It was 1:00 A.M., or thereabouts. Southampton lay in the bosom of brooding darkness as Nat Turner and his army of six crept through the woods to the home of Joseph Travis. In the yard of the house, the little band met a slave named Austin, who promptly signed on, becoming the seventh member of Nat's army. All of the men, except Nat, went to the cider press and drank. Nat, a teetotaler who was without nerves, waited. When the men returned, he pointed to the house, which they approached quietly. A ladder was propped against the chimney. Nat climbed the ladder, entered an upstairs window, came downstairs and opened the front door. Swiftly and silently, the men moved to the bedroom of Mr. and Mrs. Joseph Travis—and here, on the edge of the act, there was a last-minute attack of indecision. The men, whispering, told Nat that since the insurrection was his idea, he had to spill the first blood. Nat nodded and entered the room, armed with an old hatchet, and accompanied by Will. Without a moment's hesitation, he aimed a death blow at the head of Joseph Travis. But it was dark in the room, and the blow, which was not well-directed, glanced from the head of Travis, who sprang up, startled, and called for his wife. It was his last word. Will split his head open with the broad ax and turning, in almost the same movement, almost decapitated Sallie Travis. Two teen-agers, Putnam Moore and Joel Westbrooks, were asleep in an upstairs room. Moore was the son of Thomas Moore, and was therefore Nat's legal owner. This legal tie cost him dearly. One blow, a contemporary account said, "seems to have sufficed for [both Moore and Westbrooks], who were sleeping so close, that the same stroke nearly severed each neck." An infant, sleeping in a cradle, was overlooked. But when the band left the house, Nat remembered and invoked the terrible rule that neither age nor sex was to be spared. Henry and Will returned and slew the baby.

The insurgents appropriated four guns, several muskets, and a pound or two of powder at the Travis home. They then went to the Travis barn, where Nat formed his troops into files and tried to instill some military discipline. "I formed them in a line as soldiers," he said, "and after carrying them through all the manoeuvres I was master of, marched them off to" the home of Salathiel Francis, about six hundred yards away.

Francis, a bachelor, lived alone. Sam and Will, who were slaves of Francis's brother, Nathaniel, walked up to the front door of the house and knocked.

"Who's there?" Francis asked.

Sam identified himself and said he had a letter from Nathaniel Francis. When Salathiel Francis opened the door, Sam and Will dragged him into the yard and killed him by repeated blows on the head.

Moving swiftly now and maintaining, in Nat's words, "the most perfect silence," the rebels traveled to the home of Piety Reese, a mile and a half to the southeast. The front door was unlocked. Mrs. Reese and her son William were asleep in their rooms—they never knew what hit them. After leaving the Reese house, Nat and his army turned to the northeast and marched for several miles before reaching the home of Elizabeth Turner at sunrise. Henry, Austin, and Sam went first to the still, where they surprised and shot the overseer, Hartwell Peebles. The shot alarmed the Turner family, who hurriedly bolted the front door which Will splintered with one stroke of his axe. The rebels bolted through the opening and slew Elizabeth Turner and Sarah Newsome, who were standing, terrified, in the middle of the room.

By now, "about sunrise" on August 22, the small army had reduced the mechanics of the death march to a one-two-three routine. A general destruction of property and a search for money and guns always followed the killings. At almost every stop, additional male slaves were recruited. At almost every stop, horses and tools were appropriated. Thus, by Monday morning, the original band of seven had increased to fifteen, including nine men with horses. Nat now divided his forces, sending the six men without horses to the Henry Bryant home, leading the nine mounted men to the home of Catherine Whitehead.

As the mounted detachment approached the Whitehead home, there was a little vignette that spoke volumes about the transient nature of power. Mrs. Whitehead's son, Richard, was in the cotton field bordering the lane. Richard Whitehead was a Methodist minister; he had preached a powerful sermon on Sunday at Barnes's Church, and now he was in the field, supervising the slaves. Nat reined his horse at the lane fence and hailed the Reverend Mr. Whitehead, calling him "Dick," according to one report, and telling him, according to all reports, to "come here." This, of course, was a violation of the laws of slavery. Slaves didn't give orders to white folk, and the slaves in the field watched with considerable interest to see if the master would comply. He complied, and, said Nat, "Will, the executioner, was near at hand, with his fatal axe, to send him to an untimely grave." This was—there is no other word for it—grisly. But the system to which it was a response was worse. And it is impossible to assess Nat Turner's violence if we do not keep in mind the violent system to which it was a response.

"As we pushed on to the house," Nat said, "I discovered someone run around the garden, and thinking it was some of the white family, I pursued them, but finding it was a servant girl belonging to the house, I returned to commence the work of death, but they whom I left, had not been idle; all the family were already murdered, but Mrs. Whitehead and her daughter Margaret. As I came round to the door I saw Will pulling Mrs. Whitehead out of the house, and at the step he nearly severed her head from her body, with his broad axe. Miss Margaret, when I discovered her, had concealed herself in the corner, formed by the projection of the cellar cap from the house; on my approach she fled, but was soon overtaken, and after repeated blows with a sword, I killed her with a blow on the head, with a fence rail."

Margaret (Peggy) Whitehead was the only person slain by Nat. It would be said later that the fact that he killed only one person, and then with great difficulty, shows that he lacked heart. This is a curious view, based on a serious misreading of the evidence. In the first place, General Nat, as he was called, was the supervising general of an army of retribution, and generals seldom kill. In the second place, this was not a personal vendetta. It is agreed by almost all authorities that Nat was not personally vindictive. It was not personal vengeance he sought, but retribution and liberation. The campaign he led was therefore political in nature; and the killings he ordered, and for which he assumed full responsibility, were political and must be judged on a different scale of values. This does not excuse the killings, nor mitigate the horror of the victims. It simply states the obvious: Nat Turner was engaged in an enterprise that was more than a criminal spree or a childish attempt to prove masculinity. It is also to be observed that the victims were victims, more than anything else, of history and of the boomerang effect of a violent system they supported or benefitted from. It is not true, as so many commentators have said, that Nat unleashed a wave of violence in Southampton. The violence was already there. Slavery was violence, and Nat's acts, however regrettable they may be on a personal level, were responses to that violence and must be appraised historically, systemically, and politically.

There is another point that bears on this subject, and it has to do with the interesting fact that not a woman was insulted or molested during the day and a half that Nat commanded Southampton County. Robert R. Howison, a Virginia historian who wrote fifteen years after the event, said "it is remarkable that through the whole series of assaults, not one female was violated. Remembering the brutal passions of the Negro, we can only account for this fact by supposing the actors to have been appalled by the very success of their hideous enterprise."

If one is not a racist, this fact can be explained in a number of ways, as Thomas Wentworth Higginson indicated in his 1861 essay for the *Atlantic Monthly*. "In one thing," he wrote, "they were humaner than Indians, or than white men fighting against Indians: there was no gratuitous outrage beyond the death-blow itself, no insult, no mutilation; but in every house they entered, that blow fell on man, woman, and child,— nothing that had a white skin was spared." In this sense, one can say of Nat Turner what Harriet Beecher Stowe said of her fictional rebel, Dred: "Whom the Lord saith unto us, 'Smite,' them will we smite. We will not torment them with the scourge and fire, nor defile their women as they have done with ours. But we will slay them utterly, and consume them from off the face of the earth."

Whatever others may since have believed about the matter, Nat had no doubt about the soundness and the justice of his strategy. He maintained, as we have seen, that the poverty of his resources and the enormity of the evil he confronted made it necessary to strike with such force that potential defenders would be awed into submission. The strategy had the precise effect that Nat intended it to have. When the first mangled bodies were found on Monday morning, a nameless dread seized Southampton, and it was impossible at first to organize an effective defense. Faced with an unexpected and nameless adversary, men, women, and children panicked. Some fled to the woods and hid under the leaves. Some left the county, some left the state.

As the revolt gathered steam, large numbers of whites gathered in churches and public buildings at Pate's Hill, Cross Keys, and Branch's Bridge. Most of the white refugees were hysterical. "The least unusual occurrence," Drewry wrote, "was sufficient to produce the wildest confusion. A flock of sheep running down the road was taken for the insurgents, and in a moment women and children ... were flying to the swamps. Here they remained for two nights, sleeping upon the leaves of the forests and making use of the provisions hastily gathered as they rushed from their homes." In the general confusion surrounding the evacuation, the slaves were left to fend for themselves. The response of Drewry Bittle was typical. When news of the rebellion reached him, he hurried home and "carried his family off and left his Negroes home and directed them not to go off on any account, unless to run from the Negroes."

Wild as it may sound now, the first thought of those who could think was that the British had invaded America and were killing everything that moved. When it was finally determined that the invasion came from the slave quarters, many white men refused to join the militia, saying that it was necessary for every white man to stay at home and protect his own women and children.

All this played into the hands of Nat Turner, who pressed on, gaining recruits at almost every stop. By midmorning, he had a force of about twenty. By midafternoon, he commanded sixty.

There had never been an army like this one. There were slaves of all sizes and shapes and colors, most of them dressed in the appropriated finery of their masters and brandishing firelocks, muskets, sticks, and hatchets. There were free black men, proud and defiant, fighting side by side with their enslaved brothers. There were teen-agers and small boys, who were "placed on horses one behind each of the company." Some of these soldiers, if we can credit W. S. Drewry, wore feathers in their hats and "long red sashes around their waists and over their shoulders."

The chief lieutenants of this army were Hark, Nelson, Will, and Henry. Hark was identified in contemporary reports as "Captain Moore" and "Genl. Moore." Nelson, who claimed to be a prophet, was identified in one report as "the celebrated [General] Nelson." General Henry was the "paymaster" of the army. At least four free blacks played a part in the insurrection, and one—Will Artist—was identified as a leader. Artist, it was said, "was conspicuous among the insurgents; when pressed into service, he wept like a child, but having once tasted blood, he was like a wolf let into the fold."

For obvious reasons, biographical information on the foot soldiers is lacking. But it is worth noting that most of the soldiers were linked by years of association. Three of the insurgents—Nat, Hark, and a boy called Moses—were colleagues on the Travis plantation. And six—Sam, Will, Dred, Nathan, Tom, and Davy—were attached to the Nathaniel Francis plantation, which seems to have been a hotbed of revolutionary agitation. Some of the men, like Hark and Jack, were brothers-in-law; some, like Nathan and Ben, were brothers. There were no women among the shock troops, but women were among the most enthusiastic supporters of the insurrection. Charlotte, one of the rebellious Francis slaves, seized and attacked her mistress. So did Lucy, a twenty-year-old slave on the Barrow plantation who was romantically linked with Moses, one of Turner's boldest soldiers. The Turner army also included the young and the lame. At the trial of Nathan, Tom, and Davy, the court determined that "the oldest was not more than 15 years, the other two much younger, the oldest very badly grown." Some of the young men were detailed to hold the horses during the attack, and some of them said at their trials that they were forced to accompany Nat and "that they went unwillingly." This was a common defense at the trial, and it is worth emphasizing that the youths and men who relied on this line of defense remained with Nat until "the whole troop was dispersed."

There was something in the way these men and boys rode, there was something in their appearance, and in their blood-curdling yells, that inspired terror.

"The gait the Negroes travelled," a local man reported, "served to strike additional horror. For they never rode at less than full speed; and as their horses became tired, they pressed fresh ones." He went on to say that "the fact of their being mounted, and their irregular mode of riding, caused their number to appear much greater than it really was."

Nat, the undisputed commander of this army, rode one of the finest horses that slaveowner money could buy and carried an ivory-handled sword tipped with silver. During the latter stages of the campaign, he devoted himself almost entirely to generalship, sending one detachment to one house, a second detachment to another house, and then bringing up the rear to see that "the work of death" was well done. The separate detachments usually rendezvoused at a designated point, and Nat tells us that when he arrived at one of these points he found "the greater part mounted, and ready to start [and] the men now amounting to about forty, shouted and hurraed as I rode up."

At this juncture, the pace became faster. "I took my station in the rear," Nat said, "and as it 'twas my object to carry terror and devastation wherever we went, I placed fifteen or twenty of the best armed and most to be relied on, in front, who generally approached the houses as fast as their horses could run; this was for two purposes, to prevent their escape and to strike terror to the inhabitants on this account, I never got to the houses, after leaving Mrs. Whitehead's, until the murders were committed, except in one case. I sometimes got in sight in time to see the work of death completed, viewed the mangled bodies as they lay, in silent satisfaction, and immediately started in quest of other victims. . . ." The quest yielded victims of every imaginable sort and was punctuated by the pleas, groans, and screams of the victims. For some of the victims, the blow or bullet came suddenly, unexpectedly, and was anesthesized by a blinding explosion of nothingness. They were the lucky ones. Others saw the thing coming, had time to think about it and to die a horrible death in the mind before the bullet or axe pierced the flesh. We are a long way away from that terrible Monday, but it is impossible to read accounts of the slayings without extending to the victims that human compassion the victims—and the victims' ancestors and descendants—were unable to extend to their victims and their slayers.

In a strangely evocative phrase, Nat called this "the work of death." The work continued all day long. "Trajan Doyle. Henry Bryant and wife and child and wife's mother, Nathaniel Francis' overseer and two children . . . Mrs. Caswell Worrell and child . . . Mrs. John K. Williams and child, Mrs. Jacob Williams and three children:" they all died. So did the celebrated beauty, Ann Eliza Vaughan, and her aunt, Rebecca Vaughan, who had prepared a spread for the fox hunters and who made the fatal mistake of assuming that the thundering herd of men approaching her house were her long-awaited guests. Mrs. Vaughan and her son Richard and Ann Eliza Vaughan were shot. A Vaughan slave told a reporter that "when the work was done they called for drink, and food, and becoming nice, damned the brandy as vile stuff."

The only whites spared on that day were poor whites who owned no slaves. Governor John Floyd said later that the insurgents "spared but one family and that was one so wretched as to be in all respects upon a par with them." The same point was made by one of the rebels who said later in his confession that "Capt. Nat in passing a house where some very poor people lived said he would not kill them because they thought no better of themselves than they did of the Negroes."

Some whites escaped Nat's dragnet by hiding in holes or in secret places in their homes. Lavinia Francis, the wife of Nathaniel Francis, survived by hiding between the roof and the plastering. An unidentified twelve-year-old girl concealed herself in a fireplace from which vantage point she witnessed, undoubtedly with horror, the slaying of several persons, including her sister.

Mary T. Barrow, one of the beauties of the county and the daughter of the ill-fated Rebecca Vaughan, also escaped, but not without cost. She was, according to Drewry's account, vain about her appearance; and when word reached her house that the slaves had risen, her first thought was for appearance. While she was trying to make herself presentable for flight, her husband, Captain John Barrow, kept an anxious watch. It must have been with a sinking heart that he heard the thundering approach of Nat Turner's army. Offering himself as a willing sacrifice, he bolted the door and held off the insurgents until his wife escaped to the woods. His widow lived to an advanced age and afterwards, Drewry reports, "married a Mr. Rose, and later a Mr. Moyler."

Fate favored Mary Barrow; the same fate, with cosmic indifference, condemned others. Mary Barrow's brother George was surprised and slain on the road while he was enroute to the fox hunt. Edwin Drewry, a relative of historian W. S. Drewry, was surprised and slain in the middle

of a business transaction. Drewry and a slave named Stephen had traveled
to the farm of Jacob Williams to get a load of corn. They were standing in
the middle of the yard trying to decide "who should go for a corn measure" when Drewry heard the sound of horses and cried out, "Lord, who
is that coming?" Death was coming; and Drewry, perceiving this, ran but
was overtaken and slain.

This scene and others of similar import were witnessed by slaves and
masters. And we must pause here to note that the immediate effect of all
this was a short but meaningful revolution in race relations in Southampton. For most of Monday and part of Tuesday, most whites spoke softly
to slaves and were unusually considerate. During the same time period,
and for the same reason, there were numerous signs that most slaves, even
those who remained loyal to individual masters, felt somehow enlarged
by Nat's audacity. The spectacle of whites in the grip of wholesale panic,
the sight of powerful masters pleading and begging for mercy, the sound
of black men ordering and commanding: all this shattered—for a brief
period—the myth of white invincibility. The slaves were individuals, of
course, and they responded to this situation according to their differing
temperaments and histories. Some—the bold, the adventurous, and the
deeply aggrieved—supported Nat. Some—the timid, the cautious, the
deeply conditioned—supported their masters. As for the majority, they
did what majorities have done in every revolution: they waited on the
sidelines to see which way the wind would blow. There was nothing unusual about this. The same thing has happened in the first stages of every
revolution known to man. What is astonishing, however, and worthy of
note, is that large sectors of this wavering majority teetered—for a short
time—on the ledge of a radical commitment. There were signs of this on
all sides in Southampton on Monday, August 22. One sign, reflected in
court records and the testimony of eyewitnesses, was the large number of
slaves—in Southampton and surrounding counties—who were heard
boasting "about what they would do [to whites] if Captain Nat came their
way." Another and equally significant sign was the relatively large number of slaves who crossed the boundary of slavery after the slaying of
their masters.

For all these reasons then, Southampton on the day of the revolt was
a place of shifting sand and allegiances. The case of Lavinia Francis was
characteristic. She survived the attack, as we have seen, by hiding in a
crevice in her house. When she emerged from the hiding place, she was
surprised to find her presumably loyal slaves dividing her wedding dress

and arguing over the disposition of her goods. In the days before the revolt, Lavinia Francis could have dispersed her slaves with a glance or a word. But things had changed in Southampton, and the most important dimension to this encounter was the fact that it was recognized almost immediately, by the slaves and by the mistress, that Lavinia Francis's authority, her mystique, as mistress had disappeared. Significantly, the initiative was seized not by the mistress but by a defiant young slave named Charlotte. "I thought you were dead," Charlotte said, pulling out a dirk. "If you are not dead, you soon shall be." Charlotte's arm was stayed by a slave named Esther, who said Mrs. Francis had been kind to her and did not deserve to die. And so for the second time that day Lavinia Francis escaped death; but she had peered into the void at the heart of race relations, and life for her would never ever be the same.

At about the same time, Jacob Williams was surprised to find his slave Nelson dressed in his best clothes in the middle of the day. Williams had not heard about the insurrection; but something in Nelson's demeanor told him, as he testified later, that the slave "had some intention of attacking him." Williams decided that it was best, under the circumstances, to overlook the fact that Nelson was not working in the fields. As an extra precaution, Williams put a lot of space between himself and Nelson, going to "the woods to measure some timber." This was curious behavior for a slavemaster who didn't even know that an insurrection was in progress. But curious or not, it saved his life. Unfortunately, it did not save his family. After the slaying of Jacob Williams's wife and children, Nelson, "dressed...very clean," according to the slave cook, "came into the kitchen and asked for meat took his Mistress' meat out of the pot cut a piece off and said Cynthia you do not know me. I do not know when you will see me again—stepped over the dead bodies without any manifestation of grief." A third case showing still more clearly which way the wind was blowing was a revealing encounter between a white woman and a group of slaves on a road somewhat distant from the scene of action. The white woman, one Nancy Parsons, testified later that "she saw several Negroes standing near the road...that [Isaac] was lying some distance off outside of the field kicking up his heels—that [she] had heard of a disturbance in the County but did now know of what character—heard that the British were in the County—she asked [Isaac] if he was not afraid—[Isaac] answered that he was not—that if they came by he would join them and assist in killing all the white people."

It can scarcely be doubted, in the face of these testimonies, that the Nat Turner explosion was rending the social fabric of the Southampton slave regime. And by late afternoon on Monday, it seemed that Nat and his forces were invincible. By that time, Nat had traveled some thirty miles without meeting any opposition. Behind him was a red swath of destruction and some sixty white victims. Ahead, only three miles away, was his strategic objective, the county seat of Jerusalem (now Courtland). And here, at the gate of the James W. Parker estate on the road leading to Jerusalem and perhaps victory, events of importance unfolded. Some of Nat's men had relatives on the Parker plantation, and they naturally wanted to stop and visit. But Nat refused, saying "his object was to reach [Jerusalem] as soon as possible." The soldiers pressed the point, and Nat made the profound but intelligible mistake of permitting the larger part of his force to enter the Parker plantation while he remained at the gate with a token force of eight or nine men. This was the crucial turning point of the drama; for the visiting rebels, flushed with success and, yes, considerable portions of brandy, dallied. After a spell, Nat "started to the house for them." While he was gone, a force of about eighteen white men attacked and dispersed the guard at the gate. Thus, when Nat returned with the main body of his troops, he was faced with the first organized opposition. His response to this threat was typical. Instead of retreating, he advanced, ordering his men "to fire and rush" the whites, who stood their ground for a moment and then retreated. The black army pursued the white army for some two hundred yards, but at the last moment the whites were reinforced by additional men from Jerusalem. What happened next is described by Nat:

"As I saw them re-loading their guns, and more coming up than I saw at first, and several of my bravest men being wounded, the others became panick struck and squandered over the field; the white men pursued and fired on us several times. Hark had his horse shot under him, and I caught another for him as it was running by me; five or six of my men were wounded, but none left on the field; finding myself defeated here I instantly determined to go through a private way, and cross the Nottoway River at the Cypress Bridge, three miles below Jerusalem, and attack that place in the rear, as I expected they would look for me on the other road, and I had a great desire to get there to procure arms and ammunition. After going a short distance in this private way, accompanied by about twenty men, I overtook two or three who told me the others were dispersed in every direction."

Now, as the fate of Jerusalem hung in the balance, Nat changed directions, doubling back on his tracks to recruit additional men. He succeeded in mustering about forty, but was repulsed at a second battle at daybreak on Tuesday at the home of Dr. Simon Blunt. Hark and several other insurgents were wounded and captured at this battle.

Following the Blunt battle, the balance of forces shifted to the advantage of the whites; and Nat, perceiving this, desperately doubled his bets, sending out scouts in attempts to rally his dispersed forces. The best evidence of the power and authority of the man is the fact that his followers continued to obey him. At eight or nine o'clock on Tuesday morning, while the whites were burying their dead, a free black man named Thomas Hatchcock, accompanied by "four boys," visited the Edwards plantation and told the slaves that "Genl. Nat" had gone "towards Belfield to kill all the whites" and would return to the Edwards plantation on Wednesday or Thursday for "4 likely boys that he would take with [him]." On the same morning, and at about the same time, two slaves of Thomas Ridley—Curtis and Stephen—were riding around the county on mules, openly proselytizing for Nat. The two slaves were captured and admitted, after intense questioning and, undoubtedly, torture, that Nat had told them "to go to Newsoms and Allens quarters to get other Negroes to join them...." Asked why they accepted such a dangerous assignment, Curtis "answered that Nat...had told him the white people were too much alarmed to interrupt them." There were other recruiters in the field, notably Will Artist and his wife. Around three or four o'clock on Tuesday, Artist and his wife visited the Blunt plantation and told the slaves that the struggle was far from over. According to witnesses, Artist said "he would cut his way, he would kill and cripple as he went." This was not idle talk. Nat still had at least one organized detachment in the field. This detachment fought a pitched battle with white militia on Tuesday afternoon and suffered many casualties, including Will. Nat, unaware of this setback, continued to maneuver for position. Accompanied by two loyal aides, Jacob and Nat, he established a command post in the woods. At nightfall on Tuesday, according to his account, he sent Jacob and Nat "in search of Henry, Sam, Nelson and Hark, and directed them to rally all they could, at the place we had our dinner the Sunday before, where they would find me, and I accordingly returned there as soon as it was dark and remained until Wednesday evening, when discovering white men riding around the place as though they were looking for someone, and none of my men joining me, I concluded Jacob and Nat had been taken, and compelled to betray me. On this I gave up all hope for the present, and on Thursday night after having supplied myself with provisions from Mr. Travis', I scratched a hole under a pile of fence rails in a field, where I concealed myself. . . . "

Meanwhile, the situation grew ever so much more complicated. All labor and commerce in Southampton ground to a halt, and vast stretches of the countryside were abandoned. Many whites fled their homes, leaving the doors and windows open, and gathered in Jerusalem, whose population of 175 swelled to some 600. All this was witnessed by a number of men who left telling descriptions. A local white man, writing from Jerusalem on August 24, said "the oldest inhabitant of our country has never experienced such a distressing time, as we have had since Sunday night last. . . . Every house, room, and corner in this place [Jerusalem] is full of women and children, driven from home, who had to take to the woods, until they could get to this place. . . . " Five days later, a committee of citizens told President Andrew Jackson, in a letter of appeal, that a federal military presence was necessary. "Along the road traveled by our rebellious blacks," the letter said, "comprising a distance of something like twenty-seven miles, no white soul now lives to tell how fiendlike was their purpose. In the bosom of almost every family this enemy still exists. Our homes, those near the scene of havoc, as well as others more remote, have all been deserted and our families gathered together and guarded at public places in the county. . . . "

The situation improved somewhat with the arrival of federal and state forces. From Fortress Monroe came three companies of field artillery. From U.S. Navy ships in Hampton Roads came detachments of marines and sailors. From the state capital in Richmond and from surrounding counties came militia and material reinforcements. All in all, some three thousand federal, state, and county militia were mobilized to put down the uprising. The immediate result of this invasion by the forces of white law and order was a massacre of blacks, who were tortured to death, maimed, and subjected to other atrocities. Among those tortured was Nat Turner's wife, who was whipped at the post, contemporary news accounts said, and forced to produce his papers. Something of the spirit of the times comes out in a letter written by the Reverend G. W. Powell, who said "there are thousands of troops searching in every direction, and many Negroes killed every day; the exact number will never be ascertained." At Cross Keys, a local analyst said later, "three women, slaves of [Nathaniel] Francis, also two Negro men, slaves of Peter Edwards, Esq., were tied to a large oak . . . and shot by the enraged citizens." In their fury, some whites decapitated blacks and stuck their heads on posts along the road as warnings to future Nat Turners.

As public hysteria intensified, pulpiteers and editorial writers weighed in with words of warning and wisdom. The problem was clear to the *Richmond Enquirer*, which said on August 30 that "the case of Nat Turner warns us. No black man ought to be permitted to turn a Preacher through the country." Some citizens in Richmond and elsewhere believed the problem was more menacing. A white man who visited Norfolk and Richmond and "other parts of the State" said he heard whites "cursing the Quakers or Baptists, whom they declared would ruin the State. I FREQUENTLY HEARD IT WISHED THAT THE D-----D NEGROES MIGHT ALL BE EXTERMINATED." This wish was expressed by large sectors of white public opinion. Writing in the Richmond *Constitutional Whig* on September 3, 1831, John Hampden Pleasants put it bluntly: "Let the fact not be doubted by those whom it most concerns, that another such insurrection will be the signal for the extermination of the whole black population in the quarter of the state where it occurs." The practical implications of all this were graphically detailed by a former slave, who was quoted by Thomas Wentworth Higginson. "At the time of the old Prophet Nat," she said, "the colored folks was afraid to pray loud; for the whites threatened to punish 'em dreadfully, if the least noise was heard. The patrols was low drunken whites; and in Nat's time, if they heard any of the colored folks praying, or singing a hymn, they would fall upon 'em and abuse 'em, and sometimes kill 'em, afore master or missis could get to 'em. The brightest and best was killed in Nat's time."

In the last week of August and the first week of September, "the brightest and best" were hunted like beasts of prey in the fields and forests of Southampton. We can follow the progress of this manhunt in the dispatches of the military commander, Brigadier General Richard Eppes, and his subordinates. On Wednesday, August 24, General Eppes told Governor Floyd that "the number of insurgents were, according to the best intelligence, reduced to six—though it is not improbable that they will attempt to rally. Twelve have been taken; several have been apprehended, not of the rioters, but suspected—fifteen had been killed—the rest with General Nat Turner (a preacher and a slave) and Will Artist, a free man of color at their head, were trying to make off."

The next day, John Hampden Pleasants, a Richmond editor serving with the Richmond Dragoons, filed the following dispatch from Jerusalem:

"There are thirteen prisoners now at this place, one or more of them severely wounded; the principal of them, a man aged about 21, called Marmaduke, who might have been a hero, judging from the magnanimity with which he bears his sufferings. He is said to be an atrocious offender, and the murderer of Miss Vaughan, celebrated for her beauty. The Preacher-Captain has not been taken. . . ."

Additional prisoners were taken on Friday, according to a letter from "a gentleman" serving with another military unit, the Norfolk and Portsmouth Volunteers. He said his unit had reported to General Eppes and had "received orders to proceed to Cross Keys [where they] succeeded in making prisoners and bringing in 12 men and one woman who is said to have taken a very active part, together with the head of the celebrated Nelson, called by the blacks, 'General Nelson,' and the paymaster, Heney [sic], whose head is expected in momentarily. . . ." On Saturday, August 27, another member of the Richmond Dragoons wrote that "the war is over, and the enemy are captured, I believe, with the exception of their Chief, the notorious Capt. Nat and 2 or 3 others." This report was confirmed the next day by General Eppes, who told the governor:

"The insurgents all taken or killed, except Mr. Turner the leader after whom there is a pursuit.

"The troops will be discharged shortly."

This was an official communique, and it is probably the only official document in the history of the slave regime which frankly and respectfully refers to a slave as *Mr*. This was not an isolated phrase. The enormity of Nat's act compelled respect. On October 29, *Niles' Register* of Baltimore referred to Nat as "this distinguished leader of the blacks at the massacre in Virginia. . . ."

Although Mr. Turner remained at large, the Southampton county court began trying his alleged co-conspirators on Wednesday, August 31. The trials followed the judicial forms of slavery, but were, for all that, perfunctory. There was no jury; and the slave rebels were judged by a panel of justices of the peace, all of whom were slaveowners or allies of slaveowners. The white survivors, notably widower Levi Waller and widow Mary Barrow, and loyal slaves identified the accused. But in several instances, the testimony of prosecution witnesses was contradicted by the testimony of slaves and at least two slaveowners. It is not clear how the justices resolved the contradictions, for there was no cross-examination and the accused were not heard in their own defense.

The trials continued uninterruptedly from the last of August to late October. At twelve o'clock on Saturday, September 2, Thomas Trezevant, the Jerusalem postmaster, reported, in a letter to the Richmond *Constitutional Whig*, that "we are progressing but slowly, owing to the innumerable quantity of witnesses to be brought from different parts of the county. So far as we have gone, the testimony has been strong and conclusive as respects conspirators. No good testimony as yet to induce a belief that the conspiracy was a general one. I shall go on to detail circumstances as they occur hourly, waiting until tomorrow, up to the closing of the mail, and then will conclude with a postscript. . . ."

At three o'clock that afternoon, Trezevant added his first postscript.

"It is just reported that Billy Artist, a free man and one of the principals, has just killed himself. No doubt of his being killed, but not by his own hands; further reports that Artist is certainly dead."

At six o'clock there was another note:

"We have been rather more expeditious today; the court has just adjourned until Monday.—Condemned 14 out of 15."

The next day, just before posting his letter, Trezevant added his final postscript:

"P.S.—Sunday evening, 3 o'clock—Nothing more today. *We commence hanging tomorrow.*" [Trezevant's italics.]

The first rebels to die on the gallows were Daniel Porter and Moses Barrow. On Friday, September 9, five slaves, including Hark, Sam, and Nelson, were hanged. On Monday, September 26, Lucy—the only woman convicted—left the jail and rode on her coffin to the tree from which she was hanged.

Twenty-nine persons, including four boys, were convicted and hanged or transported. Almost all contemporary observers said the insurgents condemned by the court and the insurgents shot down in the fields died unrepentant. One white witness, quoted by historian Herbert Aptheker, said that "some of them that were wounded and in the aggonies of Death declared that they was going happy fore that God had a hand in what they had been doing. . . ." Governor Floyd said "all died bravely indicating no reluctance to lose their lives in such a cause."

While the insurgents marched defiantly to the gallows, waves of panic rolled over the South. From Baltimore, where the houses of free blacks were searched, from Dover County, Delaware, where several blacks were arrested and executed, from Frankfort, Kentucky, where rumors circulated that the slaves had captured the whole Southern coast, from Charleston and New Orleans and Macon, Georgia, came stories of insurrections and threatened insurrections.

The story from Wilmington, North Carolina, was incredible. According to an express dispatch which reached Raleigh at 10 P.M. on Monday, September 12, Wilmington had been sacked, half of the inhabitants had been slain, and an army of two thousand blacks was marching on the state capital. This report, as it turned out, was false, but a second report, received the same night, was apparently true. The second dispatch said, according to news accounts, that "the Negroes in the counties of Duplin, Bladen, Sampson and others [were] in a state of insubordination, having collected in large bodies near the line of Sampson and Johnson, murdering and burning all before them."

All this, as can be imagined, caused the greatest consternation in Raleigh, which shifted to a war footing. "The able-bodied men," one report said, "were organized into four companies to patrol the streets nightly by turns. The old men organized the Silver Grays. The fortress was the Presbyterian church. It was agreed that when the bell of the capitol rang out the women and children should hasten there for protection. They watched and waited in anxiety and fear. The news from Wilmington increased their terror."

The immediate result of all this was a bit of almost pure farce. "One night," the same account continued, "O'Rourke's blacksmith shop took fire; the capitol bell rang forth its shrill peal of alarm. It was heard from one end of the town to the other. The slumbering city was transformed into a terror-stricken multitude; the last day and the inevitable time had come; Nat Turner and his followers were upon them, for this was the signal agreed upon. Negroes were more terrified than their masters; they fled their homes, hid in shrubbery, lay down between corn rows—anything to escape destruction. The women, with hair disheveled and in night clothes, fled through the streets with ever-increasing speed for their place of refuge. It was a matter of life and death to them, and heart-felt were the thanks for deliverance when the true cause of the alarm was known."

Raleigh was not unique; there were similar scenes in cities and counties across the South. It would be said later that this was an exaggerated response to a nonexistent danger. But it was more than that. There was—without a doubt—exaggeration, but there was also a real danger, a danger that became concrete and menacing in scores of uprisings and attempted uprisings in the wake of the Nat Turner revolt. More than that, deeper than all that, was the knowledge bought by the Turner revolt, the knowledge that there was a Nat Turner or a potential Nat Turner on every plantation. No one understood this better than James McDowell, who silenced scoffers in the debate Nat Turner forced on the Virginia House of Delegates in 1832:

"Now sir, I ask you," McDowell said, facing criticis and doubters, "I ask gentlemen in conscience to say, was that a 'petty affair' which startled the feelings of your whole population; which threw a portion of it into alarm, a portion of it into panic; which wrung out from an affrighted people the thrilling cry, day after day, conveyed to your executive, *'We are in peril of our lives; send us an army for defense.'* Was that a 'petty affair' which drove families from their homes—which assembled women and children in crowds, without shelter, at places of common refuge, in every condition of weakness and infirmity, under every suffering which want and terror could inflict, yet willing to endure all, willing to meet death from famine, death from climate, death from hardships, preferring any thing rather than the horrors of meeting it from a domestic assassin? Was that a 'petty affair' which erected a peaceful and confiding portion of the State into a military camp; which outlawed from pity the unfortunate beings whose brothers had offended; which barred every door, penetrated every bosom with fear or suspicion; which so banished every sense of security from every man's dwelling, that, let but a hoof or horn break upon the silence of the night, and an aching throb would be driven to the heart, the husband would look to his weapon, and the mother would shudder and weep upon her cradle? Was it the fear of Nat Turner, and his deluded, drunken handful of followers which produced such effects? Was it this that induced distant counties, where the very name of Southampton was strange, to arm and equip for a struggle? No, sir: it was the suspicion eternally attached to the slave himself—the suspicion that a Nat Turner might be in every family; that the same bloody deed might be acted over at any time and in any place, that the materials for it were spread through the land, and were always ready for a like explosion. . . ."

The suspicion that a Nat Turner might be in every family and on every plantation: It was this suspicion that fueled the fire. And as the flames leaped from community to community, federal and state officials pressed a nationwide search for the man who started the fire. Rewards totalling $1,100 were offered for information leading to his capture, and Governor Floyd received scores of false reports that Nat had been seen or captured in Baltimore or Ohio or the West Indies.

Nat was not in Ohio; he had not drowned, as one report said, trying to cross New River—Nat was still in a cave in Southampton County, within a few miles of the scene of his first attack. For six long weeks, while the biggest manhunt in Virginia history swirled around him, he remained in the hole, leaving it only in the dead of night to scrounge for food and water and to listen at windows for scraps of information. It was a dreadful life. He was, he said later, "afraid of speaking to any human being," and he was almost captured a hundred times. But even in adversity, he maintained a sense of expectancy and discipline. To keep track of the time, he constructed a crude calendar, cutting a notch in a stick every day.

"I know not how long I might have led this life," he said "if accident had not betrayed me, a dog in the neighborhood passing by my hiding place one night while I was out, was attracted by some meat I had in my cave, and crawled in and stole it, and was coming out just as I returned. A few nights after, two Negroes having started to go hunting with the same dog, and passed that way, the dog came again to the place, and having just gone out to walk about, discovered me and barked, on which thinking myself discovered, I spoke to them to beg concealment. . . . On making myself known they fled from me. Knowing then that they would betray me, I immediately left my hiding place and was pursued almost incessantly."

Many words would be written later to celebrate the fact that Nat was routed from his first hideout by slaves loyal to the slave regime. But this fact didn't surprise Nat Turner; and it shouldn't surprise us. Every oppressive regime creates accomplices as well as rebels, and the circumstances surrounding Nat's capture indicate that there were rebels as well as accomplices in the neighborhood. The truly amazing phenomenon in this whole business, as Henry Irving Tragle observed, is that Nat managed to elude capture for six long weeks in a closely-knit neighborhood crawling with guards and searchers. There is no hard evidence on how he did this, but it is certainly reasonable to infer, as Tragle inferred, that some blacks knew or suspected that he was in the neighborhood. If so, they didn't betray him, and he remained at large until Sunday, October 30, when he was accidentally discovered and captured by a poor white farmer in a hole underneath a fallen pine tree near the residence of his late master. It was only with great difficulty, we are told, that he was conveyed alive to Jerusalem. It is said that people stuck pins into him and spat upon him along the way.

Loaded down with chains and surrounded by guards and tormentors, Nat arrived in Jerusalem—Did he remember the Bible verse that said Jesus would be taken to a city called Jerusalem and would be reviled and crucified?—at 1:15 P.M. on Monday, October 31. Two justices of the peace immediately examined him before a large gathering of officials and onlookers. Postmaster Thomas Trezevant was present and reported that "during all the examination, he evinced great intelligence and much shrewdness of intellect, answering every question clearly and distinctly, and without confusion or prevarication." Trezevant said that Nat acknowledged that he was wrong, but he must have misunderstood Nat's language, for other witnesses said Nat was unrepentant and "still pretends," as one report put it, "that he is a prophet." Nat told the examining magistrates that he had believed for a long time that he was a messenger of God and that his attack had been sanctioned by God. He was asked on that day, and later:

"Do you not find yourself mistaken now?"

Without hesitation, the answer came back:

"Was not Christ crucified?"

From the day of his examination to the day of his execution, Nat was pestered, prodded and harangued by officials and notoriety-seekers. Some whites simply wanted to see him. Others wanted to get close enough to harm him. All—officials, notoriety-seekers, and relatives of the victims— wanted to know what made him tick.

No one carried this obsession to greater lengths than Thomas R. Gray, who was, by far, the most interesting of the Southampton hangers-on. Gray was a lawyer and slaveowner. According to Tragle, he was between sixty and seventy years old and had a young wife who was between thirty and forty.

Gray was drawn to Nat by contradictory motives. As a good Southern slaveowner, he was, of course, horrified by Nat's deed. But a deed is a deed, and Gray, a man of words and a frustrated writer, was quick to recognize that Nat's deed had created so much public interest that a smart man could make some money out of it. Gray, in other words, was something of an operator, and he viewed Nat—according to all available evidence—in marketing terms that transcended the slave block.

There is some reason to believe that Gray had already conceived the idea of a book on the insurrection. Forty-four days before Nat's capture, an unnamed Southampton "gentleman well conversant with the scenes he describes" wrote a dispatch for the Richmond *Constitutional Whig* which anticipated some of the language and details of the *Confessions*. The evidence strongly suggests, as Tragle pointed out, that the Southampton gentleman was the same Thomas R. Gray who approached Nat immediately after his capture with plans for the publication of "an authentic confession" for "the gratification of public curiosity."

This was, to say the least, highly irregular. Gray had defended some of the rebels, he had access to official documents and the results of other interrogations—*but he was not Nat Turner's lawyer*. If legal forms had been followed, the court probably would have ruled that Gray's intervention compromised Nat's defense.

But neither Nat Turner nor Thomas R. Gray was concerned at this point with legal forms. They were both realists. Both knew that nothing could change the outcome, and both—for different reasons—wanted to get the message to a larger audience. The result was an unusual deal between these two improbable Southerners—a deal that insured that Nat's words and deeds would never die.

For three days, from Tuesday, November 1, to Thursday, November 3, Nat sat, in a manner of speaking, for his historical portrait. The first two days Nat talked and Gray listened. As Nat talked, Gray took notes "and having the advantage of his statement before me in writing, on the evening of the third day that I had been with him, I began a cross examination, and found his statement corroborated by every circumstance coming within my own knowledge or the confessions of others who had been either killed or executed, and whom he had not seen nor had any knowledge since 22nd of August last. . . ."

The document that emerged from these sessions does not contain, we can be sure, all Nat said or even the most important things he said. It seems also that the wily Nat, who was a master of words, used Gray as much as Gray used him. He undoubtedly wanted to shape the historical image of the revolt, and it is certainly reasonable to conclude that what he told Gray was the truth, but that he did not tell Gray all the truth he knew.

It is striking in this connection that Nat did not implicate a single

insurgent who had not been killed or tried and convicted. He didn't mention the free black insurgents, nor did he mention slaves who supported
him along the way. As a consequence, not a single slave was tried on the
basis of his "full and complete confession."

This does not mean, by any means, that the *Confessions* is questionable; it means simply that it must be approached in the spirit in which
Nat dictated it: elliptically and, yes, conspiratorially. Because of the
Confessions, we know a great deal about the workings of Nat's mind and
the details of the plot. But there is a great deal that we don't know, and
probably never will know. There is, for example, the question of names.
It is established by a great deal of evidence that General Nat and several
members of his army had adopted new names. Nat, for instance, was
said to have styled himself General Cargill. Hark Travis, as we have seen,
was referred to as General Moore. What was true of the leaders was true
also of the shock troops. To cite only one instance, Levi Waller, the
master of a slave named Davy, testified that "on Monday the 22d of
August 1831 a band of Negroes came to his house, killed all his family
but that Davy the prisoner was not at the house, he came up while
Negroes were there—dressed himself clean—drank with them—rode his
master's horse off in good spirits—was called brother *Clements* by one of
the company—left there in great glee." [Italics in original.]

What was the meaning of this? When did Davy become "brother
Clements?" More importantly, how did the other members of the band
know that he was "brother Clements?" Had they attended secret meetings together? Had they created a secret structure of code names and
code words?

The Confessions of Nat Turner is silent on this point, and it is ambiguous on the preparations that preceded the revolt. Nat tells us in
the *Confessions* that he acted almost on the spur of the moment and that
he informed only a handful of slaves. But there is evidence, as we have
seen, that additional slaves were approached in the week before the
revolt. A slave woman testified at the trials that she had heard the subject
discussed for at least eighteen months. Her testimony on this point was
vague. But she was very specific at another point, saying that "on the
15th day of August last [a week before the revolt] at a black persons
house at Solomon Parkers she heard the prisoners [three slaves named
Jim, Isaac, and Preston] say that if the black people came they would
join and help kill the white people, it was after they had been talking
some time that she went in and did not hear the Commencement of the

conversation there were several slaves present and one of them stated his master had croped him and he would be croped before the end of the year. Witnesses had heard three other slaves make use of the same declaration some time previously in the neighborhood. . . . They told her it was a secret and if she told the white persons would shoot her. . . ."

Was this witness telling the truth?

Was there more to the insurrection than Nat revealed?

We don't know. Nor do we know the ultimate objective of the attack. It has been assumed by many commentators that Nat said all he had to say on this subject in the *Confessions*. But there is internal and external evidence to show that Nat was, in part, playing the old slave game of "putting marsa on." The testimony of an unnamed white man who participated in the first official interrogation of Nat is relevant in this connection. Vaguely displeased by Nat's ambiguous responses, he pressed him on the specifics of the plan. Nat answered, as he answered in the *Confessions*, with a torrent of words about the Spirit and the Holy Ghost. The white man asked him to be specific. How did he get from the vague commands of the Holy Ghost to the concrete plan? And what precisely was the concrete plan? Nat unleashed another volley of words and the white man gave up, saying: "How this idea came or in what manner it was connected with his signs, etc., I could not get him to explain in a manner at all satisfactory—notwithstanding I examined him closely at this point; *he always seemed to mystify*." [Emphasis added.]

This is an important passage which has been overlooked by too many historians. And it is surely relevant that some of the captured insurgents, and some of their captors, said there was more to the insurrection than Nat admitted. The strategic objective mentioned most often in these reports was the Dismal Swamp. A white man, writing from the area on August 24, said flatly that "the intention of the Negroes was to reach the Dismal Swamp." If we can credit the dubious narrative Samuel Warner wrote before Nat's capture, the Dismal Swamp was also mentioned in "the confession of one of them under condemnation." According to Warner, the unnamed insurgent said there had been a difference of opinion between "the three principal leaders at the commencement" of the insurrection. One of Nat's subordinates, he said, suggested that they "might secret [themselves] in the dark recesses of Dismal Swamp, until opportunity should present to escape to the free States, or to some foreign country." But Nat, he said, "was for the total extermination of the whites, without regard to age or sex, that by so doing, they should soon be able (in imitation of the example set them by their brethren at St. Domingo) to establish a government of their own, and that he had been promised the aid of many of their enslaved brethren in North Carolina, Maryland, etc."

There were other variations on the same themes. A Southampton correspondent, quoted in the *Norfolk American Beacon* on August 29, reported that "Broadnax's servants stated their object to be to reach the free states, where they expected to make proselytes and return to assist their brethren." Perhaps the most intriguing account came from John Hampden Pleasants, who reported from Southampton that "some of them say [the object] was to get to Norfolk, seize a ship and go to Africa."

Whatever the truth of the matter, it is difficult to believe that Nat was able to persuade other slaves to revolt without revealing a plan of some kind. But the details of the plan, if it existed, were not discussed in the *Confessions* or at the trial.

The trial was held on Saturday, November 5, in the Southampton county courthouse at Jerusalem. Ten local justices of the peace were on the bench, and additional guards surrounded the courthouse "to repel any attempt that may be made to remove Nat alias Nat Turner from the custody of the sheriff—." The brief, uninformative court summary makes no mention of crowd response, but we can be sure that the courtroom tingled with suppressed excitement when Nat Turner entered "in the custody of the Jailer," and was "set to the bar." The first order of business was the assignment of "Counsel for the prisoner in his defense." The counsel assigned was William C. Parker, a local lawyer who had defended other insurgents and whose record in that regard contained nothing to inspire false hope in the breast of the defendant. In an ironic footnote, the court decided that Parker was to receive ten dollars for defending Nat and that the money was to come from the estate of his late master, who had been among the first victims of the insurrection.

The trial began with the filing of "an information" against Nat by Merriweather B. Broadnax, the counsel for the Commonwealth of Virginia. The accused, he said, was charged with the crime of "conspiring to rebel and making insurrection." Jeremiah Cobb, the presiding judge, accepted the information and put the question:

How did the defendant plead?

Nat Turner pleaded not guilty, "saying to his counsel, that he did not feel so."

The first witness for the prosecution was Levi Waller, a tragic figure who had lost all members of his family in the insurrection and who probably found some solace in his role as the principal—and indeed the only—witness against the chief of the rebellion. The witness stated, according to the stilted court summary, "that on the morning of the 22d August last between 9 and 10 o'clock he heard that the Negroes had risen and were murdering the whites and were coming. Witness sent his son Thos. to the school house, he living about a quarter of a mile off etc. to let it be known and for his children to come home. Mr. Crocker/the schoolmaster/came with the Witnesses children/Witness told him to go to the house and load the guns, but before the guns were loaded Mr. Crocker came to the still where witness was and said they were in sight. Witness retreated and concealed himself in the corner of the fence in the weeds/behind the garden/on the opposite side of the house. Several Negroes pursued him but he escaped by falling among the weeds over the fence—One Negro rode up and looked over, but did not observe him— The attention of the party he thinks were called off from him by some of the party going in pursuit of another, which he thinks they took him for but it turned out to be his blacksmith—Witness then retreated into the swamp which was not far off—After remaining some time, Witness again approached the house—Before he retreated he saw several of his family murdered by the Negroes—Witness crept up near the house to see what they were doing and concealed himself by getting into the plumb orchard behind the garden—the Negroes were drinking—Witness saw prisoner whom he knew very well, mounted (he thought on Dr. Musgrave's horse) stated that prisoner seemed to command the party— made Peter Edwards' Negro man Sam who seemed disposed to remain go with them—prisoner gave command to the party to go ahead and when they left his house—Witness states that he cannot be mistaken in the identity of the prisoner. . . ."

The next witness was Samuel Trezevant, a local justice of the peace. He was not, strictly speaking, a witness. He was brought before the court to certify Nat Turner's confession. He did this, briskly and efficiently, saying that he and James W. Parker were the "Justices before whom the prisoner was examined prior to his commitment—That the prisoner at the time was in confinement but no threats or promises were held out to him to make any disclosures. That he admitted he was one of the insurgents engaged in the late insurrection, and the Chief among them—that he gave to his master and mistress Mr. Travis and (his) wife the first blow before they were dispatched—that he killed Miss Peggy Whitehead

—that he was with the insurgents from the first moment to their disper-
sion on Tuesday morning after the insurrection took place—that he gave
a long account of the motives which led him finally to commence the
bloody scenes which took place—that he pretended to have had intima-
tions by signed omens from God that he should embark in the desperate
attempt. . . ."

This was the heart and center of the state's case. Without further
discussion or argument, Broadnax rested his case. The focus of attention
shifted then to William C. Parker. Parker knew—everybody knew—that
this was a meaningless charade. Twenty thousand angels swearing on
golden Bibles would not have saved Nat, and Parker didn't even try. He
didn't cross-examine prosecution witnesses; he produced no witnesses
for the defense—he simply submitted the case to the court without
argument.

All this, we can be sure, was watched with interest by Nat's other
legal friend—Thomas R. Gray. Gray had been busy. He had finished
editing *The Confessions of Nat Turner* "as fully and voluntarily made
to" Thomas R. Gray, and he had signed a publishing contract with a
Baltimore printer. All he needed for a publishing coup and a November
publishing date was the verdict of the court. He didn't have to wait long.
To no one's surprise, the court decided almost immediately that Nat was
guilty as charged. The sentence was pronounced by Jeremiah Cobb.

"The judgement of the court," he said, "is, that you be taken hence
to the jail from whence you came, thence to the place of execution, and
on Friday next, between the hours of 10 A.M. and 2 P.M. be hung by the
neck until you are dead! dead! dead! and may the Lord have mercy upon
your soul."

It was done. On Friday, November 11, 1831, Nat was taken from the
Southampton jail to a field near the courthouse. Oblivious to the world
he was about to leave, Nat walked with head held high to the tree marked
for the hanging. "Not a limb trembled," one witness said. Another witness said "he betrayed no emotion, but appeared to be utterly reckless
in the awful fate that awaited him, and even hurried his executioner in
the performance of his duty! Precisely at 12 o'clock he was launched
into the eternity." When Nat was safely dead, his body was dismembered,
and souvenirs, including wallets, were made from the skin. But this was
not, by any means, the end of the affair. Before mounting the gallows,
Nat made one last prophecy, saying that there would be a storm after his
execution, and that the sun would refuse to shine. And, as a matter of

fact, there was a storm in Southampton on that day. But Nat spoke a parable, and parables should not be taken literally. The storm he saw came in the generation of crisis that was the ultimate result of his act. And that crisis ended—Did Nat see it?—in the rivers of blood that veiled the American sun during the great war that ended slavery.

He Who
Is Whipped

The "Trial" of Frederick Douglass

THE chips were down, and there was no way Frederick Augustus Washington Bailey could escape the exigencies of the moment. He had been farmed out to Edward Covey, a professional Negro-breaker, and he had been broken. Now, in a wild and desolate area on the Eastern Shore of Maryland, in the year of 1834, he, a mere boy of sixteen but big for his age, was going to have to stand like a man and fight or sink down, like a stone, into the depths of perpetual self-loathing.

It was all up to him, and what made it all so terrifying was that there was no way, it seemed, that he could win, whatever he did. He was a black boy and a slave, and it was a criminal offense, punishable by summary execution, for him to raise his hand against the white man who had goaded him to the brink of madness. Worse yet, there was no space for martyrdom in slavery: the wages of martyrdom for the slave were an unmarked grave and the silence of the centuries. So, Frederick Bailey, known to history as Frederick Douglass, asked himself, in so many words,

At crossroad, Frederick Douglass arrived at Maryland farm of professional Negro-breaker.

"What difference will it make anyway?" There was no audience, no re-porters, no slave historians. He was one black boy against a mean and tough old white man on an isolated farm. What difference would it make? No one would ever know. Something in him said that, but something in him said that he would know, and that he would have to live with that knowledge for the rest of his life.

Frederick Augustus Washington Bailey lay on his back in the woods and pondered the pros and cons of the matter and the alleys and byways that had brought him to this bitter crossroad in the valley of his life.

It had started six months ago or sixty years ago or six hundred years ago. Who can say when it started, when men decided that some men were going to be masters and some were going to be slaves? Whenever it started, however it started, he had not been consulted, and he had come into the world with his heart steeled against obedience. How many times had he offended his slavemaster, Captain Thomas Auld, simply by ex-pressing human impulses? First, he had learned to read, no small offense in the eyes of slavemasters. Then he had organized a slave meeting, a harmless Sunday school meeting to be sure, but a slave meeting nevertheless. It was then that the slavemaster had decided that he was a dangerous slave who "wanted to be another Nat Turner." To prevent this and to protect his investment, Auld had decided to put him out, as he said, "to be broken."

Since Covey was a specialist in breaking the will of intractable slaves, and since he lived only seven miles from the Auld home in St. Michaels, Frederick had been dispatched to the Covey farm. That was six months ago, on January 1, 1834. Frederick remembered the day well. It was cold and windy and he had approached the Covey farm with a sense of dread.

Defending himself in struggle with Edward Covey, young black slave regained his pride.

The farm, which comprised three or four hundred acres of rented land, sat on the bank of Chesapeake Bay. The household consisted of Edward Covey, his wife, his sister-in-law, and his cousin, Bill Hughes. There were two blacks on the farm, a slave woman named Caroline, and Bill Smith, a hired slave.

The master of this entourage was a relatively poor man, unprepossessing at first glance. He was not a big man, Douglass remembered—"not more than five feet ten inches in height, I should think—short-necked, round-shouldered, of quick and wiry motion, of thin and wolfish visage, with a pair of small, greenish-gray eyes, set well back under a forehead without dignity, and which were constantly in motion, expressing his passions rather than his thoughts. . . . When he spoke, it was from the corner of his mouth, and in a sort of light growl like that of a dog when an attempt is made to take a bone from him. . . ."

In the matter of breaking men and horses, the first impression—they say—is crucial. Covey, who understood such things, made the first impression count, cutting into Frederick's consciousness with the precision of a surgeon. Looking at him that first day, Douglass knew that he had come up against something "altogether ferocious and sinister, disagreeable and forbidding. . . . I already believed him a worse fellow than he had been represented to be."

What was Covey's secret?

Why did slavemasters send their rebellious slaves to him?

And why did these once-proud rebels return to their masters "well-broken," humble, pliant, obsequious?

Frederick had not been at the Covey place for seventy-two hours before one part of the answer emerged. Thinking perhaps that he and the rebellious young slave would understand each other better if the confrontation came at once, Covey gave Frederick a task he knew he could not carry out. And when Frederick failed, Covey led him to the woods, where he leisurely cut and trimmed three shoots from a black gum tree. Then, taking his time—the waiting was a part of the treatment—he flogged Frederick until the blood came. The flogging left finger-sized welts on Frederick's back.

This was the first of a series of floggings. During the first six months of Frederick's initiation, he was beaten, either with sticks or cowskin, at least once a week. But violence was only one link in the Covey plan. The second link was severe and unremitting toil. Covey worked Frederick up to and beyond his powers of endurance, keeping him in the fields and woods from first light until darkness and occasionally until midnight. "It was never," Frederick remembered, "too hot, or too cold; it could never rain, blow, snow, or hail too hard for us to work in the field. Work, work, work. . . . The longest days were too short for [Covey] and the shortest nights were too long for him. I was somewhat unmanageable at first, but a few months of this discipline tamed me. Mr. Covey succeeded in *breaking* me—in body, soul and spirit. My nattural elasticity was crushed; my intellect languished; the disposition to read departed; the cheerful spark that lingered about my eye died out; the dark night of slavery closed in upon me, and behold a man transformed into a brute!"

As rising young abolitionist, Douglass played key role in anti-slavery struggle.

But this was not the whole story. Men cannot be broken if their tormentors cannot invade and violate their souls. They cannot be broken in the flesh if they are not broken first in the spirit. Covey knew that, and the third link in his plan was mind-control. "He had the faculty," Frederick recalled, "of making us feel that he was always present. By a series of adroitly managed surprises which he practiced, I was prepared to expect him at any moment. His plan was never to approach in an open, manly, and direct manner the spot where his hands were at work. No thief was ever more artful in his devices than this man Covey. He would creep and crawl in ditches and gullies, hide behind stumps and bushes, and practice so much of the cunning of the serpent, that Bill Smith and I, between ourselves, never called him by any other name than 'the snake.' . . . One-half of his proficiency in the art of Negro-breaking consisted . . . in this species of cunning. We were never secure. He could see or hear us nearly all the time. He was to us, behind every stump, tree, bush, and fence on the plantation. . . ."

All of this had the desired effect. At first, Frederick was sassy and somewhat unmanageable, pitting the steel of his love for freedom against

67

the steel of Covey's thrust toward slavery. But slowly and inexorably, he gave ground; and at the end of six months he did not recognize himself. He cringed in Covey's presence and went out of his way to anticipate and meet Covey's demands. Sunday was his only day of rest, and he spent it under a big tree "in a sort of beast-like stupor between sleeping and waking."

He was tempted on occasions "to take [his] life and that of Covey, but was prevented by a combination of hope and fear." Sometimes he stood on the banks of Chesapeake Bay and "with no audience but the Almighty [poured out his] soul's complaint . . . with an apostrophe to the moving multitude of ships.

"You are loosed from your moorings, and free. I am fast in my chains, and am a slave! You move merrily before the gentle gale, and I sadly before the bloody whip. You are freedom's swift-winged angels, that fly around the world; I am confined in bonds of iron. O, that I were free! O, that I were on one of your gallant decks, and under your protecting wing! Alas! Betwixt me and you the turbid waters roll. Go on, go on; O, that I could also go! Could I but swim! If I could fly! O, why was I born a man, of whom to make a brute! The glad ship is gone—she hides in the dim distance. I am left in the hell of unending slavery. O, God, save me! God, deliver me! Let me be free! Is there any God? Why am I a slave? I will run away. I will not stand it. . . . Let but the first opportunity offer, and come what will, I am off. Meanwhile, I will try to bear the yoke. I am not the only slave in the world. Why should I fret? I can bear as much as any of them. Besides I am but a boy yet, and all boys are bound out to someone. It may be that my misery in slavery will only increase my happiness when I get free. There is a better day coming."

Such were the feverish, conflicting thoughts that ran through his mind as he contemplated his unhappy state. It was only later that he realized how close he was to madness. "I was completely wrecked," he wrote then, "changed and bewildered, goaded almost to madness at one time, and at another reconciling myself to my wretched condition."

At this point, an incident took place that had a decisive impact on the future course of events. On one of the hottest days in August, Frederick collapsed while working in the treading yard. Covey, who saw everything and heard everything, dashed to the scene and told Frederick to get up and get on with the work. Frederick tried to get up but fell back again;

he had a violent headache and his arms and legs shook spastically. Without a word of warning, Covey kicked Frederick in the side and slammed a piece of hickory stick against his head, causing the blood to flow freely. "If you *have* got the headache," he said, "I'll cure you."

This, as it turned out, was a mistake. For the kick and the blow on the head pushed Frederick across the line of self-preservation. Of a sudden, he decided that it was all useless and that the only thing Covey could do was to kill him and put him out of his misery.

Perceiving this or something like this, Covey turned abruptly and walked away. Frederick lay for a spell in his blood. Then he sat up, overwhelmed by a new idea. The solution, he told himself, was to go to his slavemaster and tell him how Covey was treating him. Having made up his mind, he moved, running off across the field in the direction of St. Michaels, disregarding the threats of Covey, who gave chase. After losing Covey in the dense woods, Frederick walked for five hours before reaching the St. Michaels store of Captain Aulds, who rejected his plea and told him: "If you don't go home immediately, I'll get hold of you myself."

Sadder and perhaps a little wiser, Frederick returned to the Covey farm. As soon as he emerged from the surrounding woods, Covey darted out from behind a fence corner, with a cowskin in one hand and a rope in the other. Since it was obvious that Covey intended to tie him up and whip him, Frederick hurriedly returned to the woods, where he lay in the leaves, trying to figure out what to do about Covey and the threat that Covey symbolized.

"Life in itself," he wrote later, "had become burdensome to me. All my outward relations were against me. I must stay here and starve, or go home to Covey's and have my flesh torn to pieces and my spirit humbled under his cruel lash. These were the alternatives before me. The day was long and irksome. I was weak from the toils of the previous day and from want of food and sleep, and I had been so little concerned about my appearance that I had not yet washed the blood from my garments. I was an object of horror, even to myself. . . . What had I done, what had my parents done, that such a life as this should be mine? That day, in the woods, I would have exchanged my manhood for the brutehood of an ox."

He was still in the woods and still unresolved about his future when he was disturbed, late that night, by the approaching steps of a man. One

can imagine his relief when it turned out that the approaching traveler
was a slave named Sandy, who was on his way to visit his wife, a free
black woman who lived in the lower part of Poppie Neck.

Frederick explained his plight to Sandy, who insisted that he go with
him to the home of his wife. "It was about midnight," Douglass wrote,
"but his wife was called up, a fire was made, some Indian meal was soon
mixed with salt and water, and an ash cake was baked in a hurry, to
relieve my hunger. Sandy's wife was not behind him in kindness; both
seemed to esteem it a privilege to succor me, for although I was hated by
Covey and by my master, I was loved by the colored people, because they
thought I was hated for my knowledge, and persecuted because I was
feared. I was the only slave in that region who could read or write. . . .
My knowledge was now the pride of my brother slaves, and no doubt
Sandy felt on that account something of the general interest in me. The
supper was soon ready, and though over the sea I have since feasted with
honorables, lord mayors and aldermen, my supper on ash cake and cold
water, with Sandy, was the meal of all my life most sweet to my taste and
now most vivid to my memory." After supper, Sandy and Frederick
discussed the situation. Both, it should be noted, were persons of importance in the slave community. Frederick, as noted, was the only slave
in the region who could read and write. Sandy, on the other hand, was
an African-born priest, who was revered as a doctor and a spiritual
advisor.

It didn't take the two slave leaders long to decide that Frederick had
to go back to Covey or run away. Upon further consideration, it was
decided that escape was impossible. The Covey farm was on a narrow
neck of land, and every avenue of escape was closely guarded. There was
Chesapeake Bay to the right, and "Pot-pie" River to the left, and St.
Michaels lay athwart the only avenue of escape. There was no getting
around it: Frederick had to go back to Covey and face the music. With a
little luck, however, the music, or at least, the register of the music could
be changed. Sandy told Frederick that the root of a certain herb had
magical powers. He said that if Frederick would take it and wear it on
his right side it would be impossible for Covey to strike him. When
Frederick protested, Sandy retorted that he had carried the same root for
years, and that he had never been struck by a slaveholder.

Frederick, who had been reading European books and who was a
Christian to boot, believed it was beneath "one of his intelligence to
countenance such dealings with the devil." It seemed to him that all this

talk about roots was "very absurd and ridiculous, if not positively sinful." Sandy, who was wise in the ways of the world and young know-it-alls, gently and surgically demolished Frederick's arguments, saying in conclusion: "Your book-learning hasn't kept Covey off you."

This was a telling argument, and Frederick accepted the root and returned to the Covey farm, arriving on Sunday just as the slavemaster and his wife, dressed in their Sunday best and smiling like angels, emerged from the house. Somewhat to Frederick's surprise, Covey spoke to him as never before and asked after his health. Looking back later, Frederick said: "His manner perfectly astonished me. There was something really benignant in his countenance. He . . . seemed an altered man. This extraordinary conduct really made me begin to think that Sandy's herb had more virtue in it than I, in my pride, had been willing to allow, and had the day been other than Sunday, I should have attributed Covey's altered manner solely to the power of the root. I suspected, however, that the Sabbath, not the root, was the real explanation of the change. His religion hindered him from breaking the Sabbath, but not from breaking my skin on any other day than Sunday."

Sincere or not, Covey was punctiliously decorous all day Sunday. And he was strangely calm before daylight on Monday morning when he called Frederick to feed and curry the horses. Then, abruptly, the pendulum swung the other way. When Frederick turned his back and started climbing the stable loft, Covey pounced on him and threw him to the stable ground. Before Frederick could regain his senses, Covey pinned him and tried to slip a rope around his legs. As soon as Frederick figured out what the old Negro-breaker was up to, he gave a sudden spring with his legs, throwing Covey to the ground and defeating the plan to tie him down.

The two adversaries circled each other, lunged, and crashed to the ground. As they rolled from one end of the stable to the other, Frederick realized with a thrill that he was fighting, and fighting well. A part of his mind wondered "whence came the daring spirit necessary to grapple with a man who, eight-and-forty hours before, could, with his slightest word, have made me tremble like a leaf in a storm." He didn't know. The only thing he knew was that he was resolved to fight. "The fighting madness" had come upon him, and he found his fingers "firmly attached to the throat of the tyrant, as heedless of consequences, at the moment, as if we stood as equals before the law. The very color of the man was forgotten. I felt supple as a cat, and was ready for him at every turn. Every blow of his was parried, though I dealt no blows in return. I was strictly on the defensive, preventing him from injuring me, rather than trying to injure him. I flung him on the ground several times when he meant to have hurled me there. I held him so firmly by the throat that his blood followed my nails. He held me, and I held him."

Faced with this unexpected resistance, Covey wilted. He trembled in every limb, and his face grew pale.

"Are you going to resist, you scoundrel?" he asked.

"Yes, sir," Frederick replied, politely.

The answer disconcerted Covey, who was clearly frightened and stood puffing and blowing, unable to command words or blows.

Having become convinced that he could not conquer Frederick single-handedly, Covey called for his cousin Bill Hughes. This changed the odds, and Frederick was compelled to change his battle plan. He was compelled, he said later, "to give blows, as well as to parry them, and since I was in any case to suffer for resistance, I felt . . . that I might as well be hanged for an old sheep as a lamb. I was still defensive toward Covey, but aggressive toward Hughes, on whom at his first approach, I dealt a blow which fairly sickened him. He went off, bending over with pain, and manifesting no disposition to come again within my reach. The poor fellow was in the act of trying to catch and tie my right hand, and while flattering himself with success, I gave him the kick which sent him staggering away in pain, at the same time that I held Covey with a firm hand."

Beside himself with anxiety, Covey asked Frederick if he intended to persist in this resistance. Frederick said yes, that he had been treated like a dog for six months and he didn't intend to stand it any longer.

The words enraged Covey, who flipped Frederick over and tried to drag him to a stick outside the stable door. Anticipating the next move, Frederick waited until Covey leaned over to pick up the stick and then, "with a vigorous and sudden snatch," hurled him into the dung of the cowyard.

The sun was coming up over the eastern woods now, and the hands were gathering for work. When Bill Smith, the hired slave, arrived, he found his boss and his friend rolling and grunting, like wrestlers, in the dung and debris of the cowyard. Covey called to him immediately, but Smith affected ignorance.

"What shall I do, Master Covey?" he asked.

"Take hold of him! Take hold of him!"

"Indeed, Master Covey, I want to go to work."

"This is your work," Covey said. "Take hold of him."

Since it was no longer possible to pretend ignorance, Bill Smith screwed up his courage and spoke to the point.

"My master hired me here to work, and not to help you whip Frederick."

The subject of discussion emphasized that point, saying:

"Bill, don't put your hands on me."

"My God, Frederick," Bill replied, "I ain't going to tech ye."

With that parting shot, Bill Smith walked away, leaving Covey and the young slave to settle their own differences.

Covey made one final attempt to change the odds, calling to Caroline, a powerful slave woman who could have easily mastered Frederick. But Caroline refused. Frederick's infection was spreading; all of Covey's hands were in open rebellion.

Finally, after two hours of inconclusive struggle, Covey decided that he had had enough. Characteristically, he withdrew with a face-saving declaration. Huffing and puffing, blood trickling from scratches on his throat, he said: "Now, you scoundrel, go to your work; I would not have whipped you half so hard if you had not resisted." As a matter of fact, he had not whipped Frederick at all. And, although he dropped veiled threats from time to time, he never whipped Frederick again. Surprisingly, he did not even report the struggle to the authorities, and Frederick theorized later that "his interest and his pride" suggested the wisdom of passing the matter by in silence for "the story that he had undertaken to whip a lad and had been resisted, would of itself be damaging to him in the estimation of slaveholders."

Incomplete and inconclusive as the struggle had been, it was nevertheless a milestone in the life of Frederick Douglass. Ever afterwards, he called it "the turning point" in his life, saying: "It rekindled in my breast the smouldering embers of liberty. It . . . revived a sense of my own manhood. I was a changed being after that fight. I was nothing before— I was a man now. It recalled to life my crushed self-respect, and my self-confidence, and inspired me with a renewed determination to be a free man. A man without force is without the essential dignity of humanity. Human nature is so constituted, that it cannot honor a helpless man, though it can pity him, and even this it cannot do long if signs of power do not arise."

Douglass believed that no one could understand the effect of this struggle on his spirit who had not incurred something or hazarded something in defense of manhood or womanhood. After resisting Covey, he felt, he said, "as he had never felt before," adding: "It was a resurrection from the dark and pestiferous tomb of slavery, to the heaven of comparative freedom. . . . I had reached the point at which I was *not afraid to die.* This spirit made me a free man in *fact,* though I still remained a slave in *form.* When a slave cannot be flogged, he is more than half free."

Four years later, Frederick Augustus Washington Bailey completed his resurrection by escaping from slavery and settling in New England, where he changed his name and began his climb to fame as Frederick Douglass. As an abolitionist, editor, and national leader, he returned again and again to the lesson of the Covey fight:

Men are whipped oftenest who are whipped easiest.

Sweet Chariot

The Private War of Harriet Tubman

S HE came out of the night, silently, stealthily, mysteriously. Nobody knows how she came or when she came. But suddenly, inexplicably, she was there, on the edge of the slave quarters, singing a song old as the night and deep as the hopes of humanity.

> Hail, oh hail, ye happy spirits,
>> Death no more shall make you fear;
> Grief nor sorrow, pain nor anguish,
>> Shall no more distress you there.
>
> Around Him are ten thousand angels,
>> Always ready to obey command;
> They are always hovering around you,
>> Till you reach the heavenly land.

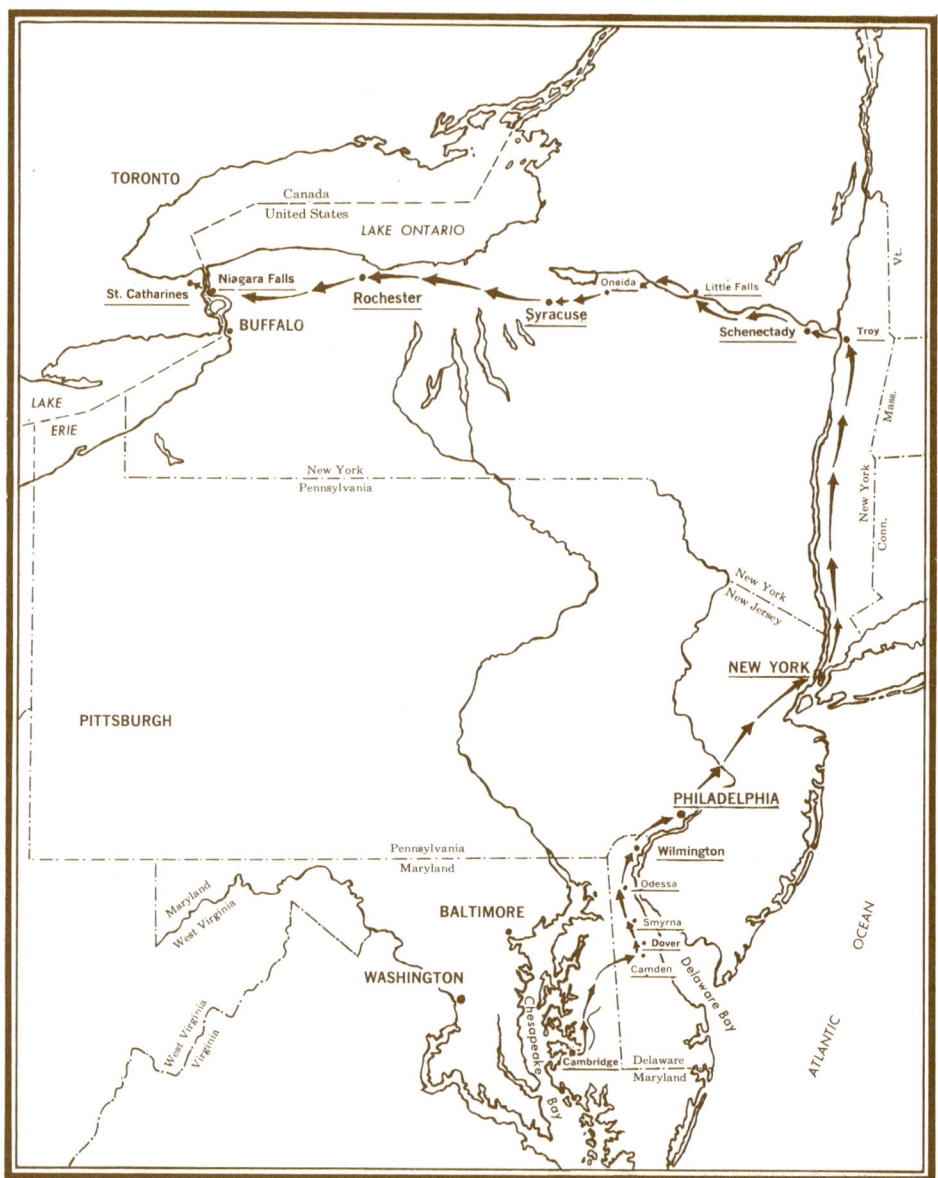

Led by Harriet Tubman, escaping slaves followed long trail (indicated by arrows) from Maryland to Canada.

The whistling wind of the cold December night carried the song across the Maryland countryside.* The slaveholders heard it, and dis-

---

* This is a historical reconstruction of the best documented of Harriet Tubman's nineteen guerrilla raids—the December, 1854, raid in the Cambridge, Md., area. The great slave rebel did not keep a journal, and this reconstruction is based on the known facts of the raids. Sometimes, she alerted slaves by rapping on the door of a slave cabin and whispering a few words before disappearing into the night.

missed it, thinking no doubt that it was just another Jesus-crazy old slave troubled by vague and incommunicative longings on the night before Christmas Eve. The slaves heard the song, probably with mixed emotions. Some, awakened unexpectedly in the night, undoubtedly expressed irritation and urged the singer to shut up. Others, one can imagine, awakened with a start and then lay in the close darkness, transfixed by the unfathomable mysteries communicated by the woman singing the song.

On typical raid, Harriet Tubman communicated with slaves by singing Spirituals.

Who was she?

How came she to the depths and the heights the song said she knew?

Of all those who heard the song, of all those who blessed and cursed the singer, only a handful knew that the song was more than a song. Only a handful knew that the song was a code, saying that the woman known as "the Woman," the woman known as "the General," the woman known as Moses, was in the Cambridge, Maryland, area, and doing business at the same old stands.

Jesus, Jesus will go with you,
   He will lead you to his throne;
He who died has gone before you,
   Trod the wine-press all alone.

In storage house, near home of her parents, abolitionist mapped plans for raid of 1854.

The words of the song rose, fell, and died away. And the men and women to whom the words were addressed, the men and women who *knew*, listened to the silence, knowing that it was time to fish or cut bait, and that the odds were with the fish. But what made the odds tolerable, or at least debatable, was the woman singing the song—Harriet Ross Tubman. She had escaped from slavery

in this very area, and had returned five times to lead out thirty or forty slaves. Now, in the Christmas, in 1854, she was back, calling for recruits. She had never lost a slave and had never failed to deliver on a promise. But nothing in this world was certain, and a slave escape was the most uncertain of the uncertainties.

William Still, "president of Underground Railroad," aided Tubman and her charges.

One may be sure that these and other thoughts occupied the minds of the slaves who waited now for the woman to give an all-clear sign. The sign would come in and through music. It was by songs that Harriet communicated her messages, and some of the songs had become so attached to her person and to her legend that it was widely believed that she had composed them. One of these songs was *Go Down Moses*. Another was *Swing Low, Sweet Chariot*. Still another was the song that broke the stillness of the night, a song "of plaintive minor strains, and unexpected quavers." There it was, again:

> Dark and thorny is the path,
>   Where the pilgrim makes his way;
> But beyond this vale of sorrow,
>   Lie the fields of endless days.

The voice in the wilderness repeated the verse twice and then was silent. This meant to the initiated that the way was clear, And, in the silence, the slaves who knew the code slipped out of their cabins and made their way to the area from which the voice had come. There, in the shadows of the trees, was the living legend. Certainly, some of the slaves were taken aback. For at first glance she didn't look like a giant-killer. Short, stout, black, with a full broad face, topped by a dashing turban, she seemed to be drowsy or disoriented. Was this the woman who had led slaves thousands of miles to freedom? Could she manage the thousand dangers that lay between Maryland and Canada? The answer was in the eyes, which were "magnetic," "fierce." And the eyes spoke for the thirty-four-year-old woman as she unexpectedly abandoned the "senile old woman" pose and assumed command, searching the faces of the potential recruits and satisfying herself that they had the guts to endure a long march. Satisfied, she designated a departure time and a rendezvous. She emphasized the time, for to her time was freedom. They would leave at the time designated or they would not leave at all: she would wait for no one. There were three other points. First: No one was to tell mother, brother, father, or sister that he was about to leave. Second: She, Harriet Tubman, was to be in complete control of the march. No one was to question her orders or her decisions. And there was to be no foolishness,

Last act in dramatic and dangerous trip was crossing bridge into Canada.

no whining or complaining on the trip. Third: There was to be no turning back. Anyone who enlisted was enlisted for the duration. It was either freedom or death. One can imagine that there was nervous laughter at this point, for it was well known that Harriet Tubman would destroy anyone and anything that endangered the lives and the freedom of her passengers. It was said that the way was sometimes so difficult and dangerous that people "who followed her would give out, and foot-sore, and bleeding, they would drop on the ground, groaning that they could not take another step. They would lie there and die, or if strength came back, they would return on their steps, and seek their old homes again. Then the revolver carried by this bold and daring pioneer, would come out, while pointing it at their heads she would say, 'Dead niggers tell no tales; you go on or die!' By this heroic treatment she compelled them to drag their weary limbs along on their northward journey."

These were the terms; and when the terms were accepted, Tubman dismissed the slaves, who returned to their cabins to sweat out the hours. While they waited, she moved noiselessly and swiftly through the night, darting in and out of the woods of Dorchester County, stopping here and there to examine and brief additional slaves.

As dawn neared, she quickened her pace. She was in a hurry. This trip was important to her. Three of her brothers were in danger of being sold and she had come South to move their cases to a higher court.

How did she know her brothers were in danger?

The word had come to her in one of her famous premonitions. She had been working in the North, saving her money for a slave strike, when, as she said later, she "became much troubled in spirit about her brothers." Acting upon this premonition, Tubman, who could neither read nor write, used a stratagem that had served her well in the past. She persuaded a friend to write a coded letter to Jacob Jackson, a literate free black who lived near the plantation where her three brothers worked. Since the authorities were monitoring the mail of Jacob Jackson, who was suspected of being involved in other slave rescues, it was necessary to use extreme caution. The letter sent to Jackson bore the signature of his adopted son, who lived in the North. The letter contained several innocuous paragraphs and the following message:

"Read my letter to the old folks, and give my love to them, and tell my brothers to be always *watching unto prayer*, and when *the good old ship of Zion comes along, to be ready to step on board*."

This was a blunder, for Jackson's parents were dead, and he had no brothers, two facts that aroused the suspicions of the inspectors who examined the mail of free blacks. The matter was discussed pro and con by the authorities, who finally summoned Jackson and asked him what the letter meant. Jackson recognized immediately that the letter meant that Harriet Tubman was coming and that he should alert her brothers, who, as she suspected, were in danger of being sold South. But nothing in his demeanor betrayed him as he read the letter slowly and then threw it down, saying: "That letter can't be meant for me no how; I can't make head or tail of it." After compounding the confusion of the inspectors, Jackson informed Harriet's brothers that she was on the way and that they should be ready at the signal to start for the North.

While these events were unfolding, Tubman was completing her preparations in the North. The trip required a certain amount of money for food, transportation, and bribes for greedy whites. There were other urgencies: a pair of stout shoes for days and nights of walking, paregoric for babies and others who could not be talked into silence, and a well-oiled revolver for various and sundry purposes. When these items were assembled in December, 1854, Tubman disappeared from her Northern haunts and reappeared in the thickly wooded forests surrounding the plantations of Dorchester County, Maryland.

And to understand the daring—and the grandeur—of her undertaking, it is necessary to step back from the details and focus a big spotlight on the woman behind the mission. Who was she? How did it happen that she was tramping through the forests of Dorchester County, Maryland, on a cold night in 1854 with her hand on a cocked revolver and fire in her eyes. The answer, in whole and in part, is slavery, which Tubman said was "the next thing to hell." She had been born in slavery in Dorchester County in 1820, one of eleven children of Benjamin and Harriet Ross and she had grown up, she said later, like "a neglected weed."

Strong of body and mind, Tubman enlisted in the war against slavery at an early age. She was only fifteen or sixteen when she placed herself between an overseer and an escaping slave. The overseer picked up a two-pound iron weight and threw it at the fugitive slave, but it fell short and struck Tubman on the head. The blow almost killed her and left a dent in her skull, a dent some scholars believe caused a constant pressure on her brain.

From that day until her death, she was bothered by "sleeping seizures." Two or three times a day, while she was working or talking, she would suddenly fall asleep. It was not a deep sleep, but it was a sleep troubled by voices and bloody visions. She saw blacks and whites fighting on slave ships, and she saw the bodies of white men lying in the blood on the decks. She saw black women leaping from the decks of slave ships with children clasped to their bosoms. She saw thundering horsemen and heard the screams of women and children as they were torn from one another. And always there were the voices, beckoning to her, saying, "Come!"

It was during this period that Harriet developed a personal relationship with spiritual forces beyond the reach or comprehension of most mortals. She talked with God, it was said, "as a man talketh with his friends." She believed that God was always with her and would let no harm befall her. The white people on the plantation, reporter Frank C. Drake said, "thought she was half-witted—*a theory she did not seek to disturb.*"

Miraculously, Harriet survived the blow to her head and to her spirit. And by the time she reached the age of nineteen she was something of a spitfire, a tough, indomitable woman who drove oxen, hauled wood, and split logs. It was said that she was a match for the strongest man on the plantation and that "she could lift huge barrels of produce and draw a loaded stone boat like an ox."

After marrying John Tubman, a free black, Harriet became increasingly obsessed with the idea of freedom. Finally, in 1849, after repeated visions in which voices told her, "Arise, flee for your life," Harriet ran away and settled in the North. And what was her reaction to freedom? "I looked at my hands," she said, "to see if I was the same person now I was free. There was such a glory over everything, the sun came like gold through the trees, and over the fields, and I felt like I was in heaven." But there was a devil in Harriet's heaven. She was free, but her people were not free. She was "a stranger in a strange land," and there could be no peace for her except in the peace and freedom of "the old folks, and my brothers and sisters." And so she came to a solemn resolve. "I was free, and they should be free also; I would make a home for them in the North, and the Lord helping me, I would bring them all there."

True to her rhetoric, she returned to the South in 1850 and rescued her sister and two children. From that moment until emancipation, she pressed a relentless private war against slavery. She worked in Cape May, New Jersey, and other Northern cities as a domestic to raise money for her raids and then swooped down on slave cabins in Maryland and other states. In 1851 she returned to the Cambridge area for her husband, but he had married another woman. Without a word, Harriet moved on, assembling a group of slaves and leading them to Philadelphia.

After passage of the Fugitive Slave Law, she moved to St. Catharines, Canada, from whence she made about two slave raids a year. By 1854 she had become a secular saint, the living legend Thomas Wentworth Higginson called "the greatest heroine of the age," the "military genius" William Still called "an adventurous spirit [who was] wholly without fear."

This was the woman who rendezvoused with a group of slaves on Christmas Eve, 1854, and set out for the Promised Land of Canada. The group included two of her brothers, Benjamin, twenty-eight, and Robert, thirty-five, and two slaves from nearby plantations, John Chase, twenty, and Peter Jackson. There was one woman, Jane Kane, twenty-two, who said her master, Rash Jones, was "the worst man in the country." Harriet ran her eyes over the group, noticing for the twentieth time that there was one absentee, her brother Henry. Where was he? What could have held him up? She looked to the left and to the right, looked up at the North Star, and then gave the word: forward. One can imagine the hurt in her heart. But it was a rule: Time was freedom, and she waited for no one. The first stop, she announced, would be the cabin of her parents forty miles to the north in Caroline County.

The Eastern Shore, with its forests and hills and rivers and creeks, was home base for Harriet, and she quickly and expertly led the group to the cabin of her elderly parents. It was late Christmas Eve when they arrived, and Harriet bypassed the cabin and established a command post in the fodder house. This was a tactical decision, which speaks volumes for the iron discipline Harriet demanded of herself and others. She had not seen her mother for five years, but her mother was given to emotional outbursts of screaming and crying, outbursts that could alert the enemy and endanger the plan. Rather than risk this, Harriet denied herself and her brothers what they desired most, the pleasure of speaking to their mother and comforting her. Without a trace of sentiment, Harriet sent two nonfamily members, John Chase and Peter Jackson, to awaken her father, who dressed hurriedly and brought food to the fodder house. Before entering the fodder house, Old Ben, as he was called, tied a handkerchief around his eyes. He was sure to be asked after the escape had he seen his children. And he wanted to be able to say with honesty in his voice that he had not *seen* them.

Despite this precaution, it was clear to Old Ben that someone was missing. Where was Henry? What had happened to him? Harriet didn't know, and his absence troubled her.

Henry was miles away, following the path left by Harriet. He had been poised to leave at the appointed hour when an emergency occurred. His wife, big with baby, had come down with labor pains, and Henry had hurried off to get the granny. After the baby was born, Henry tiptoed to the door, determined to seize what he believed was his last chance for freedom. The voice of his wife stopped him. "Where are you going, Henry?" She hadn't been told of the danger hanging over his head; but she sensed the uneasiness in him, and she knew, without knowing, that he was going to try to escape. Henry said nothing of this now, answering, as he went through the door, that he was going to see a man about some extra Christmas work. For a long time he stood outside the door, listening to the moans and sobs of his wife. And then, of a sudden, he threw open the doors and rushed to the arms of his wife. "Oh, Henry," she said. "You going to leave me. I know it. But wherever you go, Henry, don't forget me and the little children."

Henry assured her that he had no intention of leaving her and the children in slavery. Moses would come for her, he said, as she had come for him. With these words, he began his journey, and reached the fodder house at daybreak on Christmas morning.

By this time, rain was pouring down, and the little band of rebels huddled together for warmth and waited for nightfall. As they waited, they watched the mother and father through wide chinks in the boards of the fodder house. All day long, at measured intervals, the mother would come out of the cabin and look down the road to see if "the boys" were on their way. They had always come before on Christmas day, and this was a special Christmas. The pig had been slaughtered, and the bacon and sausages and chitlins were ready. What could have happened to the "boys"? Had they been sold South? Would she never see them again?

From their hiding places in the fodder house, a few yards away, Harriet and "the boys" watched, biting their lips and remaining silent. When at last darkness came, they went up to the cabin and peered through the window. "Through the little window of the cabin," Harriet told her biographer, "they saw [the mother] sitting by the fire, her head on her hand, rocking back and forth, as was her way when she was in great trouble, praying no doubt, and wondering what had become of her children." Tears streaming down their eyes, Harriet Tubman and "the boys" said "Merry Christmas" and farewell, silently, and walked into the night toward freedom.

Thus began a hazardous trip of hundreds of miles with each step a threat. The trip led northward and eastward to the Delaware line and northward to Wilmington, Delaware. Traveling by night, hiding by day, fording streams and creeks, threading the forests, always aware of the pursuers behind them and the allies of the pursuers all around them, Harriet and her passengers moved doggedly onward, following the North Star. There was no rhyme or reason to the route. It zigged and zagged and doubled back on itself. The only map was the exigency of the moment. The only road was survival. The only guide was the improvisational genius of Harriet Tubman. There was a reward of twelve thousand dollars on her head, and she probably would have been burned alive if caught. But this didn't seem to bother her as she played cat and mouse with the military might of the South. Sometimes, in response to the internal antenna which always warned her of danger, she ordered a change in the route. Sometimes she hid the group in the forest or in a ditch and went on ahead to scout the territory and forage for food or assistance. Returning, she would inform them of the lay of the land by a prearranged Spiritual code. "If I remember correctly," suffragette leader Alice Stone Blackwell said, "Harriet Tubman told me that when she was convoying parties of fugitives, she used to guide them by the songs that she sang as she walked along the roads. . . . It was when her parties of fugitives were in hiding that she directed them by her songs, as to whether they might show themselves, or must continue to lie low. . . . No one would notice what was sung by an old colored woman, as she trudged along the road."

From Maryland to Delaware and beyond, Harriet was constantly planning, improvising, and acting. Indeed, some of her fans and passengers believed she was one of the most accomplished actresses of the century. "One of her masterly acomplishments," Thomas Wentworth Higginson recalled, "was the impression of an decrepit old woman. On one of her expeditions . . . she had the incredible nerve to enter a village where lived one of her former masters. This was necessary for the carrying out of her plans for that trip. Her only disguise was a bodily assumption of age. To reinforce this, her subtle foresight prompted her to buy some live chickens which she carried suspended by the legs from a cord. As she turned a corner she saw coming toward her none other than her old master. Lest he might see through her impersonation and to make an excuse for flight, she loosed the cord that held the fowls and amid the laughter of the bystanders, gave chase to them as they flew, squawking over a nearby fence." A cool customer, Harriet—cool, confident, and fearless, never at a loss for the right gesture or the right tactic.

Most of the trip was made on foot. But with the assistance of black and white members of the Underground Railroad, the pilgrims used every mode of transport and were sheltered in buildings and homes of all sizes and shapes.

Harriet did not keep a journal of her trips, and it is not possible to list every stop she made. But on her way to Wilmington she usually passed through Camden, Dover, Smyrna, and Odessa. "At Camden, for example," as author Earl Conrad has written, "Harriet and her broods put up at the Cooper House; a regular stopover for fugitives. This gray-painted brick house was near the north entrance of the village. Negroes were concealed in a small, bunk-lined room above the kitchen. This hideout was entered by a ladder, and a round window near the peak of the roof admitted light and air. At Odessa, Delaware, the slaves often stayed at the Friends Meeting House, on the south side of the main street. It was a plain brick structure about twenty feet square, with a pitched roof and pent eaves across the gable ends. This roof covered a loft in which the blacks hid."

And so, hunted, hidden, and harried, with Harriet Tubman bullying, encouraging and leading, the pilgrims found themselves at last in Wilmington, where they were aided by the famous Underground Railroad conductor, Thomas Garrett. In a letter to J. Miller McKim of the Philadelphia Vigilance committee, Quaker Garrett said "we made arrangements last night [December 28] and sent away Harriet Tubman with six men and one woman to Allen Agnew's, to be forwarded across the country to the city. Harriet, and one of the men had worn their shoes off their feet and I gave them two dollars to help fit them out, and directed a carriage to be hired at my expense, to take them out. . . ."

In Philadelphia Harriet and her passengers were received and "examined" by William Still, the bold black leader of the Underground Railroad. Still revered Tubman and considered her the greatest of all American heroines. She was, he recalled later, "a woman of no pretensions, indeed, a more ordinary specimen of humanity could hardly be found among the most unfortunate-looking farm hands of the South. Yet, in point of courage, shrewdness and disinterested exertions to rescue her fellow-men, by making personal visits to Maryland among the slaves, she was without equal."

Still said that her success at this difficult and dangerous task "was wonderful. Time and again she made successful visits to Maryland on the Underground Rail Road, and would be absent for weeks at a time, running daily risks while making preparations for herself and passengers. Great fears were entertained for her safety, but she seemed wholly devoid of personal fear. The idea of being captured by slave-hunters or slave-holders, seemed never to enter her mind. She was apparently proof against all adversaries. While she thus manifested such utter personal indifference, she was much more watchful with regard to those she was piloting. Half of her time, she had the appearance of one asleep, and would actually sit down by the road-side and go fast asleep when on her errands of mercy through the South, yet, she would not suffer one of her party to whimper once, about 'giving out and going back,' however wearied they might be from hard travel day and night. She had a very short and pointed rule or law of her own, which implied death to any one who talked of giving out and going back. Thus, in an emergency, she would give all to understand that 'times were very critical and therefore no foolishness would be indulged in on the road.' That several who were rather weak-kneed and faint-hearted were greatly invigorated by Harriet's blunt and positive manner and threat of extreme measures, there could be no doubt. . . . So when she said to them that 'a live runaway could do great harm by going back, but that a dead one could tell no secrets' she was sure to have obedience. Therefore, none had to die as traitors on the 'middle passage.' It is obvious enough, however, that her success in going into Maryland as she did, was attributable to her adventurous spirit and utter disregard of consequences. Her like it is probable was never known before or since. . . ."

It was with this understanding that Still greeted Harriet Tubman and her passengers. Under the rules of the Underground Railroad, Still and his committee were required to examine passengers and record their names and ages. A record of his examination on this occasion survives and throws a revealing light on the background and motivations of Tubman's passengers. Here are some excerpts:

December 29th, 1854—John is twenty years of age, chestnut color, of spare build and smart. He fled from a farmer, by the name of John Campbell Henry, who resided at Cambridge, Dorchester Co., Maryland. On being interrogated relative to the character of his master, John gave no very amiable account of him. He testified that he was a "hard man" and that "he owned about one hundred and forty slaves and sometimes he would sell," etc. John was one of the slaves who were "hired out." He desired to have the privilege of hunting his own master. His desire was not granted. Instead of meekly submitting, John felt wronged, and made this his reason for running away. This looked pretty spirited on the part of one so young as John. The Committee's respect for him was not a little increased, when they heard him express himself.

Benjamin was twenty-eight years old, chestnut color, medium size and shrewd. He was the so-called property of Eliza Ann Brodins, who lived near Buckstown, in Maryland. Ben did not hesitate to say, in unqualified terms, that his mistress was "very devilish." He considered his charges proved by the fact that three slaves (himself one of them) were required to work hard and fare meagerely, to support his mistress' family in idleness and luxury. . . .

Henry left his wife, Harriet Ann, to be known in future by the name of "Sophia Brown." He was a fellow-servant of Ben's, and one of the supports of Eliza A. Brodins.

Henry was only twenty-two, but had quite an insight into matters and things going on among slaves and slave-holders generally, in country life. He was the father of two small children, whom he had to leave behind.

Peter was owned by George Wenthrop, a farmer, living near Cambridge, Maryland. In answer to the question, how he had been used, he said "hard." Not a pleasant thought did he entertain respecting his master, save that he was no longer to demand the sweat of Peter's brow. . . .

Jane, aged twenty-two, instead of regretting that she had unadvisedly left a kind mistress and indulgent master, who had afforded her necessary comforts, affirmed that her master, "Rash Jones, was the worst man in the country." The Committee were at first disposed to doubt her sweeping statement, but when they heard particularly how she had been treated, they thought Catherine had good ground for all that she said. Personal abuse and hard usage were the common lot of poor slave girls.

Robert was thirty-five years of age, of a chestnut color, and well made. His report was similar to that of many others. He had been provided with plenty of hard drudgery—hewing of wood and drawing of water, and had hardly been treated as well as a gentleman would treat a dumb brute. His feelings, therefore, on leaving his master and home, were those of an individual who has been unjustly in prison for a dozen years and had at last regained his liberty.

After the examination of Robert and the other passengers, Still and his group provided clothing, food, and money and, according to the surviving report, "they went on their way rejoicing."

From Philadelphia, Harriet and her pilgrims traveled to New York City, Troy, Syracuse, and Rochester, New York. They walked part of the way but also used boats, wagons, and even the railroad. This part of the trip was less hazardous than the journey through Delaware and Maryland; but it was still perilous, and constant vigilance was necessary to outwit lawmen and professional slavehunters, who were vested with enormous power under the Fugitive Slave Law. For this reason and for others as well, Harriet frowned on premature celebrations and insisted on maximum discipline until the group reached Niagara Falls. Then, as the pilgrims crossed Suspension Bridge into Canada, the human being behind the military commander would explode into song:

Glory to God and Jesus too,
One more soul is safe!
Oh, go and carry the news,
One more soul got safe!

As soon as her charges were settled in St. Catharines, Harriet returned to her private war, rescuing other members of her family and some two hundred and fifty additional slaves. In 1847 she carried out her most daring and dramatic rescue, freeing her mother and father who were then too old to walk far. "She brought away her parents," Thomas Garrett said, "in a singular style with a straw collar, a pair of old chaise wheels, with a board on the axle to sit on, another board swung with ropes, fastened to the axle to rest their feet on. She got her parents . . . on this crude vehicle to the railroad, put them in the cars, turned Jehu herself, and drove to town in a style that no other human being ever did before or since. . . ."

When the United States finally got around to endorsing General Tubman's war, she merged her efforts with the Union efforts, distinguishing herself as a guerrilla leader and scout. Later, when the promises of emancipation were betrayed, she went back to the front, this time as a soldier in the war against poverty and inequality. She was fighting that war in the fiftieth year of emancipation when she had her last vision. "I am nearing the end of my journey," she told the members of the AME Zion Church of Auburn, New York. "I can hear the bells a-ringing, I can hear the angels singing, I can see the hosts a-marching." Soon afterwards, on March 10, 1913, Harriet Tubman crossed her last river and went, if there is any justice in the universe, to her reward, with bells ringing, angels singing, and hosts marching.

Black and Blue

The Shootout at Chaffin's Farm

T HE name was deceptive. Chaffin's Farm was no farm or, to be more
precise, it was no longer a farm. A former producer of the raw materials of life, the farm on the outskirts of Richmond, Virginia, had
been transformed in the course of the Civil War into a producer of the
raw materials of death. The land where cattle and swine once grazed was
now honeycombed with foxholes and fortifications. The fields that once
yielded harvests of grain and vegetables now yielded harvests of corpses.

Geography defined this death farm. It lay athwart the main approaches to the Confederate capital and was the key to the defense of the
city. Whoever controlled the fortifications in and around Chaffin's Farm
controlled Richmond.*

---

* The principal Confederate entrenchments in the Richmond suburb were in and around
Chaffin's Bluff and Chaffin's Farm. The series of battles [New Market Heights, Fort Harrison,
Fort Gilmer, Laurel Hills] in the Richmond suburbs on September 29–30, 1864, is generally
called the Battle of Chaffn's Farm.

Hero of Chaffin's Farm battle, Cpl. Miles James continued to fight despite shattered arm.

By a quirk of fate, these heavily entrenched fortifications, so vital to the war effort of the defenders of black slavery, became the focal point of perhaps the greatest thrust by black soldiers in any war. In some thirty minutes of brilliant fighting on New Market Heights on a bloody Thursday morning in September, 1864, black soldiers captured the outer defenses of the Chaffin fortifications and won thirteen Congressional Medals of Honor—more Medals of Honor than were awarded to black soldiers in all the wars and years between the Spanish-American War and the Korean War.*

The charge at New Market Heights and the subsequent thrusts and parries at other Chaffin's Farm entrenchments [Fort Harrison and Fort Gilmer] grew out of and reflected the ambiguities of the Civil War which, by the fall of 1864, was grinding to a bloody climax. By this time, the Army of the James was stymied on the Petersburg line. By this time, too, black soldiers, who had fought splendidly in hundreds of battles, had

---

* From the Spanish-American War to the Korean War, black soldiers were systematically denied Medals of Honor for racial reasons.

been relegated to support roles and suicidal charges. This bothered a number of men and women, including a controversial and crafty Union general named Benjamin Franklin Butler. Butler was a New England lawyer with an instinct for dramatic gestures. He had no previous battle-field experience, and it was widely said that he was a political general who couldn't fight his way out of a paper bag. Partly to meet this charge, and partly, he said, to vindicate black soldiers, Butler conceived the idea of a surprise attack on the supposedly impregnable fortifications on Chaffin's Farm. In drawing up his plans, Butler was not unmindful of the fact that a white force commanded by General W. S. Hancock had just been repulsed at New Market Heights. Butler intended to succeed where others had failed, and he intended to succeed with an integrated force. As Butler saw it, he had everything to gain and nothing to lose. If his plan succeeded, he would establish the first Union toehold in the Richmond suburb. If he got a little luck, he would capture the Chaffin fortifications and march into the Confederate capital. Either way, he would have a

Black soldiers drove rebels from their entrenchments on New Market Heights.

laugh on critics who said he could talk but couldn't fight. Beyond all that, Butler wanted to deal with the black-white issue. He told his superior, General Ulysses S. Grant, that "the Negro troops had had no chance to show their valor or staying qualities in action" on the Virginia front. "I told him," he added, "that I meant to take a large part of my Negro force, and under my personal command make an attack upon New Market Heights, the redoubt to the extreme left of the enemy's line. . . . I said I want to convince myself whether, when under my own eye, the Negro troops will fight; and if I can take with the Negroes, a redoubt that turned Hancock's corps on a former occasion, that will settle the question." That question, of course, had long since been settled, but in this war, as in every other war, black soldiers were called upon to prove, over and over again, that they were human.

With Grant's approval, Butler drew up a plan that relied heavily on the skill and courage of black soldiers. The all-black Third Division of the Eighteenth Corps would initiate the assault at dawn with a bayonet charge up Spring Hill, which commanded the approaches to New Market Road and the intersection of New Market and Kingsland roads. The white divisions of the Tenth Corps would then proceed up New Market Road toward Richmond. Simultaneously, the white divisions of the Eighteenth Corps would advance on Varina Road, near the James River, and assault the Confederate works at Fort Harrison, near Chaffin's Bluff. The key to the plan was surprise. The black and white soldiers were to cross the James River on muffled pontoon bridges at midnight and fall on the surprised rebels at dawn.

Butler went to extraordinary lengths to insure the secrecy of the plan. All instructions were transmitted verbally and subordinates were ordered to keep the details to themselves. No one below the rank of corps commander was told the objectives or the route of march. Despite the secrecy, there was considerable speculation in the tents of the Eighteenth Corps on the south side of the James River and the Tenth Corps on the Petersburg front. An echo of this can be detected in the writings of Private A. H. Newton of the all-black Twenty-ninth Regiment of Connecticut. "I somehow had the feeling," he wrote, "that something was going on, or was going to happen, that would require one to be wise and cunning. The officers had a queer expression on their faces, and in fact all the field officers seemed to be uneasy."

The foreboding of the foot soldiers became more precise on Wednesday afternoon, September 27, when the Tenth Corps was ordered to prepare for an immediate march to an unknown destination. The soldiers were told to leave all their worldly goods except a single blanket rolled over their shoulders and a haversack with "three days' cooked rations" and sixty rounds of cartridges. Later that day, similar orders were issued to the Eighteenth Corps.

The Tenth Corps marched all afternoon and reached the banks of the James River after midnight. Meanwhile, the first detachments of the Eighteenth Corps were stealing silently across the James on pontoon bridges at Aiken's Landing. Before dawn, the first phase of the plan was complete, and the soldiers—black and white—were bivouacked in corn fields and woods on the north side of the James. There were nine black regiments in this attacking force, including the Fourth (Maryland), Fifth (Ohio), Sixth (Pennsylvania), Seventh (Maryland), Eighth (Pennsylvania), Thirty-sixth (North Carolina), and Thirty-eighth (Virginia) USCT regiments. Most of the soldiers in these regiments were former

In dress uniforms, black soldiers of U.S. Colored Troops pose for formal picture.

slaves, and most of them were seasoned veterans who had won battle stars at Wilson's Wharf, Suffolk, Petersburg, and Olustee.*

It did not take these soldiers long to realize that something big was in the works, and that the sun would bring trouble and blood. Some soldiers prayed. Some cursed. Some sang:

> Sure, I must fight if I would win,
> Increase my courage, Lord. . . .

At about 3 A.M., the black soldiers of the Third Division of the Eighteenth Corps (temporarily attached to the Tenth Corps) were marched to a point near the intersection of New Market and Kingsland roads and ordered to lie down in place. An hour passed, and then Major General B. F. Butler materialized with the orders of the day.

"At half past four o' clock," General Butler remembered later, "I found the colored division, rising three thousand men, occupying a plain which shelved towards the river, so that they were not observed by the enemy at Newmarket [sic] Heights. They were formed in close column of division right in front. I rode through the division, addressed a few words of encouragement and confidence to the troops. I told them this was an attack where I expected them to go over and take a work which would be before them after they got over the hill, and that they must take it at all hazards, and that when they went over the parapet into it their war cry should be, 'Remember Fort Pillow.' " **

Butler was a dandy with a flair for dramatics, and one can imagine the passion he invoked in this little scene, which ended with a chilling order. The soldiers were to advance in close column by divisions. There was to be no halt after they turned the brow of the hill.

The soldiers advanced, disappearing into an early-morning fog "that enwrapped them," an onlooker said, "like a mantle of death." Far to the east, the first red glow of the sun pierced the darkness, and tiny beams of light searched the faces of the candidates for death and heroism. It was 4:30 A.M., Thursday, September 29, 1864.

As soon as the men reached the brow of the hill, the enormity of the task before them became apparent. The hill plunged downwards to a creek, which drained a swamp to the left. The ground then rose at an

---

*Black regiments were officially identified as United States Colored Troops (USCT).
**Black soldiers were massacred at Fort Pillow, Tennessee, on April 12, 1864.

angle of thirty to thirty-five degrees to an abatis (heavy trees, cut down and arranged end to end, with the tops cut off and the branches sharpened and interlaced). One hundred yards from this first abatis, straight up, was a second abatis. Fifty yards from this was a square redoubt manned by some one thousand rebel soldiers, who opened fire and shouted, "Come on, darkies, we want your muskets!"

The black soldiers obliged, marching down the slope, Butler said, "as if on parade." The line wavered at the creek, where the left wing got bogged down in the mud of the swamp. There was confusion for a moment; and then, under a withering fire of artillery and musketry, the line righted itself and the soldiers splashed through the creek, holding their rifles over their heads. Having crossed this barrier, the soldiers abandoned formal maneuvers and thundered up the hill, line after line falling to the ground, Sergeant Major Christian A. Fleetwood wrote, "as hailstones sweep the leaves from the trees." On the way up the slope, the soldiers recoiled for a moment and then reformed at the call of a brave black bugler, who led them to the first line of abatis. On command, pioneer axmen sprang forward and hacked away at the abatis. The first line of axmen was cut down by enemy fire and was replaced by a second and third line. Finally, after what seemed like hours, gaping holes were opened in the abatis and the soldiers barrelled through, heads low, knees high, presenting as small a target as possible. There was only one abatis left, and it was one hundred yards away. The soldiers charged this final obstacle, vaulting over the bodies of their fallen comrades.

Now, by this time, all was confusion, and the laws of death had nullified the Jim Crow laws of the Union Army by eliminating almost all of the white company officers. Whole companies and whole columns were now under the command of black sergeants and black corporals. In the Fifth USCT, for example, Sergeant Major Milton M. Holland of Athens, Ohio, was commanding Company C; First-Sergeant James H. Bronson of Indiana County, Pennsylvania, was in charge of Company D; First-Sergeant Robert Pinn of Massillon, Ohio, was the de facto captain of Company I; and First-Sergeant Powhatan Beaty of Richmond was calling the shots in Company G. In the Thirty-eighth USCT, First-Sergeant Edward Ratcliff of James County, Virginia, was thrown into command of his company by the death of the captain and was, according to the official report, "the first enlisted man in the enemy's works, leading his company with great gallantry."

Under the leadership of these soldiers, all of whom received Congressional Medals of Honor for "gallantly and meritoriously" leading their companies after all the company officers had been killed or wounded, the Fifth USCT and the Sixth, Eighth, Thirty-sixth and Thirty-eighth regiments, many of whose companies were also led by black noncommissioned officers, reached historic heights of courage. When the color sergeant of the Fourth USCT was cut down beside him, Sergeant Alfred B. Hilton, bearer of the United States flag, picked up the regimental standard and surged forward with both colors until he was disabled by a severe wound at the second line of abatis. And "when on the ground," the official report said, "he showed that his thoughts were for the colors and not for himself." Similar feats were performed by Charles Veal, color bearer of Company D, Fourth USCT; Alexander Kelley, first-sergeant, Company F, Sixth USCT, and Christian A. Fleetwood, sergeant-major, Fourth USCT, all of whom received Congressional Medals of Honor. "I have never been able to understand," Fleetwood said later, "how Veal and I lived through such a hail of bullets, unless it was because we were both such little fellows. I think I weighed then about 125 pounds and Veal about the same. We did not get a scratch. A bullet passed between my legs, cutting my boot leg trousers and even my stockings, without breaking the skin."

In the midst of all this, Corporal Miles James, Thirty-sixth USCT, was slammed to the ground by a bullet that shattered his arm so badly that immediate amputation was necessary. Despite the pain of the gory stump on his side, Corporal James got up, loaded and discharged his piece with one hand and urged his men forward.

Led and inspired by these and other men, the Second and Third Brigades of the Third Division pressed forward, reaching the second and final abatis. Again the axmen sprang forward. Again sharpshooters leisurely picked them off. Again the fallen axmen were promptly replaced by new men, who finally breached the final obstacle. Screaming "Remember Fort Pillow!" the black soldiers rushed through the holes and swept up the hill. The astonished Confederate soldiers threw down their arms and ran, pursued by triumphant blacks, who drove them from a second line of entrenchments. The official records are not entirely clear, but it was apparently at this point that a Confederate officer leaped upon a parapet, waving his sword, and shouted, "Hurrah my brave men." Private James Gardner, Thirty-sixth USCT, rushed in advance of the Second Brigade and ran his bayonet through the officer's body to the muzzle. Another hero of the day was Private William H. Barnes, who was, the official report said, "among the very first to enter the rebel works, although himself previously wounded. . . ." General Butler said later, "As I rode across the brook and up towards the fort along this line of charge, some eighty feet wide and three or four hundred yards long, there lay in my path five hundred and forty-three dead and wounded of my colored comrades. And as I guided my horse this way and that way that his hoof might not profane their dead bodies, I swore to myself an oath, which I hope and believe I have kept sacredly, that they and their race should be cared for and protected by me to the extent of my power so long as I lived."

The capture of New Market Heights opened the front door of the Chaffin's Farm fortifications, and many rebel soldiers, finding their position untenable, fell back to the inner lines of defense. This made it possible for the entire Tenth Corps to move down the New Market Road toward Richmond. Lieutenant Colonel James F. Randlett of the Third New Hampshire Infantry (white) reported that "the enemy, discovering the success of the colored troops on my left, gave up their works without much struggle."

The situation at this point was fraught with portentous possibilities, and the leading men on both sides rushed to the battlefield. General Grant came up from City Points, and General Robert E. Lee rushed to the scene from his headquarters. As all this happened, there were wild scenes of panic in Richmond. J. B. Jones noted in a *Rebel War Clerk's Diary* that "the offices and government shops were closed and the tocsin was sounded for hours. All the local troops were hurried out to defend the city and guards on foot and horseback scoured the streets with orders to arrest every male person between the ages of seventeen and fifty and send them to Cary Street for service."

Meanwhile, the pressures on Richmond increased appreciably. As the Tenth Corps advanced on New Market Road, the Eighteenth Corps pressed the attack on the Varina Road, smashing through the rebel defenses and capturing Fort Harrison. For a brief moment, the road to Richmond was wide open. But poor communications delayed the Union advance and permitted the Confederates to reinforce the last line of defense at Fort Gilmer, some four miles from Richmond. Here, late in the afternoon, Confederate troops repulsed a charge by a white regiment, which fell back, the official report said, "in some confusion." At that juncture, the black brigade of the Tenth Corps was thrown into the fray. After the Ninth USCT attempted unsuccessfully to storm the works to the left of Fort Gilmer, four companies of the Seventh USCT were ordered to make a suicidal charge on the main entrenchments. The task, as Captain Julius A. Weiss pointed out, was virtually impossible for such a small force. The fort was some 1,400 yards away. The attacking force would have to cross an open plane and three ravines, filled with fallen trees; and it would be exposed along the whole way to enfilading fire from artillery on the left and right. Despite Weiss's protests, the four companies were ordered to prepare for an immediate assault.

The battlefield resounded now with screams and curses, punctuated by the explosion of artillery shells and the whining pitch of minie balls. "The doctors were busy sawing off legs and arms, and binding up wounds, and giving medicine to the wounded and sick," Private A. H. Newton of the Twenty-ninth Regiment, noted, adding: "[The] wounded and dying, scattered over the battlefield thick, the hurrying to and fro of the physicians and nurses; the prayers and groans and cries of the wounded, the explosion of bombs, the whizzing of bullets, the cracking of rifles; you would have thought that the very forces of hell had been set loose."

It was in this setting that Companies C, D, G and K of the Seventh USCT made one of the most gallant charges of the war, sprinting across the open plain, struggling through three ravines and reaching the great ditch which protected the fort. "[The ditch]," Captain Weiss recalled, "was some six or seven feet deep and ten or twelve wide. . . . Some one hundred twenty men and officers precipitated themselves into it, many losing their lives at its very edge. After a short breathing spell, men were helped up the exterior slope of the parapet on the shoulders of others, and fifty or sixty being thus disposed, an attempt was made to storm the fort. At the signal nearly all arose, but the enemy lying securely sheltered behind the exterior slope, the muzzles of their guns almost touching the storming party, received the latter with a crushing fire, sending many into the ditch below, shot through the brain or breast. Several other attempts were made with like result, till at last forty or more of the assailants were writhing in the ditch or silenced forever." When it became apparent that the mission was impossible, Captain Weiss and the survivors surrendered. Every soldier in the four companies, with the exception of three men, was either killed, wounded, or captured.

The successful stand of the Fort Gilmer rebels halted the Union advance, but the new Union outposts at New Market Heights and Fort Harrison were drawn daggers pointing to the aorta of the Confederacy. General Lee perceived this almost immediately and called in all available forces for a desperate counter-offensive. On the next day, Friday, September 30, Lee sent ten of the South's best brigades against the black and white Union soldiers in Fort Harrison. The *Army and Navy Journal* said that "on Friday, the 30th, about 2 o'clock the enemy made his appearance in heavy force, having been largely reinforced during the night and morning from Petersburg. In front of [G. J.] Stannard's division of the Eighteenth Corps . . . the whole of [Robert] Hoke's division is said to have been massed, General Lee superintending the attack. His object was to break through the captured entrenchment, and to separate the Eighteenth and Tenth Corps. Paine's colored division was [in position] on the left of the colored division which formed the left of the Tenth Corps. On these, about 2 o'clock, the enemy hurled themselves with great violence. He began by a furious cannonade of fifteen or twenty minutes, which was answered by our artillery. Our colored soldiers stood their ground with fidelity, and delivered a withering fire of musketry."

After the first and second charges were driven back, Lee or one of his lieutenants ordered a charge against the section of the line manned by the black veterans of New Market Heights. With a wild rebel yell, the Confederate soldiers dashed across the plain, fear and hate in their eyes. The black soldiers held their fire until the last minute and then squeezed the triggers, splattering the first and second waves. But the first and second waves were followed by other waves and the rebels finally reached the edge of the Union lines. For a long agonizing moment, free black men, freedmen and former slaves, stood toe to toe and bayonet to bayonet with the South's finest, hacking and slashing. This classic confrontation, so important to the Union and the Confederacy, held the attention of both generals and foot soldiers. So great was the realization of the danger, wrote Lieutenant R. B. Prescott, "so keen the anxiety, so doubtful the issue, that every eye was riveted upon [the scene], unmindful of the storm of lead and iron that the Confederate sharpshooters and artillery poured upon us from every available point. It seemed impossible for any to escape, but happily in a few moments, the Confederates broke in disorder and sought safety under the protecting guns of Fort Gilmer, while the Union troops shouted themselves hoarse with delight."

The meaning of this episode was clear to all the parties concerned. Union soldiers—black and white—occupied unassailable ramparts within sight and sound of the Confederate capital. And Lieutenant Prescott, cheering on the parapet of Fort Harrison, believed he could see "the beginning of the end" of the Confederacy.

*Almost Free
at Last*

The Day Slavery Died

SINCE early morning, long lines had been streaming into the Capitol and before noon the galleries of the House of Representatives were filled to overflowing. The crowd spilled over onto the floor, and the corridors and lobbies were clogged with people anxiously awaiting a decision on the future of slavery in the United States of America. That decision was going to come in a vote on a resolution authorizing submission of a proposed Thirteenth Amendment to the Constitution. Nobody knew for sure how the vote was going to turn out, but one thing was certain: it was going to be close, *very* close. The issue before the House today—Tuesday, January 31, 1865—was a substantive matter requiring a two-thirds majority. Did the antislavery forces have the votes? Had they been able to win over or intimidate or buy out the proslavery forces massed behind Tammany Hall and the Democratic party? These and other questions excited the attention of the chattering citizens as they sat, expectantly, on the edge of the benches, watching the clock and awaiting the decision of the day.

113

The day had been a long time coming. A long time before the gathering of this group, a thing called slavery, a thing of colors, of white cotton and black bodies and red blood and gold, had wormed its way into the tissues of America. The thing had spread, had compromised the white founding fathers, had grown tumors of corruption and hate and division. It had finally split the nation, and men—Yankees and Rebels, blacks and whites—were killling one another at this very moment over it. For some sixty years, this issue had convulsed the nation. Time and time again, men had tried to hide it, compromise it, finesse it. Time and time again, men had announced to themselves and to the world that it was settled forever. In 1861 another Congress had passed and sent to the states for ratification a thirteenth amendment guaranteeing the existence of slavery in America forever. The rebellion of the slave states had short-circuited the ratification process, and Abraham Lincoln had finally issued an Emancipation Proclamation, which had, as they said, settled the matter forever. But as the war drew to a close, it became increasingly clear, even to Lincoln, that nothing had been settled by the Proclamation, which was a war measure of doubtful legality and limited scope. By 1864, according to one estimate, one out of every three slaves—some 1,300,000—had been freed by the Proclamation and the events of the war. But the status of the freedmen and the status of the blacks still in slavery would be questionable once the war ended. Far more important to Northern whites was the status of the United States of America. Slavery was still a live issue in the states of the Confederacy, and it had passionate partisans in New York, Pennsylvania, Ohio, Wisconsin, and other Union states. More ominously, slavery was still entrenched in the codes and institutions and even the Constitution of the United States. And this meant that the question of the meaning of slavery could only be settled by a constitutional amendment that redefined the meaning of America. For some sixty years, this question had been nagging at the conscience of the country. Now, on January 31, 1865, it was going to be dealt with, one way or another; and some of the people assembled believed they had ringside seats for "the final and

Congressman Thaddeus Stevens of Pennsylvania led fight for passage of measure.

Huge throng gathered at Capitol to witness historic scenes surrounding the debate.

decisive conflict between slavery and freedom."

As the hour of decision approached, the House crackled with excitement. In the galleries and in the corridors, private citizens were arguing issues and principles. But on the floor, in the midst of the battle, the professionals were counting. It was a matter of arithmetic. The tally sheets listed 183 members. Two-thirds of the members were needed for passage. Who is with us, and who is against us? That was the question, the only question really, to the lobbyists and political soldiers in the trenches. Prominent among the lobbyists was a committee of substantial New Yorkers representing the Union League Club. These gentlemen had come down from New York City to argue against the dominant posture of the Democratic organization of Brooklyn and New York City. And in the minutes before the opening of the session, they surveyed the field of battle and made the following evaluation: "Hope predominated; with some almost amounted to a certainty; but even the most hopeful were conscious of a deep anxiety. . . . Up to noon of Tuesday, the proslavery [advocates] are said to have been confident of defeating the amendment, and after that time had passed one of the most earnest advocates of the measure said to [us] of the coming vote, 'tis the toss of a copper!"

Now, shortly before noon, there was not an empty seat in the House.

Henry Highland Garnet delivered sermon
in House after passage of Amendment.

The men's gallery, an eyewitness said, "was crowded with civilians and soldiers fresh from triumphs on the battlefields." The women's gallery was filled with wives and daughters of congressmen and senators and "hundreds of representatives of the benignity and beauty, the charity and culture of our land. . . ." Also filled to capacity was the diplomatic gallery. A representative of the slaves, abolitionist Henry Highland Garnet, ran his eyes over the crowd and noted with approval the presence of many blacks. "Amongst them," he said later, "were many a black brother and sister. Yes, there was the ubiquitous Negro—the universal black man—amongst the whites. Oh, it was quite a salt and pepper mixture."

The huge crowd taxed the ingenuity and patience of politicians and reporters. Noah Brooks, the Washington correspondent of a California newspaper, noted that "a mob of well-dressed women" invaded the press gallery and "for a time usurped the place of the newspaper men." There was a similar invasion of the House floor by prominent men—Supreme Court justices, cabinet members, U.S. senators, and prominent church and civic leaders—who were assigned seats left vacant by congressmen of the slave states.

It was in this setting, at twelve on the dot, that Schuyler Colfax, representative from Indiana and Speaker of the House, banged his gavel. The crowd hushed. It was high noon in the soul of America, and men and women, black and white, leaned forward, looking for a sign. There was no sign. The chaplain—William H. Channing—prayed, invoking God's blessing and help. The minutes of the last meeting were approved, and routine matters were disposed of. The proslavery forces tried to prolong the tedium by offering extraneous motions. But old Thad Stevens, the boss of the House and the best white friend black people have ever had in power, cut these maneuvers short and called for the question. The following dialogue ensued:

> Mr. [SYDENHAM] ANCONA. I ask my colleague to give way until I introduce a resolution for reference.
>
> Mr. STEVENS. I call for the regular order of business, and will yield for no purpose.
>
> The SPEAKER stated the question in order to be the consideration of the motion to reconsider the vote by which the House, on the 14th of last June, rejected Senate joint resolution No. 16, submitting to the Legislatures of the several States a proposition to amend the Constitution of the United States, and that the gentleman from Ohio [James Ashley] was entitled to the floor.

To understand the debate that followed, we must understand what happened on June 14, 1864. On that day, the House had before it Joint Resolution No. 16, which had passed the Senate on April 8, 1864, by a vote of 38 to 6. That resolution was simple and direct:

> That the following article be proposed to the Legislatures of the several States as an amendment to the Constitution of the United States, which, when ratified by three-fourths of said Legislatures, shall be valid, to all intents and purposes, as part of the said Constitution, namely:
>
> ART. XIII, SEC. 1. Neither slavery nor involuntary servitude, except as a punishment for crime, whereof the party shall have been duly convicted, shall exist within the United States, or any place subject to their jurisdiction.
>
> SEC. 2. Congress shall have the power to enforce this article by appropriate legislation.

On June 14, after considerable debate, ninety-six representatives voted for the resolution and sixty-three voted against it—ten votes shy of a two-thirds majority. Before the vote was announced, the floor leader of the antislavery forces, Congressman James M. Ashley, a Toledo, Ohio, druggist, changed his vote from yes to no. This was a parliamentary maneuver which made it possible to keep the resolution alive by a motion for reconsideration. The debate on this motion continued for the rest of the session, and it was finally decided to vote it up or down at 3 P.M. on January 31, 1865.

In the days and weeks leading up to January 31, both sides maneu-
vered to improve their position. In this maneuvering, the antislavery
forces were helped enormously by the intransigence of Southern rebels
and Union battlefield victories. The proslavery position was eroded
further by legislative action ending slavery in Maryland and Missouri
and the reelection of Abraham Lincoln on a platform calling for the
enactment of a constitutional amendment banning slavery. All of these
factors were crucial in undermining the position of the Democratic defenders of slavery. But it appears from the evidence that the key factor
was power politics. It is a maxim of civic textbooks that the good guys
win because they are supporting a good cause. But the antislavery forces
apparently decided early in the game that good causes can also be advanced by questionable methods. At any rate, it is reasonably certain that
some Democrats were persuaded to vote for the resolution or to stay away
from the House on January 31. Curiously but understandably, Abraham
Lincoln was centrally involved in this maneuvering. Although he still
favored gradual emancipation, he apparently authorized the use of his
vast patronage and pardon powers to improve the vision of wavering
Democrats.

With this background in mind, it is easy to understand the tactics of
James S. Ashley, who accepted the floor on January 31 and immediately
yielded to the gentleman from Pennsylvania—Archibald McAllister, a
"Peace Democrat" from Springfield—"to have read a brief statement."
The gentleman from Pennsylvania sent a statement to the clerk's desk
and it was read:

> When this subject was before the House on a former occasion
> I voted against the measure. I have been in favor of exhausting
> all means of conciliation to restore the Union as our fathers made
> it. I am for the whole Union and utterly opposed to secession or
> dissolution in any shape. The result of all peace missions . . . has
> satisfied me that nothing short of the recognition of their inde-
> pendence will satisfy the Southern Confederacy. It must therefore
> be destroyed; and in voting for the present measure I cast my vote
> against the cornerstone of the Southern Confederacy, and declare
> eternal war against the enemies of my country.

There was applause from the Republican side. Before it died down,
James Ashley was on his feet again, yielding again to a Democrat from
Pennsylvania—Alexander Coffroth—who announced that he, too, had

had a change of heart. He was now convinced that slavery was a threat to the survival of the country and "must soon be strangled or the nation is lost." He wanted the House to know that it was not easy for him to say this. He knew that his words would be misinterpreted. But he was acting today out of a sense of duty to his country; and if his actions today dug his political grave, he would descend into it without a murmur, knowing that he had a clear conscience and knowing there was one "dear, devoted, and loved being in this wide world who will not bring tears of bitterness to that grave, but will strew it with beautiful flowers. . . ."

Coffroth had barely completed his political epitaph when Ashley seized the floor again and offered to pull another Democratic rabbit out of his hat. But a Democrat complained that he was monopolizing the floor and farming it out "to whomever he pleases." The Speaker explained that Ashley had a right to use his time as he pleased. But in the maneuvering that followed, William H. Miller, a proslavery Democrat from Pennsylvania, won the floor for five minutes. Miller said he had listened to the complicated arguments on the legality of the proposition but "no member has yet satisfactorily met the great question at the bottom of the proposition." And what was the great question at the bottom? That question was the Negro. "Abolish slavery, and no man among them has pretended to show what we are to do with the freedmen, except that, as good Christians, it will become our duty to feed and clothe them. The true philanthropists and taxpayers of the country are equally interested in knowing what is to be done with the elephant when we get him."

It was not the elephant that worried the next speaker. What worried him was the donkey. The Democratic Party—Anson Herrick of New York City said—was losing ground because of its "seeming adherence to slavery," and this proposition presented "a desirable opportunity for the Democracy to rid itself at once and forever of the incubus of slavery." It was plain to him that "if the Democratic Party would regain its supremacy in the Government of the nation it must now let slavery slide!" This view was contested by James S. Brown, a former mayor of Milwaukee, who said that the proposed resolution was injurious to Democrats and Republicans, slaveholders and slaves, blacks and whites. It was "mischevious in so far as it would tie the hands of the President in so regulating the mode of abolishing slavery as not to precipitate upon the country three million ignorant and debased Negroes, without the slightest preparation for liberty or power on the part of the Government, by a system of apprenticeship or otherwise, to require them to labor."

At this point, with his fortunes rising, Garvey issued a call for an International Convention of the Negro Peoples of the World. Plans for the convention were carefully crafted, and the organizing committees spent months going over the details. All the while, week after week, Garvey stagemanaged the preparations, sending recruiting teams of singers and actresses and lecturers to Cuba, Jamaica, and Panama, dispatching Black Star ships to areas of maximum visibility.

The convention opened on Sunday, August 1, with three religious services at Liberty Hall, a low, zinc-topped structure at 114 West 138th Street. According to the *New York Times*, the "upper portion of Manhattan, from between Cathedral Heights, and the Hudson River, was practically taken over by the delegates," who reportedly came from almost every state in the Union and twenty-five countries on four continents. There was only a handful of delegates from the black civil rights establishment, but William Monroe Trotter of Boston was there. So also was William C. Matthews, a leading Massachusetts Republican who was later elected UNIA general counsel.

Before the afternoon service, the delegates and UNIA members staged a silent march through Harlem. During the parade, large handbills were distributed announcing a "monster" rally at Madison Square Garden and proposing the election of "a President of Africa, a leader for the Negro people of America and a leader for the Negro people of the world."

The rally was scheduled for the next day, which dawned clear and cool with temperatures in the sixties. By midday sun beamed over Lenox Avenue and the temperature was in the seventies. This was a good sign, and thousands lined the streets, waiting for the big parade which was scheduled to precede the rally. There was, as usual, a brief period of anxious waiting and watching, and then the first units came into view. At a distance the marching men looked like soldiers. As they came closer the crowd discovered with a shudder of delight that they were, in fact, soldiers, members of Garvey's embryonic army, the African Legion. The Legionnaires were smartly dressed in dark blue uniforms. They were unarmed, but this was a mere detail, which the imagination corrected. They had been long and brilliantly trained by their commander, E. L. Gaines, a former U.S. Army captain; and they moved along Lenox Avenue with dash and precision, conscious of the impact they were making.

The Legionnaires were followed by a fifty-piece band, contingents of table. Stiles demanded a roll call vote. A current of excitement ran through the chamber: the real struggle was about to begin. The clock on the wall said 3:20.

The clerk called the roll and announced that the motion to table had been defeated by a vote of 111 to 57, with 14 members abstaining. There was something for everybody to consider in this. The antislavery forces had prevailed in the first skirmish, but the vote against tabling was less than the two-thirds required to pass the amendment. A second test vote on a motion to reconsider the vote of June 14 was carried by a similar margin, 112 to 57, with 13 members abstaining. Thus, the issue was clearly posed, and after months of debate and seventy-eight years of evasion, the House of Representatives of the United States came at a few minutes before 4 P.M., on January 31, 1865, to the main question, which was the passage of a resolution sending the Thirteenth Amendment to the states. The yeas and nays were called for, and the final vote began, an eyewitness said, "in profound silence." As the clerk called the names of the members in a dull drone, representatives and visitors gathered in groups around Republican and Democratic tally clerks. When a Connecticut Democrat, James E. English, unexpectedly voted yes, there was a burst of applause. Similar demonstrations greeted the yes votes of three New York Democrats—John Ganson, William Radford, John B. Steele— whose defection from the Democratic ranks meant, Noah Brooks noted, "that the Rubicon was passed and the resolution was safe." The clerk added the names and whispered the results to the Speaker. There were 119 yeas, 56 nays, and 8 absentions. Every Republican member of the House was present and voted yes. Eleven Democrats crossed the line and voted with the Republicans, thus ensuring the passage of the proposition by a razor-thin margin. If three of the members recorded in the yes column had voted nay, the amendment would have been doomed.

Sobered perhaps by this thought, Speaker Colfax rose in the hushed House and announced in a grave voice: "The constitutional majority of two thirds having voted in the affirmative, the joint resolution is passed."

For a moment, reporter Noah Brooks noted from the press section, "there was a pause of utter silence, then a burst, a storm of cheers, the like of which no Congress of the United States ever saw. Strong men embraced each other with tears. The galleries and spaces stood bristling with cheering crowds; the air was stirred with a cloud of women's handkerchiefs and cheer after cheer, burst after burst followed. . . ."

Standing in the midst of this tumultuous outpouring of emotions, an-

other reporter, the correspondent of the *New York Tribune*, was moved
to exclamation points. When the Speaker announced what "the audience
quickly interpreted to be THE MIGHTY FACT THAT THE XXXV-
111TH AMERICAN CONGRESS HAD ABOLISHED AMERICAN
SLAVERY," he wrote, the "tumult of joy that broke out was vast, thunderous, and uncontrollable" and all gave way "to the excitement of the
most august and important event in American Legislation and American
History since the Declaration of Independence. . . . God Bless the
XXXV111TH Congress!"

The cheering and weeping and backslapping continued for at least
ten minutes. Finally, Ebon C. Ingersoll caught the eye of the Speaker
and moved "in honor of this immortal and sublime event . . . that the
House do now adjourn." The motion was carried and the House adjourned at 4:20 P.M. after a sore loser—Benjamin G. Harris of Maryland
—forced a roll call vote. As the representatives and visitors streamed out
of the House, they were greeted by a thunderous salute fired by three
batteries of regular artillery on Capitol Hill "to notify all who heard
that slavery was no more."

This message, which was, to say the least, premature, sped across the
country and set off demonstrations, parades, and artillery salutes. The
next day the *New York Tribune* headline said:

FREEDOM TRIUMPHANT.

COMMENCEMENT OF A NEW ERA.

DEATH OF SLAVERY.

The Constitutional Amend-
ment Adopted.

Grandest Act Since the Declaration
of Independence.

The *New York Times* was no less enthusiastic, calling "the adoption
of this amendment [the] most important step ever taken by Con-

gress. . . ." The *Times* added: "With the passage of this amendment the Republic enters upon a new stage of its great career. It is hereafter to be, what it has never been hitherto, thoroughly *democratic*—resting on human rights as its basis, and aiming at the greatest good and the highest happiness of all its people." Similar words appeared in the *New Orleans Tribune*, the first black daily newspaper in America. The *Tribune* called for full citizenship rights for freedmen and urged blacks to remember the event with an annual holiday of thanksgiving. "The Constitutional Amendment offered by the Congress to the ratification of the Legislatures of the several states will mark a new period in American history," the *Tribune* said. "By the oppressed race it will always be remembered as an act of justice, as the just recognition of an old debt by the legal representatives of the American people. No event can more properly be made the object of a grand and national celebration."

In New Orleans and other cities across the country, blacks and whites organized mass meetings to celebrate passage of the amendment. On February 4 a huge meeting was held in Boston's Music Hall. The high point of the evening was a powerful rendition of "Sound the Loud Timbrel," led by the Reverend Mr. Rue, pastor of the black Methodist Church. "It was a scene," William Lloyd Garrison, Jr. wrote later, "to be remembered—the earnestness of the singer, pouring out his heartfelt praise, the sympathy of the audience, catching the glow and the deep-toned organ blending the thousand voices in harmony. Nothing during the evening brought to my mind so clearly the magnitude of the act we celebrated, its deeply religious as well as moral significance than, 'Sound the loud timbrel o'er Egypt's dark sea. Jehovah has triumphed, His people are free.' "

The season of celebration reached a climax eight days later with a memorial sermon delivered by Henry Highland Garnet to senators and representatives in the House chambers. This was the first time a black man had spoken in the House, where so many whites had spoken so often to blacks and for blacks. There was thus a peculiar symbolism in Garnet's presence as well as his words—a symbolism Garnet emphasized by dwelling not on the victory won but on the work necessary to make the victory real. Was this presumptuous? Where would all this end? Where and when would the demands of the reformers of this and coming ages end? Garnet, a Presbyterian minister who had escaped from slavery in Maryland, answered:

"When all unjust and heavy burdens shall be removed from every man in the land. When all invidious and proscriptive distinctions shall be blotted out from our laws, whether they be constitutional, statute, or municipal laws. When emancipation shall be followed by enfranchisement, and all men holding allegiance to the government shall enjoy every right of American citizenship. When our brave and gallant soldiers shall have justice done unto them. When the men who endure the sufferings and perils of the battle-field in the defence of their country, and in order to keep our rulers in their places, shall enjoy the well-earned privilege of voting for them. When in the army and navy, and in every legitimate and honorable occupation, promotion shall smile upon merit without the slightest regard to the complexion of a man's face. When there shall be no more class-legislation, and no more trouble concerning the black man and his rights, than there is in regard to other American citizens. When, in every respect, he shall be equal before the law, and shall be left to make his own way in the social walks of life." Then, "and not till then," Garnet said, "shall the effectual labors of God's people and God's instruments cease." Garnet said "we ask no special favors, but we plead for justice. While we scorn unmanly dependence; in the name of God, the universal Father, we demand the right to live, and labor, and to enjoy the fruits of our toil."

And so, in conclusion:

"The nation has begun its exodus from worse than Egyptian bondage; I beseech you that you say to the people, *that they go forward.*' With the assurance of God's favor in all things done in obedience to his righteous will, and guided by day and night by the pillars of cloud and fire, let us not pause until we have reached the other and safe side of the stormy and crimson sea."

Even as Garnet spoke, state legislators were racing one another for the honor of being the first to ratify the amendment. The first legislature across the line was Illinois on February 1, followed closely by Rhode Island and Michigan on February 2, and Maryland, New York, and West Virginia on February 3. Ten months later, on December 18, 1865, Secretary of State William H. Seward announced that the requisite number of states had acted and that the Thirteenth Amendment was therefore an integral part of the U.S. Constitution. It was over—over in the sense that an operation to remove a cancer is over, over in the sense that there was no way to tell—then or now—whether malignant cells had entered the bloodstream of the patient and would lead, despite everything, to death.

Black and White

The People's Convention

NOTHING quite like this had ever been tried before, and nothing remotely approaching it has happened in America in all the years since. To the surprise of just about everybody—and to the outrage of some—a people's assembly, an assembly consisting for the most part of former slaves and poor whites, was convening in the elegant Charleston Clubhouse for the purpose of writing a constitution and framing a civil government for the state of South Carolina. This was no assembly of lawyers and businessmen and power-brokers speaking for the people. Here for the first time—and the last time—in America was an official state assembly of people speaking for themselves. Here also for the first time—and the last time—in America was an official state assembly with a black majority. There were, or there would soon be, 124 delegates in this hall, and at least 76 of them were black. This was a new and unprecedented thing in the history of the white Western world, and there was an understandable air of excitement in Charleston as the delegates gathered for the opening session.

The excitement had been building since the first of the year, and the streets of Charleston on this day—Tuesday, January 14, 1868—were filled with jubilant blacks. There were huge throngs of former slaves on the Battery, which had been the special preserve of white aristocrats in the days of slavery. On King Street and Market Street, blacks paraded to and fro, rejoicing and sampling the first fruits of freedom. The crowd was densely thick on Market Street near the site of the convention, the Charleston Clubhouse.

Like the Battery, like the City Hall, like every important stone and building in Charleston, the Clubhouse had become a symbol in a complicated crisis of legitimacy. It was, contemporaries said, "one of the handsomest buildings in Charleston," and the grounds were still filled with "choice shrubbery." For more than a decade, this building had been the center of Charleston high society. Here, in what some people called the good old days, aristocrats and slaveowners, the *New York Times* said, "entertained their guests and each other in a style of elegant hospitality." Now, in an extraordinary turnabout, this building was to become the setting of the first official act of the new regime. And this, more than anything else, had raised the ire of the old aristocrats, who were charging that the site had been selected as a deliberate act of provocation. "This sentimental grievance," according to the same *New York Times* dispatch, "seemed to be the worst aggravation of the whole proceedings in the eyes of the natives. . . . A stranger unacquainted with the circumstances of the case, might suppose that the choice of locality was expressly intended to humiliate the quondam 'swells.'" The men of the new regime denied this, saying that the Clubhouse had been sold to a Union man and that it had been selected because it was cheap and available. Whatever the truth of the matter, the Clubhouse was a singularly handsome backdrop for the opening drama of the new age. The grounds had been manicured, and the large hall in the interior had been renovated to accommodate the needs of new men and new times. Since there was no gallery in the hall, a wooden railing, or bar, had been erected to separate the spectators from the delegates.

It was in this aristocratic setting, and in an atmosphere of charged emotions, that the South Carolina Constitutional Conventional met on January 14, 1868, at noon. A large crowd of spectators, predominantly black, were on hand for the opening ceremony, and white reporters noticed, with some surprise, that the black spectators "kept perfect order and spat around as naturally as any white native." Inside the railing, the delegates circled one another warily and moved in and out of last-minute caucuses. One white reporter noted that the white delegates were "sandwiched between delegates in every stage of nigritude [sic]." This reporter and others also noted that the black delegates were well-dressed. Indeed, the "get-up" of the convention, as Charleston newspapers put it, was so respectable that hostile whites charged that the blacks had gotten "some clothes out of the [Freedmen's] bureau." The only discordant note, appropriately enough, was provided by a black delegate who turned up in a grey Confederate overcoat he had purchased in a second-hand clothing store. This infuriated local whites, who interpreted the gesture as a studied insult to the Confederate dead.

To the surprise of some reporters, who expected bedlam, and to the dismay of some whites, who expected blacks to make fools of themselves, the opening session was as conventional—and as dull—as the opening of any other legislative or quasi-legislative body. Of the ninety-two delegates who attended the first session, more than sixty were black. There were five blacks and four whites in the Charleston delegation, four blacks and one white in the Orangeburg delegation, four blacks and three whites

Harper's Weekly drawing depicted "The First Vote" of freedmen who reconstructed South.

Among leaders of Reconstruction process in South Carolina were (left to right, above) J. H. Rainey, F. L. Cardoza, Jonathan J. Wright, and (below) Robert Smalls, R. H. Cain.

in the Edgefield delegation, three blacks and one white from Marion, and three blacks and one white from Richland. Chester County was represented by three blacks. There were all-black delegations from Horry, Lancaster, and Marlboro counties.

It was apparent to all those present that this was a new departure in the history of race relations and the history of American democracy. And to measure the impact of this convention, one must look first at the world context in which it occurred.

This gathering was the product of a revolutionary cycle which began with Appomattox and climaxed in a bitter constitutional struggle between President Andrew Johnson and Congress. In the course of this struggle, it became clear to some men that the only way to preserve Northern war gains and check the resurgence of the planter aristocracy was to enfranchise the former slaves, who constituted a majority in two states and a formidable force in every Southern state. Most Northern whites had profound doubts about the wisdom of black enfranchisement but reluctantly gave their assent when Southern whites refused to make even minimal gestures toward a recognition of the new state of affairs. The general outcome was a series of Reconstruction acts, which divided the South into military districts and authorized the creation of new governments based on all male voters. Carrying out the letter, if not the spirit of these acts, Union military commanders ordered new registrations and supervised elections for delegates to the new constitutional conventions. The first constitutional convention opened in Montgomery, Alabama, on Tuesday, November 5, 1867. Seventeen days later, on November 22, forty-nine blacks and forty-nine whites assembled in Mechanics Institute in New Orleans. In the first weeks of December, constitutional conventions opened in Richmond, Virginia, and Atlanta, Georgia. And as 1867 turned the corner of 1868, black and white delegates began to assemble in Raleigh, North Carolina, Little Rock, Arkansas, Jackson, Mississippi, and Charleston, South Carolina.

The number of black delegates in these conventions ranged from a low of eight in Arkansas to highs of forty-nine (50 percent) and seventy-six (61 percent) in Louisiana and South Carolina, respectively. Thus, the South Carolina convention was the only assembly with a clear black majority. This was due, in part, to the sheer weight of numbers. There were 415,000 blacks and 289,000 whites in South Carolina, and there were black majorities in twenty-one of the thirty-one counties. In Georgetown, for example, there were 13,388 blacks and 2,773 whites. The same general situation obtained in Beaufort (29,050 blacks and 5,399 whites), Sumter (17,805 blacks, 7,463 whites), Charleston (60,693 blacks, 28,204 whites).

South Carolina blacks had the numbers, but numbers count only when there are leaders and cadres who make them count by educating and organizing people. By singular circumstance, South Carolina had an unusually gifted pool of black leaders. Some of these leaders came from the relatively large free black population of Charleston, Columbia, and Orangeburg. No less important in the unique South Carolina equation was a cadre of Northern-born blacks, some of whom settled in Black Belt counties after completing service in black Union regiments. Of equal and perhaps greater importance was the fact that the Sea Islands and other coastal areas were liberated early in the Civil War and became a magnet for missionaries, who helped sow the seeds of assertion and organization. Particularly important in this regard were the missionaries of the Northern Methodist Church and the African Methodist Episcopal Church.

All these forces and factors helped to strengthen the cohesion of South Carolina blacks, who had a clear comprehension of their interests and a network of organizations long before the war ended. The clearest example of this was the vote for the constitutional convention. Of the 81,000 registered black voters, 68,875 went to the polls in November, 1867—and 68,875 voted in favor of holding a constitutional convention. In other words, every black who cast a ballot voted for the constitutional convention. This happened only two years after the end of slavery in the face of a withering campaign of intimidation and harassment; and it was a demonstration of a level of consciousness and unity black Americans have not matched since.

From the time of the voting through the convention and beyond, the black masses of South Carolina vibrated with revolutionary passion. By the thousands and the tens of thousands, they attended huge open-air political rallies and endorsed demands for equal rights, education, and land. As the holiday season neared, the demands of black South Carolinians became more precise. Contemporary witnesses said there was a general feeling that the Day of Judgement had arrived and that at long last the bottom rail would finally be placed on top. In November and December, tens of thousands of blacks walked off plantations and wandered down the dusty roads, rejoicing. Many blacks, we are told, refused to sign labor contracts for the new year. Some refused all work, preferring, it was said, to wait for the land and freedom they believed the new convention would bring.

If hope heightened the interests of blacks, fear of what might happen caused the greatest consternation in aristocratic white circles. A white man traveling in South Carolina in these days heard bitter complaints on all sides. In a revealing letter to the *New York Times*, he relayed the message white Southerners had asked him to spread in the North. " 'Blood is thicker than water,' they say," he wrote, "and when the Northern people shall once be fully acquainted with the real state of things here, they will never permit that we of the Caucasian race like themselves—we, as it were, of the same flesh and blood—shall be trodden down and domineered over by" blacks. The white people this writer talked to were opposed to universal suffrage for both blacks and whites, saying that "whether [the Negro] is as fit for universal suffrage as the uneducated Irish, is an open question. The fact is, however, that the uneducated Irish ought never to have had it, and two wrongs will never make a right."

Thus spoke unreconstructed South Carolinians as they prepared for a fate some considered worse than death. Some of the old slaveowners, believing apparently that the world was about to come to an end, packed up and left the state. Other whites buried their heads in the sand and tried to pretend that the convention was not happening. Still others were moved to hysteria by the thought of former slaves, "semibarbarians," they said, ruling their former masters. What was the world coming to? How and where would it all end? It would end, some whites said, "in dire deeds of riots, rape, robbery, incendiarism and bloodshed."

Counterrevolution by Ku Klux Klan and terrorists overthrew Reconstruction regimes.

It would end, former governor Benjamin Perry said, in "a war of races," in "the most terrific war of extermination [of blacks] that ever desolated the face of the earth in any age or country."

To prevent this disaster, Perry and other whites appealed to Congress and Northern whites, asserting in various petitions and resolutions that the white people of South Carolina were an oppressed minority who were victims of "the maddest, most unscrupulous, and infamous revolution in history."

Revolution: it was a word that came easily to the lips in a time that author Henrietta Buckmaster called "the most revolutionary year in American history." This was not a rhetorical flourish. From January 1, 1868, to the opening of the South Carolina Constitutional Convention the following events occurred:

Sunday, January 12, 1868: Benjamin Franklin Butler, a Massachusetts politician and former Union General, spoke, according to press reports, to an "enormous mass of Negroes" at "the African Church" in Richmond on the subject of "their equality, if not supremacy, to the white races."

Monday, January 13: Secretary of War Edwin M. Stanton, who had been ousted by President Johnson, was reinstated by Congress. Press reports said the excitement in Washington, D.C. was at "fever heat" and that the air was thick with rumors of coup d'etats and revolutionary uprisings.

Tuesday, January 14: A black man, Francis E. Dumas, was narrowly defeated for the Republican nomination for governor of Louisiana. Dumas refused to accept the lieutenant governor post, saying "that he would not occupy any subordinate position in the party."

There were other and equally significant currents. According to a *New York Times* editorial, some radical Republicans were demanding the naming of Frederick Douglass or some other black for vice-president on the Republican ticket in the forthcoming presidential campaign.

All these fears, all these hopes, all these pressures converged on the seventy-six black men and forty-eight white men who assembled for the South Carolina convention. Who were these men? The answer is that they were average men with larger than average political passions dictated by their attachment to competing social groups. From the first day of the convention to its tumultous ending, the delegates were vexatiously divided into two large groups, one white, the other black, both riven by internal tensions relating to place of birth.

The dominant group—the black group—was composed of seventeen Northern-born delegates and some fifty-nine Southerners. Thirteen of the black delegates were ministers, eleven were schoolteachers, nine were Union war veterans. "Beyond all question," the *Charleston Daily News* said, "the best men in the convention are the colored members." This was a polemical thrust, designed, in part, to humiliate the white associates of the black Republicans. But there is corroboration for the statement from another source. In a dispatch of January 21, the *New York Times* correspondent said "the colored men in the Convention possess by long odds the largest share of mental calibre. They are the best debaters; some of them are peculiarly apt in raising and sustaining points of order."

Thirty-eight of the fifty black Southerners were former slaves. Since it was a crime for these men to read and write before 1865, it is hardly surprising that there were no university graduates among them. But this does not mean that they were deficient in the requisite political skills. Almost all of the former slaves were literate. Most were artisans (carpenters, blacksmiths, shoemakers, tanners, and carriage makers), ministers, and businessmen. One of the former slaves—Calvin Stubbs—was now a teacher. Another—Robert Smalls—was a ship captain who had gained national fame by sailing a Confederate steamer out of the Charleston harbor and delivering it to the Union Navy.

The social and political skills of the black delegates who were free before the war were no less real and tangible. At least twelve of the Southerners were from the free black colony of Charleston. Most of these men came to the convention after serving in outlying areas as Freedman's Bureau teachers or aides. Three of the Northern-born blacks —William J. Whipper, Robert Brown Elliott, and Jonathan Jasper Wright—were lawyers.

There was the same range of skills in the white group, which was also divided into sub-groups of Northern-born and Southern-born contingents. Twenty-seven of the forty-eight white delegates were native white Southerners. Certain of these men were poor, but others, notably Thomas Jefferson Robertson and Albert Gallatin Mackey, were well-to-do and had close connections with the prewar ruling class.

Most of the white Southerners had, according to their own testimony, good intentions, but almost all of them were limited by the racial and class biases of the time. It is only fair to add that some of the poor whites were radicals with advanced economic views. Among their number was Solomon George Washington Dill, a native white South Carolinian who seems to have envisioned a radical reconstruction of the state based on a coalition of poor whites and poor blacks.

There remains finally the group of Northern-born whites who were generally lumped together by the pejorative word *carpetbagger*. The word was imprecise and unjust. Most of the Northern-born whites were missionaries, former Union Army officers, or Freedman's Bureau officials who had settled in the state before the beginning of Radical Reconstruction. Some of these men were now businessmen and planters. Others were ministers of black churches, teachers in black schools, or publishers of black newspapers.

The white delegates were a diverse group, with sharply varying views on the dominant issues of the day. We see them unavoidably through the lenses of white reporters, who apparently believed that they were traitors to the white cause. There was, for example, James M. Runion, a Baptist preacher who was described in contemporary dispatches as "a smooth sanctimonious fellow, who ranted fiercely against everything 'Yankee' during the war, served as a chaplain, and then took the test oath that he had not given aid or comfort to rebels." A preacher of a different stripe was Benjamin Franklin Whittemore, a Northern Methodist minister from Massachusetts, "stout, burly, with a strong voice, vigorous style, and sledge-hammer movement." He was hated, it was said, by whites in Darlington County, who charged that he had organized and armed blacks, creating "a whirlwind he cannot now control." The white delegation also included C. C. Bowen, a lawyer and former Confederate officer who became a radical after the war; and Charles P. Leslie, a businessman from New York, who was described as "a sharp, shrewd worker, full of humor and temper, thin as a slab, and a conservative, who didn't believe 'a Negro is as good as a whiteman.'"

These were the men—black, white, poor, rich, Southern-born, Northern-born—called to Charleston to remake the legal foundations of the state. An onlooker with the gift of prophecy would have focused on twelve of these men, for they would go far and would symbolize in their intertwined careers the limitations and possibilities of the new order. No man better than William Beverly Nash, for example, symbolized the depth of the changes brought about by the Reconstruction measures. Six feet tall, "black as charcoal, handsome of face and commanding of figure." Nash was a middle-aged former slave who quoted Shakespeare and was said to be the most popular black in the state. He was a brilliant stump speaker and a leader of the Republican party in the capital city of Columbia, where, only three years ago, he had been a slave waiter in a hotel.

Francis Louis Cardozo, a tall, handsome, portly man, then thirty-one, came from a different social milieu. He had been born free in Charleston, the son of a Jewish merchant and a black woman, and had been educated abroad at the University of Edinburgh and the London School of Theology. A minister, he had returned to the state after the war and was now principal of Avery Institute, the largest black school in the state. Cardozo was the best educated man—black or white—on the floor. He would later become the black anchor of the Republican administration, serving successively as secretary of state and treasurer.

High state offices would also go to two black lawyers—W. J. Whipper and J. J. Wright. Whipper, a flamboyant and somewhat erratic personality, was born free in Pennsylvania. He came to South Carolina with the Union Army and remained to practice law in the provost courts. An able parliamentarian, and the son of black pioneer William Whipper, he would seize the convention floor on every opportunity to push two of his major interests, women's suffrage and the abolition of capital punishment.

Jonathan Jasper Wright, a very different personality, was also a native of Pennsylvania. A dark-skinned man, almost six feet tall, he would soon become the first black on the South Carolina Supreme Court. He believed, contemporary press accounts said, "in nothing less than equal privileges with the white race."

A spectator with the gift of foresight would have noticed these men, and he would have given special attention to the six blacks the state would send to the U.S. Congress in the next ten years. Four of these men —Joseph H. Rainey, Alonzo Ransier, Robert C. DeLarge, and Robert Smalls—were native South Carolinians.

Rainey, the first black to serve in the U.S. House of Representatives, was born in slavery but grew up in freedom in Georgetown after his father purchased the freedom of the family. A light-skinned man of medium height, then thirty-five years old, he was a barber and the son of a barber.

Another native, also destined for major state and federal offices, was Alonzo Jacob Ransier, who was born free in Charleston and worked as a shipping clerk there before the war. Ransier was thirty-four. He would later become the first black lieutenant governor of South Carolina and would then move on to Congress. Robert Carlos DeLarge, a tailor and a native of Aiken, South Carolina, would also go to Congress. He was only twenty-five but was already well known in freedmen's circles as a professional parliamentarian. It would be said later that he was perhaps the most active black delegate and "the best parliamentarian" on the floor. The fourth member of this group was the celebrated Robert Smalls, who had a fanatically loyal following in the Beaufort area.

Similarly touched by destiny were two newcomers—Richard Harvey Cain and Robert Brown Elliott. Cain, who was pastor of the huge Emanuel AME Church, was a man of dramatic presence and power—tall, black, with big magnetic eyes and luxuriant side whiskers. A graduate of Wilberforce, he came South in 1865 as a missionary and was now alderman of the city of Charleston. He would go from this convention to the state senate and the U.S. House of Representatives and would end his days as a venerable bishop of the AME Church.

It was obvious, even on the first day of the convention, that Cain would scale the heights. But it would have been more difficult to predict the future of Robert Brown Elliott, who later outdistanced all his contemporaries and became the most powerful black man in South Carolina. Elliott was a free black who had been handsomely educated. He would sit in this hall for sixteen days without opening his mouth and then, taking the floor for the first time, would make his mark. A white reporter who interviewed him shortly after the convention opened said "he was very black, but very well spoken, and bitter as gall."

On his way up, Elliott would cross swords with two ambitious and controversial white men who came to the convention with private agendas. One of these men was Franklin L. Moses, Jr., a former Confederate diehard who converted to Republicanism after the war and now preached and, some said, practiced social equality. He would later become governor of the state and would do much to destroy Republicanism by extravagance and dishonesty. Another future governor was Daniel H. Chamberlain, a graduate of Harvard and the Yale Law School, and a former lieutenant in the Fifth Massachusetts Colored Cavalry. A little below average height, prematurely bald, with the mien of a scholar or a professor, Chamberlain was a cold, methodical man, painfully ambivalent on the issue of race. He too would help destroy Republicanism, not by extravagance, but by collaboration with conservative Democrats.

A markedly different fate awaited two of Chamberlain's fellow delegates who would not live to see another new year. The first man, Solomon George Washington Dill, was a native white radical who identified with the plight of poor whites and poor blacks. Within four months, he and his black guard—Nestor Peony—would be shot to death in his home by white terrorists. A similar fate awaited Dill's black colleague, Benjamin Franklin Randolph, a tall and courageous Northern Methodist minister who would be shot to death in broad open daylight at Hodges Depot in Abbeville County.

Damned men, ambitious men, far-seeing men, men with hidden agendas, men with visionary dreams, men on the lookout for the main chance: such are the men who compose all assemblies, and such were the men who inaugurated the new order in South Carolina. The first event of the new order—the opening of the Constitutional Convention—was sober and undramatic. In fact, the *New York Times* correspondent went so far as to say that the proceedings were "utterly devoid of interest." Here, as in so many other instances, the *New York Times* correspondent was wrong. The preliminary proceedings, like the preliminary proceedings of any other legislative body, were dull. But they were not, by any stretch of the imagination, without interest. As a matter of fact, part of the drama of the day was in the dullness, was in the fact that the freedmen and former slaves adapted themselves so quickly to the parliamentary routine. This naturally disappointed notoriety-seekers, who came to see a show and were confronted instead with a serious, sober and revolutionary attempt by the poor and the oppressed to seize the instruments of power.

Either by inadvertence or arrangement, the first session opened without a flourish or even a prayer. By unanimous consent, Thomas Jefferson Robertson, a wealthy white South Carolinian who now espoused the doctrine of equal rights, was named temporary chairman. Robertson gave a brief and decorous speech, saying that the delegates had assembled "for the purpose of restoring our State to her proper relations in the Federal Union." To that end, he urged the delegates "to frame a just and liberal Constitution, that will guarantee equal rights to all, regardless of race, color or previous condition. . . ."

There then followed an interesting and dramatic incident. By unanimous consent, a black man, William J. McKinlay of Orangeburg was chosen temporary secretary. McKinlay, a teacher and a well-to-do scion of the free black colony of Charleston, read the order convening the body and called the roll of delegates. Immediately after that, Benjamin Franklin Whittemore seized the floor and moved that the convention proceed to permanent organization. Robert Carlos DeLarge rose to a point of order and said that the first order of business was the appointment of a committee to examine credentials. There was a brief and pointed debate, and—another interesting event—DeLarge prevailed. A committee of thirty, with roughly the same number of blacks and whites, was appointed and retired to consider credentials. After a brief adjournment, the committee returned with its report, which was adopted. A few minutes later, after meeting for something like four hours, the convention adjourned until Wednesday at twelve noon.

Thus ended the opening session of one of the most extraordinary experiments in American history. The session, as reporters noted, was not visibly dramatic. But the drama of this day was not on the surface but in the inner details, a fact that was obvious to everyone, including the reporters who complained about the tedium of the time-consuming debate on credentials. The sight of black men, of freedmen and former slaves, standing in the hall of power, speaking to and for a whole state; the sight of a black majority controlling and shaping the affairs of blacks and whites; the sight of white men, conscious of that power, working with black men and debating with them and deferring to them—all this unleashed possibilities that were breathtaking in scope and dimension.

If there were any doubts on this score, they were dispelled at the second session on Wednesday. This time the delegates began by invoking the blessings of God. Prayer was offered by the doomed Benjamin Franklin Randolph, who asked "Almighty God, Creator and Ruler of the universe" to help the delegates and show them the way.

After disposing of routine business, the convention elected a permanent president—Albert Gallatin Mackey, a highly respected white native and a former grand master of the Masons. His election was the first of a number of compromises designed to appease white public opinion. This strategy was based on the idea that it was necessary for blacks to forego the immediate exercise of visible power in order to give whites time to adjust to the new order. Mackey was the first fruit of this policy, which would later lead blacks into some dangerous and ultimately disastrous alliances.

We can see this quite clearly now, with the benefit of hindsight. But the sharp curves on the road ahead were visible to almost no one in the wave of emotion and good feeling that followed the unanimous election of Dr. Mackey. A. J. Ransier, the future lieutenant governor and congressman, moved that a committee of three be named to escort Mackey to the chair. The temporary president appointed two blacks—Ransier and R. C. DeLarge—and one white—B. F. Whittemore—to escort the permanent president to the platform.

After the applause died down, Mackey formally accepted the honor, saying that the convention was "marked by two peculiarities, which has distinguished no other Convention that preceded it in South Carolina— peculiarities which demand for it the commendation of every lover of liberty and respecter of human rights." In the first place, he said, "it is the first Constitutional Convention in this state, in the selection of whose members, the ballot box, the true palladium of rational liberty, has been made accessible to every man who was not disqualified by legal or political crime. In the call for the five South Carolina conventions which have preceded it, and which were held in 1776, in 1777, in 1790, in 1860, and in 1865, but a portion of the people were permitted to exercise the elective franchise, because slavery, that vile relic of barbarism, had thrown its blighting influence upon the minds of the people, and for the noble doctrine that governments were constituted for the good of the whole, was substituted that anti-republican one, that they were intended only for the benefit of one class at the expense of another. But in the call for this body, every true man who could labor for the support or fight for the defense of the commonwealth has been invited to a representation. Manhood suffrage has for the first time been invoked to convene a body which is to make the fundamental law for all. This is, then, truly and emphatically a people's Convention—a Convention by the representatives of all who have minds to think—and to think for themselves, or muscles to work—and to work for themselves."

With these words ringing in their ears, the delegates completed the organization and began the serious work of writing a constitution. As in all bodies of this sort, the real work was done off the floor in standing committees. Three of these committees were chaired by blacks. R. C. DeLarge was chairman of the committee on franchise and elections. Francis Louis Cardozo headed the committee on education. S. A. Swails, a war hero and a leader of the party in Williamsburg, guided the deliberations of the committee on rules and regulations. There was substantial

black representation on all committees, and the assistant secretary, en-
grossing clerk, doorkeepers, sergeant-at-arms and messengers of the convention were black.

For fifty-three days, the delegates assembled punctually at noon. "A
colored attendant," a white witness wrote, "pushed forward an earthen
spittoon, weighing perhaps a quarter of a ton. The production of this
national institution seemed to be the signal for coming to order."

As these scenes unfolded within the walls of Charleston Clubhouse, there
was a rising tide of hysteria in white circles. For a short while, many
aristocrats believed, or pretended to believe, that the machinery of government was so complex that blacks could not make it work. When it
became apparent that the black and white delegates were going to write
a good and perhaps a great constitution, the white diehards changed their
tactics and denounced the delegates in strident tones, saying, among other
things, that "an ignorant and depraved race" had been placed "in power
and influence above the virtuous, the educated and the refined."

There were similar but more moderate complaints in influential
Northern circles. In an editorial, printed on Friday, January 17, three
days after the opening of the convention, the *New York Times* said it
was for emancipation and "some" protection for blacks but was opposed
to putting into the hands of blacks "the absolute shaping of our national
policy and the decision of our destiny for many years to come." Under
the Radical Reconstruction plan enacted by Congress, the paper said,
"the Negro vote will decide the political complexion of six or eight, and
probably all of the Southern states; and this, it is assumed, will decide
the Presidential election and the policy of the nation for a good many
years to come. If this programme be carried out we shall not only have
given the late slaves their freedom, but shall have conferred upon them
the power of shaping the policy, the laws, the destiny of our Republic
in this crisis of fate."

The same querulous tone marked dispatches to the *Times* from its
Charleston correspondent, who said that there was not a drop of racist
blood in his veins but that the sight of the South Carolina convention
made him uneasy. "Twist and distort the fact as you may," he wrote,
"declare that the convention now in session is the legitimate result of
the action of Congress. . . . look at it in any light, and yet the truth must
be confessed—it is a Negro convention. Negroes are in the majority,

Negroes rule the House, Negroes control the committees. The people who sent them here are Negroes, holding a majority outside of 45,000, and are the people for whom the chief benefits of legislation are intended."

Indifferent to this and other attacks, the South Carolina delegates continued their work, formulating proposed sections of the Constitution in committee sessions and debating them in open sessions. The debates were serious, passionate, and sometimes acrimonious, particularly on the crucial issues of equal rights, education, and land and tax reform. Finally, after meeting for fifty-three days, the convention approved the new constitution and adjourned in the midst of "great cheering applause."

The new constitution, which was overwhelmingly approved by the electorate, was an excellent document. "The learning of the leaders [of the convention]," historian Francis B. Simkins wrote, "bore fruit in a constitution written in excellent English and embodying some of the best legal principles of the age. In letter it was as good as any other constitution the state has ever had, or as most American states had at that time." The new constitution protected the rights of all South Carolinians and extended to women and poor whites fundamental rights denied them by the leaders of the old regime. Over and above this, the new constitution gave South Carolina its first statewide public school system, and it specified that all public schools and colleges "shall be free and open to all children of this State, without regard to race or color."

All things considered, this was a brave beginning, which was compromised finally and destroyed by a violent white counterrevolution and the bad faith of men who did not believe in democracy or the human potential of either poor blacks or poor whites. For all that, the beginning was important and it remains, even today, a high-water mark in the quest for a government of, by, and for all the people in the United States of America.

Sunrise at
Harpers Ferry

Prelude to Protest

THEY came out of the mist, walking barefooted on the rocks and stones. They came silently, purposely, self-consciously, a long, thin, defiant line of poets, professors, protesters, and dreamers. On and on they came, up and down the side of the great mountain, past, one of the poets noted, "the gnarled old oaks," the "sombre-foliaged pines," and "the crimson banner" of the sumac. The line twisted and turned and halted finally before a battered old brick building in an open field. And there, as the dawn broke in explosions of brilliant light, the marchers performed a curious ceremony. First, they prayed. Then they marched single file around the building, singing the "Battle Hymn of the Republic." The march and the building and the hymn were symbolic. For in this building in 1859, John Brown had made his last stand against slavery. And now, forty-seven years after John Brown's stand and one hundred years after his birth, more than one hundred members and friends of the new Niagara movement had gathered at Harpers Ferry,

149

At 1904 unity conference, Booker T. Washington and W. E. B. DuBois made an unsuccessful attempt to settle their ideological differences.

West Virginia, to summon the spirit of Brown and his black and white followers in a new challenge to the massed might of a new form of slavery.

The Harpers Ferry gathering was the first national public meeting of the Niagara movement, which had been founded a year before at a secret conclave on the Canadian side of Niagara Falls. The movement had only a handful of active members on this day—August 18, 1906—and there were men and women, black and white, who heaped scorn on their "whining" and "melodramatic" gestures. But history does not scorn the dramatic gestures of men and women who are willing to live and die for their ideas. And it is generally agreed today that Jesse Max Barber, the poetic editor, was right when he said in 1906 that this movement and this meeting marked "the beginning of a new epoch in the history of Negro-Americans." For on the foundation erected at this meeting rose the NAACP, the marches and demonstrations of the fifties and sixties, and the whole modern protest movement. Looking back thirty-five years later, W. E. B. DuBois, the guiding spirit of the movement, said that "[we] had in significance if not numbers one of the greatest meetings that

150

American Negroes have ever had. We made pilgrimage at dawn barefooted to the scene of Brown's martyrdom and we talked some of the plainest English that has been given voice to by black men in America."

The plain English followed the marching and can only be understood in the light of the markers on the road to Harpers Ferry. The first marker on that road was the violent revolution that overthrew the Black Reconstruction regimes and nullified the Fourteenth and Fifteenth amendments to the U.S. Constitution. The response to this sociopolitical disaster was lukewarm in both black and white leadership circles. There were, at first, shouts of defiance. But as the years wore on, and as the spirit of racism marched across the soul of America, radical energies ebbed in both black and white leadership circles. The grand outcome was the complete collapse of the old abolitionist spirit and the emergence of a number of black leaders who counselled accommodation and called for a moratorium on protest and "whining." The most talented of these leaders was Booker Taliaferro Washington, the Tuskegee Institute president who

Meeting in a tent on the Canadian side of Niagara Falls in 1905, Niagara militants charted a militant racial strategy.

Leaders of Niagara Movement included (left to right) W. E. B. DuBois, William Monroe Trotter, and Jesse Max Barber.

also deprecated higher education for blacks and blamed, or seemed to blame, blacks for their own plight. When Washington combined all the elements of the new gospel of accommodation in one eloquent speech at the Atlanta Exposition of 1895, he was hailed as a new messiah by some blacks and almost all whites. There were dissenters, notably John Hope, the Atlanta educator, and novelist Charles W. Chesnutt. But Washington, who was a superb politician, quickly amassed enormous power that made it difficult and even dangerous to speak out against his policies. Through the good offices of political patrons like President Theodore Roosevelt, he virtually controlled patronage in black America. Through the good offices of economic patrons like Andrew Carnegie, he had veto power over the allocation of certain educational and philanthropic funds. Nor was this all. To the dismay of his adversaries, he controlled a large discretionary fund that enabled him to subsidize friendly black newspapers and to buy out or harass hostile black newspapers.

Washington critics—and there were many—watched his growing power with alarm. But the critics lacked resources and were ineffective until the convergence of three forces changed the balance of power. The first force was the increasing audacity of a system of racism which went, in the last decades of the nineteenth century, from triumph to triumph. The second was the increase in the number of black college graduates. The third force was the rising tide of color consciousness which spawned, in the first decades of the twentieth century, protest movements of lawyers and intellectuals all over the Third World. No one understood these forces better than one of the black college graduates, W. E. B. DuBois of Fisk and later Harvard. In a germinal book, *The Souls of Black Folk*, he said "the problem of the twentieth century is the problem of the color line. . . ." In the same book, which was immediately hailed as a milestone in American literature and race relations, DuBois, who was teaching at Atlanta University, criticized Washington, saying that "so far as [he] apologizes for injustices, North or South, does not rightly value the privileges and duty of voting, belittles the emasculating effects of caste distinctions and opposes the higher training and ambition of our brighter minds—so far as he, the South, or the nation, does this—we must unceasingly and firmly oppose them."

The temblors set in motion by *The Souls of Black Folk* traveled swiftly through black America, dividing intellectuals into Washington and DuBois parties. Between these two parties, James Weldon Johnson wrote, "there were incessant attacks and counterattacks; the [accommodators] declaring that the [militants] were visionaries, doctrinaries, and incendiaries: the [militants] charging the [accommodators] with minifying political and civil rights, with encouraging opposition to higher training and higher opportunities for Negro youth, with giving sanction to certain prejudiced practices and attitudes toward the Negro, thus yielding up in fundamental principles more than could be balanced by any immediate gains. One not familiar with this phase of Negro life in the twelve- or fourteen-year period following 1903 . . . cannot imagine the bitterness of antagonism between these two wings."

Although DuBois tried at first to maintain a position of moderation above the field of battle, his position was undermined by events surrounding the so-called Boston Riot, which was organized and led by his old schoolmate, William Monroe Trotter, editor of the *Boston Guardian.* Trotter, like DuBois, was a descendant of an old free black family and, like DuBois, was a graduate of Harvard University. But Trotter, unlike DuBois, was impetuous. Raised on the myths of the old abolitionists, he made himself over into an image of the old abolitionists, dedicating himself and all he had to a root-and-branch destruction of Booker T. Washington and his policies. Week after week, he denounced Washington in the columns of his paper. But his attacks attracted little attention until the summer of 1903 when Washington unwisely accepted an invitation to speak in Boston, one of the centers of the anti-Washington party. There were rumors all over town that "something" was going to happen at the meeting, and the Columbus Avenue AME Zion Church was packed on the night of July 30 when Washington got up to speak. As soon as Washington opened his mouth, he was interrupted by shouted questions from Trotter and his associates. In the uproar that followed, four persons, including Trotter and his sister, Maude, were arrested. Trotter later served a thirty-day sentence at the Charles Street Jail, an ordeal that he turned to his political advantage.

Of minor importance in itself, the "Boston Riot" was nevertheless a far-reaching event that marked a turning point in the racial history of the period. Before the "riot," it had been virtually impossible to get front-page coverage of the seething ideological controversy in the black community. But the events surrounding the "uprising" in the Columbus Avenue Church were so dramatic that it was impossible to keep them off the front page. The result was that large sectors of the public were informed for the first time that some blacks were dissatisfied with "their" leader. Of much more immediate consequence was the fact that the "riot"—as Trotter may have foreseen—pushed W. E. B. DuBois off the fence. By coincidence—or had Trotter planned it?—DuBois arrived in the city immediately after the "riot" for a long-scheduled visit with the Trotter family. When he got off the train, he discovered that his host was in jail. After an investigation of the facts, DuBois came down hard on Trotter's side. "I did not know beforehand of the meeting in Boston," he wrote later, "nor of the projected plan to heckle Mr. Washington. But when Trotter went to jail, my indignation overflowed. I did not always agree with Trotter then or later. But he was an honest, brilliant, unselfish man, and to treat as a crime that which was at worst mistaken judgement was an outrage." Reminiscing thirty-seven years later, DuBois said that he immediately assumed leadership of the anti-Washington party. In fact, his conversion was more protracted and was mediated by one other event, the abortive black unity conference of 1904. This secret conference was held in New York's Carnegie Hall on January 6–8, 1904, and was called by Washington. The purpose of the conference was to bring both wings together to "try to agree upon certain fundamental principles and to see in what way we understand or misunderstand each other and correct mistakes as far as possible." The idea, all hands agreed, was excellent. The execution, however, raised serious questions. In the first place, the list of invited delegates was heavily weighted in Washington's favor. (DuBois estimated later that twenty-two of the twenty-eight delegates were safely in the Washington camp.) In the second place, Washington controlled the administrative machinery, and the expenses of the conferees were paid for by one of his white benefactors, presumably, Professor Herbert Aptheker said, Andrew Carnegie. To make matters worse, several prominent whites, including Andrew Carnegie, came to the meet-

ing and patronizingly lectured the black conferees on the virtues of
Booker T. Washington. The end result was surprising to almost no one.
"It was a conference," DuBois said, "carefully manipulated. There was
no confidence and no complete revelation. It savored more of armed truce
than of understanding. Those of us who represented the opposition were
conscious of being forced and influenced against our will.... Numbers
of rich and powerful whites looked in upon us and admonished us to be
good, and then the opposition between the wings flamed in bitter speech
and charge. Men spoke with double tongues saying one thing and meaning
another. And finally there came compromise and an attempt at constructive effort which somehow no one felt was real. I had proposed a Committee of Twelve to guide the Negro race but when the committee was
finally constituted I found that it predominantly represented one wing
of the controversy and that it was financed indirectly by Andrew Carnegie, and so I indignantly withdrew and the Committee of Twelve never
functioned but died leaving only a few pamphlets...."

Whatever the reasons for the collapse of this venture, the paradoxical
result was that a conference called to create unity sealed the divisions in
the black community and led to the founding of the Niagara movement.
The first organizational moves were made not by DuBois but by a forgotten protest leader, Attorney Frederick L. McGhee, of St. Paul, Minne-
sota. McGhee, an influential Catholic layman, called for formation of an
NAACP-type organization based on sustained protest and litigation.
Similar ideas came from William Monroe Trotter and Dr. Charles E.
Bentley, a prominent Chicago dentist. "The honor of founding the organization," DuBois said later, "belongs to F. L. McGhee, who first suggested it; C. E. Bentley, who planned the method of organization and
W. M. Trotter, who put the backbone into the platform." To DuBois's
list one should add, of course, the name of W. E. B. DuBois, who issued
in June, 1905, a "private and confidential" call for selected black men
to meet "in the vicinity of Buffalo, New York," in July, 1905, "to in-
augurate a permanent national forward movement." The call was signed
by fifty-nine men from sixteen states and the District of Columbia.

In the first week of July, in the midst of a deepening crisis (a race
riot in New York City and the lynching of seven blacks and one white in
Watkinsville, Georgia), DuBois went to Buffalo and "hired a little hotel
on the Canada side of the river at Fort Erie, and waited for the men to

attend the meeting. If sufficient men had not come to pay for the hotel, I should certainly have been in bankruptcy and perhaps in jail. . . ." Although several persons dropped out at the last moment, presumably because of pressure or fear of pressure from the Washington camp, twenty-nine men from thirteen states and the District of Columbia showed up, and the conference proceeded as planned, though apparently not in the Fort Erie Beach Hotel hired by DuBois. Jesse Max Barber, editor of the Atlanta-based *Voice of the Negro*, was there, and he said later that "officially speaking the meeting was held at Buffalo, but in reality all of the sessions were held under a tent at Fort Ontario."

The twenty-nine men attending the three-day conference (July 11–13) were a varied lot linked together by a passionate belief in equal rights, "aggressive, manly" protest and higher education for blacks. Ten were lawyers;* six, including two of the lawyers, were teachers;** five, including one of the educators, were ministers;*** three were editors;**** and two, including one of the lawyers, were government clerks. The list of delegates also included one dentist, Dr. Bentley, businessmen like Alonzo F. Herndon, founder of Atlanta Life Insurance Company, and artists like Robert Bonner.

It has been generally assumed or implied that the Niagara militants were Northern-born graduates of Ivy League colleges. Certain of the founders, including Trotter and DuBois (who attended Harvard after graduating from Fisk), were identified with Ivy League colleges, but most of the college graduates attending the session were from black institutions like Howard (Richards, Hart, Carter, Miller), Atlanta University (Kershaw, Morgan), Lincoln Institute, Missouri (Bradley), Knoxville (McGhee), and Virginia Union (Barber). An additional point of

---

* Clement G. Morgan, a former alderman of Cambridge, Mass.; W. H. Richards, professor of law, Howard University; W. H. H. Hart, professor of law, Howard University; Lafayette M. Kershaw, U.S. Department of Interior; William Justin Carter, former assistant attorney general, Dauphin County, Penn.; George W. Mitchell, a prominent Pennsylvania attorney; Isaac F. Bradley, former assistant prosecuting attorney, Kansas City, Kans.; B. S. Smith, former alderman, Kansas City, Kans.; Frederick L. McGhee, St. Paul, Minn.; George H. Woodson, Buxton, Iowa.

** Dr. H. L. Bailey, Washington, D.C., public school system; Rev. J. L. R. Diggs, president of Virginia Theological Seminary and College; Richard Hill, Nashville public school system; W. H. Richards and W. H. H. Hart, Howard University; W. E. B. DuBois, Atlanta University.

*** Rev. W. H. Scott, Woburn, Mass.; Rev. Garnet R. Waller, Baltimore, Md.; Rev. Byron Gunner, Columbia, S.C.; Rev. George Frazier Miller, Brooklyn, N.Y.

**** William Monroe Trotter, *Boston Guardian*; Jesse Max Barber, *Voice of the Negro*; Harry C. Smith, *Cleveland Gazette*.

significance, frequently overlooked, is that some of the delegates had not attended college (H. C. Smith), or even high school (A. F. Herndon).

Whether they came from universities or the streets, the delegates were firm supporters of higher education and racial militancy. All, or almost all, believed in absolute human equality. All, or almost all, maintained a militantly aggressive posture in their daily lives. A striking case in point was Attorney McGhee, who was said to be the first black lawyer west of Illinois. In a long and successful career, he demanded and received respect from a large black and white clientele. When a white lawyer objected to doing business with "a damned nigger," Attorney McGhee spat in his face.

Most of the delegates were somewhat conventional in economic and social matters. Most were Republicans, but at least one, Attorney McGhee, was a Democrat. Two, W. E. B. DuBois and the Reverend George Frazier Miller, the Episcopal priest from Brooklyn, were socialists.

Republicans, Democrats, socialists, Baptists, Methodists, Episcopalians, Congregationalists, Catholics: these were the men who met in a tent in Canada and grappled with the black agenda within sound of the roaring waters of Niagara Falls. After three days of meeting and an afternoon off for sightseeing at the Falls, the delegates formed, a contemporary report in the *Washington Bee* said, "a national organization called 'The Niagara Movement'; with a General Secretary, a General Treasurer, and an executive committee, composed of State Secretaries, who are in turn the heads of the State Committees." DuBois was elected general secretary, and George H. Jackson of Cincinnati was named treasurer. The delegates also issued an address to the nation. In this address, and in its constitution, the Niagara movement took a stand on eight principles:

1. Freedom of speech and criticism
2. An unfettered and unsubsidized press
3. Manhood suffrage
4. The abolition of all caste distinctions based simply on race and color
5. The recognition of the principle of human brotherhood as a practical present creed
6. The recognition of the highest and best training as a monopoly of no class or race
7. A belief in the dignity of labor

8. United effort to realize these ideals under wise and courageous leadership.

These principles constituted, in the eyes of Jesse Max Barber and other founders, "the colored man's declaration of independence." How did the founders propose to achieve their goals? The founders proposed a systematic campaign of agitation, litigation, and pamphleteering. Writing in the *Voice of the Negro* in 1906, co-founder J. Max Barber said "this movement will seek to implant high ideals in the minds of our young people, and will further seek to educate public sentiment up to a position where it will be more healthy and robust on the race question. The methods to be pursued are many and will be readjusted as occasions may demand. Among them will be the method of distributing very widely pamphlets and leaflets on human rights. Committees will in various ways reach our political gatherings and place the cause of the race before them." To doubters, who said that "the ideals [were] impossible of realization" and that "we can never gain our freedom in this land," DuBois answered: "We certainly cannot unless we try. If we expect to gain our rights by nerveless acquiescence in wrong, then we expect to do what no other nation ever did. What must we do then? We must complain. Yes, plain, blunt complaint, ceaseless agitation, unfailing exposure of dishonesty and wrong—this is the ancient, unerring way to liberty, and we must follow it."

The Niagara platform called for agitation, but it also called for work, listing eleven things "we as black men must try to do: 1) To press the matter of stopping the curtailment of our political rights, 2) To urge Negroes to vote intelligently and effectively, 3) To push the matter of civil rights, 4) To organize business co-operations, 5) To build school houses and increase the interest in education, 6) To open up new avenues of employment and strengthen our hold on the old, 7) To distribute tracts and information in regard to the laws of health, 8) To bring Negroes and labor unions into mutual understanding, 9) To study Negro history, 10) To increase the circulation of honest, unsubsidized newspapers and periodicals, 11) To attack crime among us by all civilized agencies. . . ."

Acting upon the letter and the spirit of these tasks, the Niagara militants tried to create not a mass movement but, in modern terms, a cadre organization. In his year-end report, the General Secretary listed two hundred members and added: "No attempt has been made to drum up a membership, to force men in for the sake of numbers, or to do anything inconsistent with a thoughtful, dignified attempt to unite in one National organization men who think alike. At the initial Niagara meeting it was decided that for the first year a membership of about 150 persons would be as large a body as probably could easily work together in harmony and effective co-operation, and that at any rate the membership should not exceed 200." Writing at a somewhat later date, Jesse Max Barber made the same point and added: "[the Niagara movement] is the tiny piece of leaven which we expect to leaven the whole lump. . . . We have reached the leaders of the people and depend upon them to reach the masses. Still we will never be satisfied until every black man in this country knows that he is not tethered to some kind of sub-human super-animal world. . . . "

The initial response to the emergence of the Niagara movement was predictable. There was general condemnation in white America and considerable criticism in black leadership circles. The general idea behind most of the criticism was that the Niagara movement was composed of a small group of "grumblers" and "whiners" who were envious of Booker T. Washington and ashamed of their race. Barber heatedly denied this, saying: "A few pompous ignoramuses have broken out into long-faced homilies about the movement being started to oppose Dr. Booker T. Washington. No assertion could be more groundless. The conference was greater than that; it was too great to devote its deliberations to any one man. Mr. Washington's name was called but twice during the whole conference, and both times the secretary ruled that we had gathered to consider principles and not men."

This disclaimer didn't satisfy the Washington camp, which moved to the attack, using spies and provocateurs in an abortive attempt to smash or disrupt the movement. Despite this opposition, the movement gained ground. In a report of January, 1906, General Secretary DuBois said the Niagara movement had done "five things:

1. It has established strong local organizations in seventeen of the thirty states in which it is represented and is rapidly organizing the other thirteen.
2. It has inaugurated an annual and simultaneous celebration throughout the nation, of the work of the great abolitionists.

3. It has joined in the celebration of [William Lloyd] Garrison's 100th anniversary.
4. It has encouraged the free unsubsidized Negro Press.
5. It has aroused and focused public opinion throughout the nation and put new life into all the older Negro organizations."

It was in this atmosphere of ferment that the Niagara members traveled to Harpers Ferry to honor John Brown and to hold their first national convention. More than one hundred men and women attended the public sessions, which were held at Storer College, August 15–18, 1906. "All day Wednesday [August 15]," an Associated Press dispatch said, "each train brought delegates and visitors till the ample dormitories of Storer College were filled." The first public session was held that night in the auditorium of Anthony Hall and was addressed by Storer President Henry T. McDonald and other dignitaries. At a working session the next morning, status reports were delivered by state secretaries. Summaries of two of these reports have been handed down to us and throw a revealing light on civil rights agitation at the beginning of the modern protest movement. "It is hard to tell," editor Barber wrote, "which state organization—that of Illinois or that of Massachusetts—did more work last year. Both states did good work. Dr. Charles E. Bentley as Secretary of the Illinois branch of the Movement gave a very interesting report of the work in his state. The first constructive work of the Illinois State organization was the securing of the appointment of a colored man on the new charter committee for the city of Chicago. This appointment was secured from Mayor [Edward F.] Dunne after the colored people had been turned down by a Republican governor and legislature. Certain newspapers in Chicago were calling upon the charter convention to separate the races in the public schools. Dr. Bentley and his associates managed to secure the appointment of three men as the Education Committee whose views they know. A Committee from the I. B. Niagara movement has secured from the Education Committee the assurance that a law will be incorporated in the charter prohibiting the separation or segregation of the races in the public schools. It was interesting to see how the N.M. managed the 'Clansmen' in Chicago. When Thomas Dixon went to Chicago with his new play he met very little notice. The Niagara Movement was responsible therefor. The opinions of the Chicago colored people varied all the way from bomb-throwing to injunctions. Jane Addams of the Hull House was consulted. She sympathized with the colored people and called a conference of all the prominent dramatic critics of Chicago. The conference decided to take no notice of the play.... 'The Clansman' went to Chicago, stayed seven weeks and left without a line of advertising save that it paid for and a few unfriendly literary criticisms of one or two papers.... When Chicago abolished her justice shops and police courts and instead established municipal courts, Niagara Movement men succeed in having one of her number appointed as one of the judges."

The report from Attorney Clement G. Morgan of Massachusetts was, according to Barber, equally encouraging. The two great fights of the Massachusetts Niagara branch were "against the Warner Amendment to the rate bill and against the appropriation of money by the Massachusetts legislature to the Jamestown Exposition, unless Virginia should stipulate that all citizens of Massachusetts regardless of color should receive the same treatment on the Exposition grounds. The Massachusetts men probably deserve the credit for the death of the Warner Amendment. They did not quite succeed in their fight on Jamestown Jimcrowism but they fought right nobly."

The most dramatic session of the four-day convention was John Brown Day, which opened with the morning of pilgrimage and ended with major addresses by General Secretary DuBois and the Reverend Reverdy C. Ransom, pastor of the Charles Street AME Church in Boston. DuBois, according to the *Washington Bee*, gave "an analytical study of the whole question of slavery." It was a weighty speech, read with scholarly precision from a manuscript, and it evoked thought but very little emotion. When DuBois finished, the chairman, Attorney W. Justin Carter of Harrisburg, Pennsylvania, introduced Ransom, calling him "the thunderer." Ransom lived up to his name, bringing the militants to their feet with stinging criticisms of Booker T. Washington and the Republican party. "The large audience applauded him to the echo," the *Washington Bee* said, "the applause frequently interrupting the speaker for several minutes."

Sure of his audience, in great voice, Ransom zeroed in on the raging ideological dispute in Black America. There were, he said, two classes of blacks. "One counsels patient submission to our present humiliation and degradation; it deprecates political action, ignores or condones the usurpation and denial of our political and Constitutional rights, and preaches the doctrine of industrial development and the acquisition of property, while it has no word of protest or condemnation for those who visit upon us all manner of fiendish and inhuman indignities."

This class, Ransom said, was wrong, tragically wrong. "The other class believes that it should not submit to being humiliated . . . it believes in money and property but it does not believe in bartering its manhood for the sake of gain; it believes in the gospel of work and industrial efficiency, but it does not believe in artisans being treated as industrial serfs, and in laborers occupying the position of a peasant class. It does not believe that those who toil and accumulate will be free to enjoy the fruits of their industry and frugality if they permit themselves to be shorn of political power. . . . "

Put that way, the choice between two classes was clear, and Ransom at once deduced the consequences, urging all honest men and women to ally themselves with the Niagara leaders of the second class.

When the future AME bishop finished, "the audience stood up," the *Bee* reporter said, "in prolonged applause, and sang John Brown's Body."

There then followed another electric moment, which brought tears to the eyes of many. Two of the great names of history were invoked with the introduction of Lewis Douglass, the son of Frederick Douglass, and Henrietta Evans, the sister of Sheridan Leary, a black guerrilla who was killed while fighting with John Brown at Harpers Ferry, and the aunt of John Copeland, another black Brown supporter who was hanged at Harpers Ferry. "The audience crowded forward," the press report said, "as the venerable Mrs. Evans seated in an arm-chair on the platform" spoke in a feeble but defiant voice of "the self-sacrifice of her kinsmen in dying as they did for the race."

It was a moving and perhaps instructive moment, and the meeting ended in a revival spirit. Men and women, the *Voice of the Negro* reported, "who had attended the New England antislavery meetings fifty years ago said that they had witnessed nothing like the enthusiasm in that meeting since the dark days of slavery. Women wept, men shouted and waved hats and handkerchiefs. . . . "

From this great height, the delegates descended on the next day— Saturday—to the dangerous and sobering level of black reality. The debates on this issue were, Niagara chroniclers tell us, serious and impassioned. A graphic account of the internal ferment can be found in a reminiscence written on the twenty-fifth anniversary of the founding of the NAACP by J. B. Watson. "I was a member," he wrote, "of the second Niagara Movement at Harpers Ferry in the summer of that year—and what a meeting! No group of Negroes before or since have I found to be so honest and sincere—so fervent, determined and direct. Irreconcilable.

Uncle Harvey Johnson was there from the Druid-Hills Baptist Church in Baltimore. Dr. Johnson was always afire. Good old fighting, Catholic McGhee was there from St. Paul. On the pilgrimage to John Brown's tomb, McGhee walked with bare feet over jagged stones.... Reverdy Ransom was then at the pinnacle of his powers as an eloquent pleader. His speech on that occasion probably is his masterpiece. Too bad the Bishopric had to lay hands on him. Episcopal Priest Waller and his Baptist preacher brother [Garnet R. Waller] were there. What a mixture in one family of thought. I recall very well Priest Waller's red and sweaty face as he emerged from a committee room exclaiming with unction, 'How that fellow does swear.' DuBois was in the committee room. In the whole meeting DuBois insisted on having his way and had it as usual. Monroe Trotter was there snorting and gnashing. John Hope took to the meeting a cruse of oil in case of troubled water, but found he needed a tank of heavy viscosity. Though he, himself, at times forgot his oil, I believe Hope would go down as the pacifier of the meeting if there was one. Mary Church Terrell was there in her prime. Sutton E. Griggs strode about the grounds with a large book on abstruse philosophy under his arm. Hershaw, Tom Johnson and who-all. It would take all night to name and evaluate them all. All those, who, in the last twenty-five years, have employed organized, legitimate protest, more or less have followed in the wake of the Niagaras." Unknown to Watson, one of their number was a spy from the Booker T. Washington camp. The Washington spy, Richard T. Greener, former U.S. Consul to Vladisvostock, made a splendid impression, giving one of the major addresses.

Before the conference ended, the delegates added several new departments, including a Women's Department and a Pan-African Department, and admitted women to full membership. DuBois was reelected general secretary and George H. Jackson was reelected treasurer. The conference ended on Saturday night with the adoption of another address to the nation. This address, which DuBois wrote in a "tumult of emotion," is an extraordinary document which deserves detailed consideration.

In detail [it said] our demands are clear and unequivocal. First, we would vote; with the right to vote goes everything: freedom, manhood, the honor of your wives, the chastity of your daughters, the right to work, and the chance to rise, and let no man listen to those who deny this.

We want full manhood suffrage, and we want it now, henceforth and forever.

Second. We want discrimination in public accommodation to cease. . . .

Third. We claim the right of freemen to walk, talk, and be with them that wish to be with us. . . .

Fourth. We want the laws enforced against rich as well as poor; against Capitalist as well as Laborer; against white as well as black. We are not more lawless than the white race, we are more often arrested, convicted and mobbed. We want justice even for criminals and outlaws. We want the Constitution of the country enforced. . . .

Fifth. We want our children educated. The school system in the country districts of the South is a disgrace and in few towns and cities are the Negro schools what they ought to be. We want the national government to step in and wipe out illiteracy in the South. . . .

These are some of the chief things which we want. How shall we get them? By voting where we may vote; by persistent, unceasing agitation; by hammering at the truth; by sacrifice and work.

We do not believe in violence, neither in the despised violence of the raid nor the lauded violence of the soldier, nor the barbarous violence of the mob; but we do believe in John Brown, in that incarnate spirit of justice, that hatred of a lie, that willingness to sacrifice money, reputation, and life itself on the altar of right. And here on the scene of John Brown's martyrdom, we reconsecrate ourselves, our honor, our property to the final emancipation of the race which John Brown died to make free.

Needless to say, these words were not heeded, then or later. But they expressed real grievances which have not yet been redressed in America. The failure of America to deal with these grievances was not due to the lack of ardor of the Niagara militants, who continued to hold meetings at abolitionist landmarks, going from Harpers Ferry to Boston and from Boston to Oberlin. "We may expect a future session at Appomattox," critic Kelly Miller wrote, "so prone is the poetic temperament to avail itself of episodal and dramatic situations."

There was no meeting at Appomattox. After a series of internal explosions between DuBois and Trotter partisans, the movement dwindled in effectiveness and merged, for all practical purposes, with the founding cadres of the NAACP. By that time, the energies of the accommodation movement were ebbing and a climate had been created for the modern protest movement. The seeds for this and later development were sown by the Niagara founding fathers, and it was no small achievement for twenty-nine men who dreamed impossible things in a small tent near the roaring waters on the Canadian side of Niagara Falls.

Eagle in the Air

Jack Johnson
and the Great White Hope

N O other single event dug so deep into world consciousness until the Lindbergh flight seventeen years later.

More reporters covered it than covered the Russo-Japanese War.

More words were written about it in American newspapers than were written about the Republican convention in 1908, and more space was devoted to it in British newspapers than was devoted to the major events of the Boer War. An official of the telegraph company said that except for the San Francisco disaster of 1906 no greater volume of words had been handled for a single event in the history of telegraphy. "Perhaps no other event," the *Freeman* of Indianapolis said, "has held so universally the gaze of mankind."

This was an exaggeration, but it was understandable at the time. For this event mesmerized the world; and before it was over, scores had been killed or maimed in race riots, the foreign offices of governments had issued position papers, and the U.S. Congress had passed a law making it a federal crime to show moving pictures of it.

The cause of all these words, all this excitement, all this passion, was not a political crisis or a natural catastrophe—it was a prize fight, the 1910 contest between Jack Johnson, the first black heavyweight champion, and Jim Jeffries, the great white hope of the Western world. But this was obviously more than a prize fight. It was the first great modern happening; it was the first great media morality play. Johnson had captured the championship, whipped all available white talent and thumbed his nose at the deepest values of the white populace. There he was, resplendent, triumphant,

John Arthur (Jack) Johnson won heavyweight championship in 1908.

smiling his famous "golden smile," and leaning on a gold-tipped walking cane, with a blonde on each arm. Such a black, in 1910 (and 1992) was obviously a threat to the social order. Such a black, as Professor Al-Tony Gilmore has argued, was obviously a "Bad Nigger," the very incarnation of the deepest fears of white men. Such a black had to be defeated and humiliated, dramatically and publicly. Thus it was that millions of men and women convinced themselves that their honor, their virtue, and their sense of reality depended on the outcome of the struggle that matched Johnson and Jim Jeffries, who was said to be invincible. Thus it was that the Johnson-Jeffries fight was invested with a cosmic significance. This was no simple clash of two men; it was a clash of elemental forces. It was about sin and redemption. It was about the forces of evil and the avenging blonde warrior. It was Gotterdammerung. It was Revelation. It was Captain Ahab and the white whale, Bigger and Mary, Hemingway and the white snows of Kilimanjaro, Rudyard Kipling and the lesser breeds outside the law.

And it was real. On Monday, July 4, 1910, in Reno, Nevada, a dusty little frontier town in the Wild West, the Avenging Warrior and the black champion were going to climb into a ring and fight for forty-five rounds or until one of them was maimed or beaten into unconsciousness. How could the world resist such a drama? How could one fail to understand the prefight headline in the *Chicago Tribune:* RENO NOW CENTER OF THE UNIVERSE.

Behind this headline and the state of mind it reflected were years of controversy centering on the person and personality of John Arthur (Jack) Johnson, who is still considered by many experts to be the greatest boxer in the history of prize fighting. And to evaluate exaggerations that seemed obvious to the men of that day, we must back up a few years and consider the long road that carried Jack Johnson to Reno and the center of the universe. Johnson was born on March 31, 1878, in Galveston, Texas. He seems to have deplored the inadequacies of the Jim Crow environment of Galveston. At any rate, he quit school at the age of twelve and ran away from home, traveling by box car to the East Coast, before returning to Galveston, where he did odd jobs and ended up on the docks as a longshoreman. In his years of roaming, and in his years on the docks, he acquired certain fighting skills as a simple function of his need to survive. He later drifted by easy stages into the boxing business, which was illegal then almost everywhere. Boxing was not an easy life, then or now. Johnson fought in open fields, in smoky stags, in barns. He fought in battle royals, going into the ring with five or six blacks who entertained whites in vicious battles that continued until only one man was standing. Sometimes he fought two opponents in one night; sometimes he fought two major fights on successive days. It was a hard life, and an exacting life, for the penalty of failure was not a lost battle, but a lost life. Johnson lost few fights and climbed to the top of his chosen profession, acquiring polish and a formidable style on the way. He was then and later a master of defensive technique. And he was fast. He was so fast, a friend said later, "that he could block a punch and hit you with the same hand."

By 1904 Johnson was one of the greatest boxers in the world. He had defeated the major black heavyweights and was issuing challenges to heavyweight champion Jim Jeffries, who drew the color line and refused to meet him. Undaunted, Johnson fought wherever he could and continued to press his suit. All the while, week after week, he was attacked and ridiculed in the white press.

Bold, independent, unconventional, Johnson had acquired certain personality traits that made him a controversial figure in black and white

America. He loved fast horses, fast cars, and fast women—not neces-sarily in that order. He spent money freely on expensive champagne, tailored suits and handmade shoes, and gave no thought to tomorrow or what people thought of him. In this period, and later, he was in and out of traffic courts, controversies, gambling houses, and bordellos.

He was a curious man, John Arthur Johnson, full of quirks and odd contradictions. He had a brilliant mind, a natural flair for drama, and an apparently deep appreciation of art, culture, and history. But there was a raging fire within him. He was fascinated by speed and the limits of the possible, and he couldn't resist dramatic gestures which expressed his contempt for the white social order and his desire to tempt fate. There is no really satisfactory personal biography of the man, but he seems to have been engaged in an inchoate and individualistic war for his right to live exactly as he pleased. One story gives the measure of the man. "At one period of my gambling activities," he tells us, "I had prospered sufficiently to engage a drawing room to New York, but before the train departed I lost every cent I had. I had prepared to board the train penniless. A friend, Frank Sutton, knowing my predicament, in-sisted on lending me some money, but I refused to take it." Sutton insisted, and Johnson finally accepted one dollar. He got on the train, gave the porter a fifty-cent tip, bought two cigars with another quarter and tossed the last quarter to a newsboy at Grand Central Station as he walked into New York City, carefree and unafraid.

This was the man—cool, flamboyant, defiant—who captured the imagination of the world with a brilliant three-year campaign for a shot at the heavyweight championship. When, in 1905, Jeffries retired unde-feated, Johnson laid siege to Tommy Burns, the new champion. Burns tried to ignore the black challenger and scurried from continent to con-tinent with Johnson in hot pursuit, issuing challenges and capturing headlines. Finally, after a great deal of public pressure and a public declaration in favor of the fight by Edward VII and a reputed private declaration by President Roosevelt, Burns gave in and the fight was scheduled for Sydney, Australia, on the day after Christmas in 1908. Johnson, fighting brilliantly and coolly contemptuous of the jeering white mob, cut Burns to pieces and the police stopped the fight for humanitarian reasons in the fourteenth round. For the first time in history, a black man was the official heavyweight champion of the world.

This had immediate consequences in sports and political circles, and a worldwide search began for white hopes. The literary leader of this ath-

Jack Johnson and second wife, Etta, were photographed at race track around 1910.

Scenes from Reno fight reflect excitement of crowd and coolness of Johnson, who clowned and joked with ringsiders.

Fight between Johnson and Jim Jeffries, the former heavyweight champion, captured world attention.

letic posse comitatus was Jack London, a famous American author with advanced social views and retarded racial reflexes. London covered the Sydney fight for the *New York Herald*, and his story from ringside became the literary testament of the White Hope movement. Here is the meat of the London story:

The fight! There was no fight! No American massacre could compare to the hopeless slaughter that took place in the Sydney Stadium....

Johnson play-acted all the time. He played with Burns from the opening gong to the finish of the fight....

'Hit here, Tahmy,' he would say, exposing the right side of his unprotected stomach, and when Burns struck, Johnson would neither wince nor cover up. Instead, he would receive the blow with a happy, careless smile, directed at the spectators, turn the left side of his unprotected stomach and say, 'now here Tahmy,' and while Burns did as directed, Johnson would grin again, chuckle and smile his golden smile....

But one thing now remains, Jim Jeffries must now emerge from his Alfalfa farm and remove that golden smile from Jack Johnson's face.

Jeff, it's up to you. The White Man must be rescued.

Jeffries, who seems to have had good instincts, despite his virulent racism, resisted this pressure for several years. In the interim, Johnson easily disposed of various and sundry white hopes and became a major attraction on the vaudeville circuit in America, Europe, and Canada. He traveled with a large entourage of valets, secretaries, and blondes.

The white public, and, to tell the truth, large sectors of the black public were offended by stories of Johnson speeding through the streets of Paris, London, and Chicago in big crimson racing cars filled with white women. There were other points of aggravation. Johnson, it was said, had no gratitude. What this meant was that Jack Johnson was Jack Johnson's manager, a point Johnson emphasized from time to time by dismissing uppity white managers.

Johnson battered Jeffries into submission in 15th round of scheduled 45-round fight.

It was against this background and in a climate approaching hysteria that Jim Jeffries announced that he was returning to the ring to redeem the honor of the white race. Johnson was delighted, not so much, one gathers, by the racial implications as by financial predictions that a Johnson-Jeffries fight would bring the winner the largest amount of money ever paid to an artist or entertainer for a single appearance or exhibition. This was a powerful inducement to both Johnson and Jeffries, and a match was speedily arranged for San Francisco. When the governor of California yielded to the antiboxing lobby and banned the fight, promoter Tex Rickard shifted the battle to Nevada, the only state in the union where boxing was legal. The fight was scheduled for Monday, July 4, 1910, in Reno, which had some ten thousand inhabitants.

As July approached, large segments of white and black America whipped themselves into a frenzy of anticipation. The white world was almost unanimous in support of Jeffries, who reportedly could not be hurt and who could, some said, kill a man with one blow. These assertions did not disturb the black community, which was solidly behind Johnson. In a famous cartoon on the front page of its February 4, 1910, edition, the *Chicago Defender* pictured Johnson in a ring with Jeffries, who was surrounded by phantom figures labeled "Race Hatred," "Prejudice," "Negro Persecution." The ringside was packed with what the cartoon called "Jim Crow Delegates." The caption of the cartoon said: "He Will Have Them All To Beat." In this cartoon, and in a barrage of front-page comment leading up to the fight, the *Defender* expressed the point of view of the overwhelming majority of blacks, who were hemmed in by segregation and discrimination and desperately needed someone or something to cheer for. The world of the *Defender,* and of the *Defender* readers, was a world of violence and humiliation and intimidation. It was a world in which the *Defender* reported [on March 19] that "100 Negroes [Are] Murdered Weekly in the United States by White Americans." It was a world in which, as the *Defender* reported on April 1, the town fathers of Muskogee, Oklahoma, could decide that "Negro women may walk on the walks, but Negro men must keep to the streets."

This was the world, a world of triumphant white supremacy, in which the drama of the Johnson-Jeffries fight unfolded. It was this world that whites were defending and blacks were attacking in and through the person of John Arthur Johnson. Almost everyone recognized this. As John Callan O'Laughlin said in a story in the *Chicago Tribune* on the day of the fight, there was a fear abroad that the spectacle of Johnson whipping white men would give blacks dangerous ideas. If [Johnson] gains the victory," O'Laughlin wrote, "it will increase the confidence [blacks] feel in themselves and, some persons fear, cause them to be less respectful of the power of the whites." This fear, he said, was especially pronounced in the South. "If Johnson wins, the Negroes in the Southern states are likely to regard his victory as evidence of their ability to defeat the white man when fighting on equal terms. They may be encouraged to acts which formerly they would not dare commit."

All these fears converged on the little town of Reno, which was a swirling mass of humanity by the last week of June. Never before had so many people from so many places come together for an athletic or entertainment event. There were sports and big money men from America, England, Canada, Australia, India, China, Cuba, Brazil, and Burma. There were hoboes, miners, cowboys, cattle herders, businessmen, politicians, touts, pickpockets, and prostitutes. The population of the town had more than doubled, and special trains were arriving daily from the East Coast and the West Coast. The main street, Centre Street, was virtually impassable; and the lobby of the Golden Hotel, where the big spenders were staying, was a solid mass of wall-to-wall people. By now, the last week in June, the saloons were crowded, and men were standing four and five deep around roulette, faro, and crap tables. The most celebrated crooks in America were already in attendance, and others were expected. Cincinnati Slim was there; and the Sundance Kid, according to rumors, was on his way. Also on the way were some of the leading men of the industrial directorate. Payne Whitney of New York and a party of Wall Street magnates were said to be on their way in four private railroad cars.

These and other reports titillated the crowd, which had nothing to do except wait and gamble and trade rumors. The bookies in front of the Palace and Sagebrush clubs were shouting odds of 10 to 6 on Jeffries, but betting was light. The foci of attention at this point were the training camps of the two fighters on the outskirts of town. Jeffries and his entourage were at Moana Springs on the Truckee River, and Johnson and his white wife and his managers and trainers were at Rick's Roadhouse, about four miles from town.

The two camps reflected the personalities and life styles of the two fighters. Jeffries's camp was tight and tense; Johnson's was loose and open. Jeffries was moody and secretive; Johnson was affable and available to all. Jeffries shunned the crowds, insulted reporters and disappeared for long stretches; Johnson welcomed spectators, dazzled them with his speed and entertained them with his wit. He trained hard, gambled hard, and entertained friends at night with his bass fiddle. The camp of Jeffries, the *Freeman* reported, "is said to more resemble a funeral, while that of his opponent is more like a picnic."

Everything indeed suggests that Jeffries discerned the outlines of the disaster ahead. It was there in plain daylight for all to see, but race blinded the pundits and reporters. The *New York Times* reported accurately that Jeffries was uptight, but attributed it to his possession of "the worrying qualities of the white race." One man with an eye to see and enough character to speak was Governor Denver S. Nickerson, who said after watching Johnson work out, "I have never seen a man who can whip Jack Johnson as he stands today, and I am forced to bet on him."

Governor Nickerson's observation did not noticeably alter the odds, for the weight of expert opinion was on Jeffries's side. Tommy Burns watched the two fighters work out and announced for Jeffries. So, surprisingly, did Sam Langford, the great black heavyweight who was engaged in a bitter feud with Johnson. Langford also organized a caravan of blacks, who drove out to Moana Springs to tell Jeffries that not all blacks backed Johnson.

If we can rely on the almost unanimous opinion of an army of reporters and athletic experts, Johnson acted in this period like he didn't have a worry or an enemy in the world. This was, by any standard, one of the most incredible demonstrations of coolness under fire in the history of athletics, or anything else. For Johnson was virtually alone in hostile territory; and he had, as he knew, millions of enemies and at least one real worry: the threat of death by a trained enemy agent or a crazed bigot. At least one attempt had already been made to poison him, and extraordinary precautions had been taken to prevent a second attempt. His food was prepared by a trusted friend, who never bought supplies twice at the same store. Johnson was also protected by a number of armed policemen, who guarded his private quarters and walked sentry at night. And although Johnson was genial and accessible to all comers, he was no fool. He walked around Reno with a loaded pistol in his pocket and kept a revolver on his bedstand at night.

There was nothing melodramatic about these precautions, for Reno was rife with rumors that someone was going to shoot Johnson before, during, or after the fight. The most widely circulated report was that scores of men were going to draw and shoot Johnson down if he knocked Jeffries out. Taking note of these reports, promoter Tex Rickard called a press conference on the eve of the fight and announced unprecedented security arrangements. There would be special deputies inside and outside the arena and all men would be searched at the gate. As an added precaution, liquor would not be sold and pop bottles would be confiscated.

As might have been expected, this announcement, coming on the eve of the fight, heightened tensions instead of diffusing them; and by Sunday, July 3, Reno and every hamlet and city within reach of the telegraph were pressure cookers of conflicting rumors, reports, and expectations.

Now, as the countdown began, men began to prepare for the day of judgement according to their different lights and means. By Sunday night, an army of men and women were en route to Reno by train, buggy, and car. On the same night, thousands of blacks were praying for Johnson in special church services, and arrangements were being made to bring spiritual forces into play. The Negro Holiness church of Hutchinson, Kansas, for example, had erected a large tent and had announced that it would hold special services on Monday. The pastor said that most of the twelve hundred black inhabitants of Hutchinson would pray and sing Spirituals until Johnson won, "if it takes all night." As an added precaution, the pastor had made secular arrangements to have the results of the fight telegraphed into the tent round by round. Similar services were planned for Denver, Chicago, New York, New Orleans, Washington, and other cities. But there were strong dissenters. The Reverend William D. Cook, pastor of Chicago's historic Quinn Chapel, was critical of this alliance between God and Mammon. "Pugilism," he said, "is brutish and beneath the notice of Christians. Neither Johnson nor Jeffries are representative of the highest type of the race to which they belong." There was truth in this, but it was not the kind of truth blacks or whites were seeking on the first Sunday in the month of July, 1910. And so, even as Cook spoke, thousands of black Chicagoans were getting ready for a huge victory celebration. The same thing was happening in Pittsburgh, where blacks were so confident that they had hired a hall and a band for "a victory celebration."

This day, July 3, was a Sunday, but betting was heavy in Pittsburgh and other cities. In Reno, Tom Corbett, the leading oddsmaker, predicted that at least three million dollars would change hands after the fight. In the black communities of Chicago, Galveston, and other cities, blacks were betting heavily. Some blacks were mortgaging their homes; some were discounting their paychecks for weeks in advance; some were borrowing or pawning clothes and jewels to get money to put down on Johnson. Some of this activity was stimulated by a telegram Johnson sent to his brother. The telegram said, in effect: BET YOUR LAST COPPER ON ME.

They were still betting in Chicago and Galveston and New York and London and Berlin, in thousands of cities and hamlets all over the world, when the sun cleared the mountains surrounding Reno on Monday, July 4. Jack Johnson got up early and consumed a huge breakfast of three scrambled eggs, four lamb chops, and a side order of rare steak. At the Jeffries camp across town, the mood was somber. Jeffries ate sparingly, taking a little fruit, toast, and tea.

As a matter of course, both camps issued victory statements. Johnson, as usual, was more articulate. How did he feel on the morning of the greatest fight of his career? "I'm just like a kid," he said, "on Christmas morning."

The fight was scheduled to begin at 1:30, but a crowd estimated at twenty-five thousand began to move in waves toward the arena at 10 A.M. The entire rolling stock of the Reno transportation system consisted of two cars, and most of the spectators walked down the dusty road or followed the railroad tracks. It had been almost impossible to get food or bathing water in Reno on this morning, and most of the ticket-holders were unshaven, unwashed, and suffering from hangovers.

When the first wave arrived at the arena, which was about three-fourths of a mile east of the station and close to the railroad tracks, carpenters were still hammering and putting on the finishing touches. The arena was an eight-sided structure set down in the center of the Reno valley, which was surrounded, Arthur Ruhl of *Collier's* noted, by "brown mountains with patches of yellow and olive-green and exquisite veils of mauve and amethyst, and at their top, blazing white in the clear air, patches of austere snow." The seats were plain unpainted pine, which rose tier after tier from the center. The only difference between the fifty dollar planks in front and the ten dollar planks in the rear was that the fifty dollar planks were planed smooth.

When, at noon, the gates were opened, lines of people stretched away from the arena for half a mile. There was only one entrance, and there was a stampede to get in. This created a tense and ugly movement, which promoter Rickard resolved by knocking holes in the fence and taking cash from all comers. The crowd rushed in, ran the gauntlet of security guards and spread fanwise to the various sections. The lemonade sellers and other vendors began to hawk their wares, and the arena was soon a din of screaming, shouting, milling spectators. The blazing desert sun dominated the proceedings, and most of the male spectators wore wide-brimmed hats and green reading shades.

The arena was three-fourths filled an hour before the scheduled starting time. At 12:30 it was packed with some eighteen thousand ticket holders and some two thousand persons who had paid five dollars for the privilege of standing on the top tier. While the crowd waited, various celebrities—Governor Nickerson, Bat Masterson, monologist Frank Fogarty and former heavyweight champion John L. Sullivan—arrived and self-consciously accepted cheers. During the cheering, Johnson's wife, Etta Duryea Johnson, slipped into the arena and took a seat down front. She was, a reporter noted, "attractively gowned" and wore an enormous picture hat. As whispers sped through the crowd, some men stood on their seats and gawked at her.

Shortly before 1 P.M., the Reno band entered the ring and played "America" and "Dixie." The spectators stood up and waved small American flags.

By 1:45, the crowd was getting restless, and Billy Jordan, a famous announcer of the day, climbed into the ring and introduced the leading fighters and has-beens. These pleasantries and diversions continued until 2:27 when there was a commotion in the northeast corner. The spectators came to their feet, jostling and shoving, and presently Jack Johnson came into view, wearing a flowing black and white silk robe which reached to his feet. He was smiling his famous "golden smile," so called because of its warmth and the large number of gold teeth it exposed. Johnson, surrounded by aides and handlers, most of whom were white, received perfunctory applause, and some jeers. He scaled the second rope, stepped into the ring and raised himself to his full height, beaming. He was thirty-two years old and in perfect physical condition, a little over six feet tall, weighing some two hundred pounds and wearing blue tights.

At this point, Sam Berger, a Jeffries aide, approached Johnson and offered to flip a coin for corners. Johnson, who was a master of the grand put-down, waved him away contemptuously, saying: "You can take any corner you want. Any corner is good enough for me." Berger chose the southeast corner. This meant that Jeffries would have the sun at his back.

Johnson swept regally across the ring, installed himself in the northeast corner and looked into the sun. What was he thinking at this moment? "As I looked about me," he said later, "and scanned that sea of white faces I felt the auspiciousness of the occasion. There were few men of my own race among the spectators. I realized that my victory in this event meant more than on any previous occasion. It wasn't just the championship that was at stake—it was my own honor, and in a degree the honor of my race. I was well aware of all these things, and I sensed that most of that great audience was hostile to me." Despite the "sun and the jeering mob and the occasional thought that there might be a gunman somewhere in that vast array of humanity," Johnson was not unduly disturbed. "I was cool," he said, "and perfectly at ease. I never had any doubt of the outcome."

Johnson's reverie was broken by a wild whoop in the back of the arena. Jim Jeffries, the great white hope, was on his way. The crowd came to its collective feet, screaming, shouting, cheering. Jeffries, who was thirty-five and weighed about 230 pounds, came down the aisle like an emperor, preceded by Bob Armstrong, a black sparring partner, who held aloft a great circular five-foot paper shade. Jeffries wore a light gray business suit over his blue tights and a golf hat on his head. He slipped through the ropes, jumped up and down on the platform, and glared at Johnson's corner. "I had a seat," Arthur Ruhl said, "directly opposite him, and I can unhesitatingly state that I have never seen a human being more calculated to strike terror into an opponent's heart than this scowling brown [the great white hope had a brown suntan!] Colossus as he came through the ropes, stamped like a bull pawing the ground before his charge, and, chewing gum rapidly, glared at the black man across the ring. If looks could have throttled, burned and torn to pieces, Mr. Jack Arthur Johnson would have disappeared that minute into a few specks of inanimate dust."

Johnson was neither intimidated nor disconcerted by the look. He seemed to be amused by the huge cheer that Jeffries received. Somewhat to the surprise of the spectators, he joined in, clapping his hands and beaming.

Johnson was the first to strip. As he did so, a strange thing happened: the crowd gasped. "There was," the *New York Times* man said, "a sigh of involuntary admiration as his naked body stood in the white sunlight." Rex E. Beach, a prominent novelist who was covering for a syndicate of newspapers, noted the same phenomenon, saying that as Johnson "stepped forth for the lenses to register his image he was a thing of surpassing beauty from the anatomist's point of view. He had none of that giant play of brawn and muscle that Jeffries displayed a moment later, but instead a rounded symmetry more in line with the ideals of the ancient Greek artists. His head, though slightly larger than an ostrich egg, was of the same shape and shaved to an equal smoothness. From crown to sole he was a living life-size bronze, chiseled by the cunning hands of a master."

The seconds and photographers fussed over the fighters for a few minutes, and then the referee, promoter Tex Rickard, announced that the fighters would not shake hands. At 2:44 P.M. he ordered the ring cleared. At 2:45, the gong sounded. The Fight of the Century was on.

As the sound of the gong reverberated through the Reno arena, there was a gasp and then silence. In the silence, Jack Johnson and Jim Jeffries shuffled to the center of the ring and circled each other, warily. Jeffries was chewing gum, and Johnson was smiling. Both men were alert, cautious. Around and around they went, moving clockwise and then counterclockwise. As this continued, there was an almost palpable feeling of disappointment. The spectators expected an immediate explosion—what they got was a probing operation, with both fighters feinting, bluffing, and jockeying for position. This continued for fully ten seconds, and then Johnson landed the first blow, a straight left to the mouth. The two men clinched, and Jeffries pumped furiously on the inside. Almost casually, Johnson blocked the blows and, resting his head on Jeffries's shoulder, smiled and nodded to friends at ringside. It went on like this until the end of the round. At the sound of the gong, Johnson patted Jeffries on the shoulder with the palm of his glove and told him to cheer up.

A reporter sitting at ringside made a note on his pad: "The first round is uneventful and furnishes no intelligent line on the fight." He was wrong. There was, to be sure, little or no dramatic action in the round. But there was a lot of action. The action, however, was internal, visible only to the eyes of the initiated. Hugh E. Keough of the *Chicago Tribune* saw it. Jeffries's plan, he noted, was to rush Johnson and overwhelm him, adding: "He was not there half a minute before it occurred to him that it would be better to break out a new line of thought. Jeffries saw that the graven image in front of him was not afraid and it puzzled him. He had been made to feel that this big lump of charcoal with gleaming teeth had a yellow streak and weak kidneys." The first few seconds of the round disabused Jeffries of that notion, and a kind of desperation was born in him. For he knew now that he was in for a long, interesting, and possibly disastrous afternoon.

The action in this and succeeding rounds was relayed by telegraph to millions gathered in bars, coliseums, and private clubs, from one end of the world to the other. In every city of any consequence, bulletins were being flashed to yelling multitudes, who crowded around bulletin boards or strained to hear blow-by-blow accounts read over megaphones.

In Washington, D.C., some thirty thousand were assembled before bulletin boards. In Kansas City, some fourteen thousand were following the action in Convention Hall. In Chicago, ten thousand were in front of the *Chicago Tribune* building at Dearborn and Madison streets. In New York City, thirty thousand thronged Times Square and followed the fight on the *New York Times* bulletin boards.

This mania was not confined to America. It was past midnight now in London and Berlin, but excited crowds were milling around newpaper offices and fashionable hotels. If we can believe contemporary reports, returns were being telegraphed to every club of prominence in the United States and Canada. In Long Island, at the Edgemere Club, the interested patrons included William K. Vanderbilt and Howard Gould. At the same time, but in vastly different circumstances, the prisoners of the Cook County (Chicago) jail were receiving the fight returns. The telegraph key was being operated by a telegrapher who happened to be an inmate at the time.

In Chicago, in New York, in San Francisco, in London and Berlin, there was a certain sameness in the responses of white auditors. The *New York Times* reported that the crowd in Times Square went wild when Jeffries scored a point, "but when the bulletin showed that the Negro had delivered a telling blow, there were no cheers, just a murmur." The same phenomenon was observed in Chicago, where a *Chicago Tribune* reporter said that "throughout the description of the battle, they were ever pulling for the white man, cheering every time that he landed a blow on his opponent, and maintaining silence when the Negro landed one of his punches."

There were few blacks in these crowds, which were hostile to Johnson and resented any demonstration on his behalf. In New Orleans, a black man—the newspapers said he was "demented"—couldn't resist a liberating shout for Johnson and was manhandled and driven from the crowd. There were no "unpleasant" incidents in Times Square, we are told, for the "few Negroes" there were not demonstrative. This was not the case in Chicago, Johnson's adopted hometown, where blacks were for Johnson and didn't care who knew it. When a white woman in the *Tribune* crowd made an uncomplimentary remark about Johnson, a black woman grabbed a handful of hair and swung on her.

To prevent hassles of this kind, many blacks had arranged for special telegraph connections to bars and theaters, where they could give vent to their true emotions. And as the early rounds unfolded, more than two thousand blacks, including Johnson's mother, Mrs. Tina Johnson, were crammed into the Pekin Theater in Chicago. There was a telegrapher in the wings; and after each round the proprietor, Robert Motts, came on-stage and read the results to wildly cheering men and women.

The Pekin crowd had something to cheer about in the second round, which was, in some respects, a replay of the first. Jeffries came out in his famous crouch, with his left arm extended before him like an antennae. In the old days, this pose had struck terror into the hearts of his opponents. But if he thought he could bluff his way through this fight, he was sadly mistaken, a point Johnson underlined by leading again with a hard uppercut to the chin. Jeffries countered with a left to the body and took another blow to the face. They clinched, and the referee pulled them apart. Jeffries crouched and waited for Johnson to come in. Johnson smiled, declining. They sparred around for a while and clinched again. After the break, Jeffries waded in, and Johnson landed a wicked left hook to the left eye, causing it to flush. At the end of the round, Johnson threw his head back and laughed out loud. This puzzled ringsiders, who wondered why he was happy. It was the general consensus of the experts that the round was dull and that neither fighter had struck a good blow. Which only goes to show that it is not wise to give too much weight to "expert" opinion. The experts said the round was dull. In fact, the round had decided the fight, which was almost over. Johnson had exceptionally well-developed back muscles and powerful arms, and his blows were harder than they seemed. And, as it turned out, one of his blows, the little-noted left hook to the eye, had done irreparable damage to Jeffries's face and psyche. The blow did not travel far, but it landed with such force that it paralyzed the right side of Jeffries's face and sent needles of pain through his body. Jeffries would say later that the blow "affected the vision in my right eye and I could see two colored men in the ring before me."

There were moments in succeeding rounds when it seemed that Jeffries was fighting four colored men. For in the third round, Johnson seized the initiative and imposed a new rhythm on the fight. Jeffries continued to charge, flailing his arms and punching the air. But his blows lacked steam, and Johnson sidestepped and counterattacked with deadly efficiency. Puzzled, feeling vaguely that something had gone wrong, Jeffries rushed around the ring like a bull. Johnson led him like a clever matador, sidestepping his charges and stabbing him with lefts and rights. As Johnson worked, he chatted with friends and reporters at ringside and joshed Jeffries and his chief second, Jim Corbett. Corbett heard him tell Jeffries at one point: "Let me see what you got. Do something, man. This is for the *cham*-peenship."

After the third round, Johnson treated Jeffries, the Associated Press reported, "almost as a joke. He smiled and blocked playfully, warding off the rushes of Jeffries with a marvelous science, now tucking a blow under his arm, again plucking it out of the air as a man stops a baseball." Toward the end of the fourth round, a big sporting man who had bet ten thousand dollars on Jeffries shouted: "He'll kill you, Jack." Johnson stung Jeffries with a left and shouted over his shoulders: "That's what they all say."

In the fifth round, Jeffries rushed out in a low crouch. When Jeffries's seconds shouted to him to stand up, Johnson said, "I'll straighten him up in a minute."

The crowd, enraged, shouted: "He'll straighten you up, nigger."

Johnson smiled and answered with a left and right to Jeffries's battered face. At the end of the round, Johnson leaned over the ropes and spoke to John L. Sullivan, the former heavyweight champion.

"John," he said, "I thought this fellow could hit."

"I never said so," Sullivan replied, "but I believe he could have six years ago."

"Yes," Johnson nodded, "five or six years ago ain't now, though."

Relentlessly, throughout the sixth, seventh, and eighth rounds, Johnson increased the pressure, landing blow after blow on Jeffries's damaged eye. At the end of the sixth round, Jeffries' right eye was closed and his nose was bleeding. The seconds worked hard at the end of the sixth and seventh rounds, but this seemed to irritate Jeffries, who waved them away.

"Come on, Jeffries!" Johnson taunted at the beginning of the eighth. Jeffries came on and got a hard left in the eye for his pains. As soon as the blow landed, Johnson waved to Jim Corbett and asked: "Did you see that one, Jimmy?" Prompted by some lingering hope, Jeffries continued to rush, but he was taking a terrific beating, and the odds at ringside were now even money on Jack Johnson.

In the next three rounds, Johnson kept Jeffries's head bobbing constantly, hitting him almost at will. His famous short-arm punches were working like pistons, and he was scoring effectively with hooks and uppercuts. Near the end of the eleventh round, he turned Jeffries's head clear around with a whistling left to the jaw. In the twelfth round, he put on such a dazzling display of speed and defensive ability that the hostile crowd actually cheered him. By the end of the round, Jeffries was bleeding from the lip and nose, and his legs were unsteady. As he turned to go to his corner he spat up a large quantity of blood and gasped for air. At this point, one of Jeffries's friends left his ringside seat and fled the arena, crying.

It had been clear for some time now that Johnson could put Jeffries away anytime he wanted. Why didn't he? This question would be debated at length in coming days. The white manager Johnson dismissed on the eve of the fight charged bitterly—and Johnson denied—that Johnson had agreed to let the fight go a certain number of rounds for the benefit of the movie cameras. Nat Fleischer, the boxing expert, offered another explanation. It was Johnson's style, he said, to punish opponents who insulted him. He liked, Fleischer said, to teach these opponents a lesson by cutting them up and making their punishment as severe and protracted as possible.

Whatever the reason, Johnson toyed with Jeffries for two more rounds. At one point in the fourteenth, he tauntingly exposed his stomach and invited Jeffires to hit him. The blow, when it came, was feeble, and Johnson showed no sign of pain or distress. At this point, as John L. Sullivan noted in a dispatch to the *New York Times*, "Jeffries was a sight to behold. He was cut in six places and he was still going after Johnson. Johnson brought home lefts across and they always caught Jeffries on the face. Jeff's arms seemed like lead, and he could barely raise them, let alone hit Johnson."

When the gong for the fifteenth round sounded, Jeffries's face was puffed and bleeding, and his legs were wobbly. Blindly, he stumbled after the elusive Johnson, sometimes crouching low with his left hand stuck out in front of him, sometimes standing erect. But crouching or standing, he was an easy target for Johnson, who waited until he was in range and chopped his face to pieces. Instinctively, Jeffries clinched. As he broke away, Johnson pivoted and sent a left and right to the jaw. Jeffries stumbled against the rope. Johnson pounced on him, shooting lefts and rights. Jeffries reeled away. Johnson shot a left from the hip straight to the jaw and Jeffries crashed to the floor for the first time in his career. The crowd, stunned by the fury and suddenness of the attack, came to its feet, soundlessly, and watched with horror as Jeffries staggered to his feet. Johnson pounced. A left, a right, and another left landed on Jeffries's chin, and he stumbled backwards, falling through the ropes and landing on the overhanging platform.

"Stop it!" the spectators screamed. "Stop it! Don't let him be knocked out!"

The referee ignored these pleas, and Jeffries's seconds and some of the reporters pushed him back into the ring. Slowly, as if out of a fog, he got to his feet and reeled around the ring. Johnson stalked him, measured his distance and swung. The great white hope crumbled and went through the ropes again. The timekeeper raised and lowered his arm, "one, two . . ." He had reached the count of eight when Jeffries's handlers came into the ring to get him. It was 3:41, fifty-six minutes after the fight began. Tex Rickard put his hand on Johnson's shoulder and declared him the winner.

While Jeffries's handlers were ministering to him, Johnson swept through the crowd and went to his training quarters. He had earned some $190,000, roughly equivalent to $1 million today.

Of all the improbable aspects of this improbable drama, the oddest was that no one lifted a finger to harm Johnson. The undisputed champion of the world went to his quarters, changed clothes, collected his wife and ordered his chauffeur to drive slowly through the center of Reno. Johnson and his white wife sat in the back seat of the open touring car.

In an extraordinary gesture of sang-froid (some called it gall), Johnson made a speech from the car and held a reception in front of the Golden Hotel where, according to press reports, thousands of white men filed by to shake his hand. He left Reno that night at 9:50 in a private railroad car equipped with a phonograph, piano, and buffet. All this was noted in the press, and it was agreed that, whatever else might be said of Johnson, no one could deny that he had style.

As the train rolled across the country, white America went into something approaching national mourning. The first telegraphic message—

FLASH/JOHNSON WINS IN THE FIFTEENTH ROUND—was re-
ceived with shocked disbelief by the millions following the bulletins. Almost without exception, the white crowds received the news with mur-
murs of disappointment and then filed away with the solemnity of a
funeral procession. There was, the *New York Times* said, in a revealing
dispatch, an almost universal feeling of "personal loss."

The *Times* could have added that there was an almost universal
feeling of "personal triumph" in the black community. When Robert
Motts walked onto the stage of Chicago's Pekin Theater to read the flash,
the smile on his face said all that needed to be said, and the crowd
exploded in cheers and screams.

Within seconds, State Street from Twenty-fifth to Thirty-fifth was a
surging mass of screaming blacks, shouting, "Jack, Jack, J-A-J." There
were similar celebrations in Pittsburgh and other large Northern cities
where there were enough blacks to risk the expected white retaliation. In
the West Indies, in South America, wherever the telegraph reached and
the risks were acceptable, blacks demonstrated and danced. In Port-of-
Spain, Trinidad, a large crowd gathered at the telegraph office and, a
reporter said, "the colored people held a jollification."

In all these places, and in Chicago as well, there had been doleful
predictions that a Johnson victory would trigger white wrath. Within
hours after the flash, the predictions came true in a rash of riots and
skirmishes in almost every major American city. In Washington, D.C.,
the *Washington Bee* reported that "white ruffians showed their teeth and
attacked almost every colored person they saw upon the public streets."
In New York City, young hoods of the Hounds of Hell and Pearl Button
gangs roamed the streets, attacking and beating blacks. In one New York
area, whites barricaded the doors and windows of a tenement house, set
it on fire and tried to cremate the black tenants. In another area of the
city, a group of whites accosted a black man who was buying a newspaper. "What do you think of the fight?" they asked. The black man
replied with consummate diplomacy, "I'm neutral." The whites shouted,
"Let's kill the coon." The black man drew a wicked-looking stiletto and
held the whites off until police arrived.

The most colorful encounter of the night occurred in Brooklyn,
where a white man named John Dermody heard Edward Coleman tell his
dog to "lie down there, Jeffries."

Dermody told Coleman, "You have your nerve to call that dog Jeffries. Why don't you call it Johnson?"

Coleman looked Dermody in the eye and said: "Because Johnson is black and this dog is yellow." Before the fight ended, Brooklyn police had a minor riot on their hands.

This episode might be considered trifling, but it was characteristic of scores of other incidents that were reported all over America. In Mounds, Illinois, blacks shot up the town and killed a black constable. In Uvaldia, Georgia, there was a shoot-out between blacks and whites. In Keystone, West Virginia, blacks seized the town and disarmed the police.

So it went almost everywhere—in Little Rock, Roanoke, Philadelphia, Wilmington, New Orleans, Atlanta, St. Louis, Omaha, and Louisville. In smaller towns in the South, whites unleashed a virtual reign of terror. Many years later, Benjamin E. Mays, the celebrated educator, recalled the atmosphere in Ninety-Six, South Carolina. "White men in my county," he wrote, "could not take it. A few Negroes were beaten up because a Negro had beaten a white man in far-away Nevada."

By midnight on July 4, 1910, at least eleven persons had been killed. Or, to be more precise, at least eleven persons had been reported killed. No one knows, and no one will ever know, how many blacks were killed on that July night because a black man whipped a white man in a prize fight in Nevada.

Since most of the victims of the violence were black, certain men— black and white—suggested that Johnson had done blacks a disservice by whipping Jeffries. A distinguished black intellectual, Professor William Pickens of Talladega, disagreed. He was opposed, he said in a *Chicago Defender* article to "pugilism," but he believed that Johnson had done "missionary work" in defeating Jeffries. As for the casualties, "it was a good deal better for Johnson to win and a few Negroes be killed in body for it, than for Johnson to have lost and all Negroes to have been killed in spirit by the preachments of inferiority from the combined white press. It is better for us to succeed, though some die, than for us to fail though all live."

While blacks and whites fought and died in his name, Jack Johnson sped across the country, making ceremonial stops at selected sites. At Cheyenne, Wyoming, the soldiers of the famed Ninth Cavalry turned out en masse to greet Johnson, who stood on the steps of his private railway car, shaking hands with the men and bowing to their wives. An escort of six soldiers presented a woman and an infant, who had been named Jack Arthur Johnson. John Arthur (Jack) Johnson gravely shook hands with his tiny namesake. When the train pulled out, a dozen soldiers got on their steeds, and, riding as hard as they could, followed the train for about a mile, waving their caps and cheering.

It was a grand gesture, reminiscent in some ways of some of the tributes tendered Johnson's hero, Napoleon. Johnson watched the stirring scene for a moment and said: "It is a great thing to make so many people happy."

Johnson had occasion to remember these words when the train pulled into the Chicago and Northwestern station in Chicago. The station was packed, and the streets were lined with some twenty thousand blacks who had declared an unofficial holiday in his honor. When Johnson appeared, the crowd, a *Chicago Tribune* reporter said, "went stark staring mad," shouting over and over again, "Oh, you Jack Johnson!" The next night Johnson was honored at a testimonial and banquet organized by what the *Chicago Tribune* called "the Negro Elite." When Johnson was introduced, men and women stood on their seats and cheered for five minutes. Johnson, obviously overwhelmed, responded with a speech. "Ladies and gentlemen," he said, "it gives me great pleasure to appear before you this evening as the undisputed heavyweight champion of the world. But before I mention fighting or go on any further I want to impress on you that I don't want my friends to be like the French. When Napoleon was winning battles he was loved by his people, but when he lost, he lost his friends. I want my friends to love me just the same if I lose or win a battle tomorrow or if it be a year hence...."

Considering the fact that Johnson was at the peak of his glory, and that the time of his troubles was still far ahead, these were powerful words. For the people were cheering because they believed the war had been won. And Johnson was saying, at least on one level, that he and the forces he represented had only won one battle in a long and continuing war in which defeat and even destruction were possible. He could not have been more right, for the war continued on many fronts. The U.S. Congress and several foreign governments, including South Africa and Cuba, banned the fight film; and Johnson was later convicted, on dubious testimony, of violating the Mann Act by transporting a white woman across state lines for immoral purposes. Before sentence could be executed, he jumped bail and wandered across the face of the earth, telling vaudeville audiences that his only crime was the crime of whipping Jim Jeffries. To complicate matters further, Etta Duryea—Johnson's wife—committed suicide. In 1915 he was "defeated" by Jess Willard in a championship fight in Havana, Cuba. Johnson claimed that his "defeat" was part of a deal in which he was promised immunity from prosecution in the United States. Unfortunately for Johnson, the deal, if there was such a deal, fell through, and his self-imposed exile continued until 1920, when he returned to the United States and served a year and a day in the federal penitentiary.

After this ordeal, Johnson picked up the threads of his career and tried, unsuccessfully, to get a match with the new heavyweight champion, Jack Dempsey. In 1926, at the age of forty-eight, he fought his last serious contest, defeating a ranking young white heavyweight in fifteen rounds. In the thirties and forties, he lectured, performed in sideshows and did whatever was required to pay for the champagne and racing cars he had become accustomed to. He was returning from a sideshow engagement on June 10, 1946, speeding up a highway near Franklinton, North Carolina, when his luck ran out. A big truck crossed the center line, and Johnson reacted, but his reflexes were not what they were on July 4, 1910, and the big Lincoln Zephyr careened across the road and smashed into a power pole. They carried him back to Chicago and put him into the ground beside the tragic Etta Duryea Johnson in an exclusive white cemetery on the North Side. His body lies there today, surrounded by the tombs of the Pullmans and Palmers and McCormicks, and the memory of his spirit haunts the Republic.

Storm Warning

Marcus Garvey's Hour of Triumph

ARLEM was used to spectacles.

The city within a city was young then, but it had seen it all, and heard it all, or at least Harlemites thought so, back there in the days when the leaves were new on the Lenox Avenue trees.

Harlem was used to dreams and dreamers.

It was hemmed in, imposed upon, *imprisoned* by an intolerable reality. And it attracted, and would attract, thousands of men and women who claimed, in one way or another, to have the key to the doors of the prisons. Hustlers, charlatans, radicals, nationalists, tea-readers, men on white horses, men on black horses, messiahs, mahatmas, prophets fresh from the wilderness: Harlem had seen everything, and heard everything. But Harlem had never seen anything like this. Right before the startled eyes of thousands of spectators, a new nation, a mighty new black nation, was unfolding itself, flexing its muscles, marching down Lenox Avenue, bands blaring, children singing, the sharp swords of soldiers gleaming in the sunlight. There had been thousands of parades in the Harlems of America, but there had never been a parade like this one, before or since. The line of march seemed endless. There were twelve bands, regiments of real black soldiers, contingents of real black officers and real black sailors from real ships, all of them resplendently attired, all of them erect and proud, swathed in a riot of colors and costumes and flags. It made the heart beat faster. It brought a lump to the throat. It forced reluctant tears from cold, cynical eyes. There they were, in broad open daylight, the soldiers of the African Legion, the women saviors of the Black Cross Nurses, and contingents of marching black brothers and sisters from almost everywhere, from Cuba and Costa Rica and Panama and Trinidad and Liberia and Canada. This clearly was no ordinary parade: this was the marching of a new world spirit. And the word went forth from Harlem on this day—Monday, August 2, 1920—that a new force was loose in the black world.

What was the meaning of this?

Who was behind it?

The answer to the second question was easy. The leader, the creator and the orchestrator of the new force was Marcus Garvey, who seemed to be everywhere on this day, leading the parade in an open touring car, reviewing the parade from an improvised stand, gesturing, waving, commanding scores of aides, who gave him the deferential attention usually reserved for monarchs and emperors. He was not a man, Garvey, to hide his light under a bushel. And on this day he was royally attired in a satin mantle of red and black. He was accompanied, the Baltimore *Afro-American* reported cautiously, "by Prince Deniyi, said to have come from Africa, clad in blue and white silk and satin, and others with gold braid and bright uniforms." Who was this man? He was one of the dreamers, one of the shooting stars that streak across the Harlem sky from time to time, leaving a train of brilliant sparks and hopes. What perhaps is most astonishing is that he had arrived in New York only four years before this his day of triumph. Like all the dreamers that preceded him, and like all the dreamers that followed him, he had talked big, and Harlem had listened and smiled. But now he was showing them, and his critics were shaking their heads in wonder and admiration.

Never one to give up an advantage, or to let the attention of his audience wander, Garvey followed up this master stroke with a series of dazzling moves that changed the tone of race relations in America. That night, before some twenty-five thousand screaming followers in

Marcus Garvey attracted national attention with colorful uniforms, nationalistic message.

Madison Square Garden, the thirty-three-year-old president-general of
the Universal Negro Improvement Association (UNIA) opened the first
International Convention of the Negro Peoples of the World. This convention sat for thirty days and thirty nights, and Garvey sustained the
excitement and drama of the opening night. Speaking before a second
monster rally at Carnegie Hall, he underlined the meaning and implication of the unfolding drama. "The Negroes of the world say, 'We are
striking homewards towards Africa to make her the big black republic.'
And in the making of Africa a big black republic, what is the barrier?
The barrier is the white man; we say to the white man who now domi-
nates Africa that it is to his interest to clear out of Africa now, because
we are coming 400,000,000 strong, and we mean to retake every square
inch of the 12,000,000 square miles of African territory belonging to us
by right Divine. . . ."

What did all this mean concretely?

It meant, Garvey said, black pride, black power, and black self-
reliance. To some men then, and to some men today, it meant "Back to
Africa," a mass migration of African-Americans to the fatherland. It was
argued persuasively then, and it has been argued persuasively since,
that this was a misunderstanding of Garvey, who, it is said, was only
calling for the liberation of Africa and the migration of *some* African-
Americans. Whatever he was calling for, it was apparent to all in August,
1920, that Garveyism meant black militancy. From now on, Garvey told
the delegates, "the first dying to be done by the black man . . . will be
done to make himself free." And "if we have any charity to bestow, we
may die for the white man." But "as for me," Garvey said, as men and
women rose to their feet screaming, "I think I have stopped dying for
him."

This was clear enough, and ominous enough, and it went substantially beyond the traditional posture of black protest leadership. But
talk was cheap. What did Garvey plan to do? The answer or answers to
this question are not entirely clear, even today. Substance and shadow
were so inextricably intertwined in the Marcus Garvey crusade that it is
hard to say what was real and what was illusion. And it is impossible to
understand this complex personality without a recreation of the events

Black Cross nurses and other contingents of Garvey empire led Harlem parade.

At Liberty Hall in Harlem, Garvey received deferential attention of aides.

that led him out of the obscurity of a West Indian island to such a position of power that for a short time he stood in the center of the worldwide racial drama.

The path began in St. Ann's Bay on the northern coast of Jamaica, where Garvey was born on August 17, 1887. The youngest of eleven children born to artisan Marcus Garvey and his wife, Sarah, he was raised in a stern, stable environment dominated by British colonialism. He attended local elementary school and later moved to Kingston, where he mastered the trade of printing. All who knew him then agree that he was proud and ambitious. A contemporary, J. Coleman Beecher, said "he was fiercely proud of being black. He carried a pocket dictionary with him and said he studied three or four words daily, and in his room he would write a paragraph or two using these words."

By the age of twenty, Garvey was a master printer and foreman of one of the largest plants on the island. But he lost this job when he helped organize a printers' union strike. After an unsuccessful venture as an editor, he left Jamaica and drifted from one port to another. He worked for a while in Costa Rica, then in Panama, then in Ecuador, always studying, always agitating, always dreaming. In 1912 he went to London, and there, in the pre-World War I years, all the strands came together. Associating with African agitators like Duse Mohammed Ali and reading the tracts and books of African protest leaders, he began to glimpse the possibilities of a new world order. Then, by accident, he came across a copy of Booker T. Washington's biography, *Up From Slavery*. "I read *Up From Slavery* by Booker T. Washington," he said, "and then my doom—if I may so call it—of being a race leader dawned upon me....I asked: 'Where is the black man's Government? Where is his King and his kingdom? Where is

202

his President, his country, and his ambassador, his army, his navy, his men of big affairs?' I could not find them, and then I declared, 'I will help to make them.' "

Without losing any time, Garvey returned to Jamaica, "determined," he said, "that the black man would not continue to be kicked about by all the other races and nations of the world." His brain "was afire," he said, with the possibility of "uniting all the Negro peoples of the world into one great body to establish a country and a Government absolutely their own." On August 1, 1914—the eighty-first anniversary of emancipation in the West Indies—Garvey organized the Universal Negro Improvement Association, an organization designed to "reclaim the fallen" and "to establish a Universal Confraternity among the race." The organization attracted few members; and Garvey, enraged by the indifference and hostility of "some of these colored men on the island who did not want to be classified as Negroes," ranged far and wide in search of support. After corresponding with Booker T. Washington, he decided to seek recruits and support in America. On March 23, 1916, he landed in New York.

He could not have picked a more agreeable place or a more agreeable time. There were some eighty thousand blacks in Manhattan, which was, as Claude McKay said, "a vast humming hive" of newcomers from the South and the West Indies. Racial tensions had reached the crisis point in Harlem and Black America, and every train brought new migrants, who were swarming to the big cities of the North in an unprecedented mass migration. These migrants, threatened by new and explosive forces, brought new hopes and new fears. The first great war "to make the world safe for democracy" had disillusioned and radicalized black soldiers and large segments of the black population. There was, at the same time, a sharp white backlash in

The beginning of the end of Garvey dream came in 1925 when he was convicted of using the mail to defraud.

the white community, which was demoralized by the war and terrified
by the new forces unleashed by the war. One result of all this was a
nationwide resurgence of the Ku Klux Klan. Another was the development of a national mood of nativism and racism. From the time of
Garvey's arrival to his moment of triumph, America was wracked by a
rising tide of lynchings, racial confrontations, and riots.

All this—the race riots, the new mood of black militancy, the uproot-
ings of the migrations, and the resurgence of the Klan—was grist for the
mill of Garvey, who came for a visit and looked around and decided to
stay. He was only twenty-eight years old then, but years of traveling and
reading had sharpened his skills, and his desire. One of the first American blacks to meet him, John Bruce, was so impressed that he could still
recall the fire and force of the man years later. "He was," he said, "a little,
sawed-off, hammered down black man, with determination written all
over his face, and an engaging smile that caught you and compelled you
to listen to his story." Garvey told his story wherever he could find a
listener. He harangued crowds on street corners and in small halls. He
traveled from city to city, observing, recruiting, preaching. Slowly, painfully, he recruited a handful of men and women in the West Indian
community and moved out from this base to the untapped reservoir of
migrants from the South.

To Southern migrants, to West Indian immigrants, to anyone who
would listen, Garvey preached a new doctrine of black regeneration and
black renaissance. "When Europe was inhabited by a race of cannibals,"
he said, "a race of savages, naked men, heathens and pagans, Africa was
peopled with a race of cultured black men, who were masters in art,
science and literature; men who were cultured and refined, men who,
it was said, were like gods. . . . Why then, should we lose hope? Black
men, you were once great; you shall be great again. Lose not courage,
lose not faith, go forward."

Contemptuous of traditional black organizations, Garvey attacked
W. E. B. DuBois, Asa Philip Randolph, and other black leaders. Prayers
and petitions, he said, would never solve the race problem. The only
solution, he said, was power, black power, solidly rooted in a free and
united Africa.

At home in his own skin, Garvey insisted that other blacks accept
their skin color. Black, he said, in so many words, was not only beautiful,
it was also redemptive. So stating and so believing, he gave a positive value
to everything black and tried to give his listeners a new sense of their

potentialities. Time and time again, he pulled men and women to their feet with the words, "Up, you mighty race, you can accomplish what you will."

What made all this enormously effective was Garvey's organizational ability and his flair for dramatics. Garvey had great histrionic gifts and a genius for bold and flamboyant gestures. More than any other black leader, he excelled in mass organization. More than any other black leader, he knew how to attract and hold the attention of large masses of people. It is not surprising, therefore, that the organization he formed was more, and less, than an organization. The Garvey organization was a revival, a show, a way of life. It had life in it. It moved, it attracted the eye, the ear, and the heart. There was a flag, red (for the blood shed by the race), black (for the color of the race), and green (for the hopes of the race). There was an African court of knights and ladies, there were high-sounding titles for the faithful, and there were Liberty Halls in major cities, where members gathered on Sunday to hear the word preached. From these halls radiated concentric circles of expression that enclosed the faithful in a total medium. The organization had a police force, a small army of African Legionnaires, a Royal African Motor Corps, and contingents for children and women. Of equal and perhaps greater importance was the string of shops, restaurants, and small businesses organized by Garvey. His biggest coup, however, was the organization in 1919 of the Black Star Shipping Line. When, in November, 1919, the first ship of the line, the *Yarmouth*, sailed from the 135th Street pier under the command of a black captain, Garvey critics, critic W. E. B. DuBois said, were "compelled" to admiration.

The ships, the businesses, the color and the pageantry had the effect Garvey intended it to have, and blacks by the thousands flocked to his banner. In 1920 Garvey claimed four million members, but objective observers said the number was closer to five hundred thousand. By that time, the Garvey newspaper, the *Negro World*, was one of the largest black weekly newspapers in America.

A revealing account of the Garvey operation at this peak moment has been transmitted to us by Captain Hugh Mulzac, who was a master on the *Yarmouth*, which was rechristened the S.S. *Frederick Douglass*. As he approached the UNIA headquarters at 56 West 135th Street, he discovered "a line more than one hundred yards long waiting to enter." He added: "There were jobseekers and supplicants, stock-owners-to-be, and a few hero worshippers who simply wanted to tell Mr. Garvey how proud they were of him for what he was doing for the race. Since I had an appointment, I walked past and up the stairway leading from the first floor to the second, and the second to the third. There in the topmost office was a counter stacked with bundles of bills of small denominations—the savings of thousands of earnest, hard-working folk who had come to buy five-dollar shares of stock in the Black Star Line.

"Off this room was Mr. Garvey's office. As I entered he rose from his desk and gave my hand a fierce shake.

" 'Glad to see you, Mulzac,' he said, giving me a piercing look from his deep black eyes set in a fleshy but well-formed face. 'Sit down, sit down,' he ordered and started to unfold his dream before I had even obeyed his command.

"Garvey was a short, stocky man of pure African descent. As he expounded, taking off every few moments in a flight of oratory, his black eyes flashed and his quick fingers drove home each point. At one moment he was wildly castigating white men for their cruelty and hypocrisy, and the next extolling the greatness of ancient African civilizations and recounting the unlimited wealth of the 'mother continent.'

"Throughout our half-hour meeting, during which he outlined the greatest 'Back-to-Africa' movement the world has ever seen, I sat transfixed with awe."

Another and more critical view of the Garvey operation was written by James Weldon Johnson. "Meetings at Liberty Hall," he wrote, "were conducted with an elaborate liturgy. The moment for the entry of the 'Provisional President' into the auditorium was solemn; a hushed and expectant silence on the throng, the African Legion and Black Cross Nurses flanking the long aisle and coming to attention, the band and audience joining in the hymn, 'Long Live Our President,' and Garvey, surrounded by his guard of honor from the Legion, marching majestically through the double line and mounting the rostrum."

Some of Garvey's flights into theatrics, as this quote indicates, provided ammunition for critics, who said Garvey was a vain and shallow man with a Napoleonic complex. Garvey's defenders claimed, however, that he was forced to adopt questionable means in order to attract and hold the masses.

Personality apart, it was clear to critics and defenders that Garvey was more than a showman. And as the tide of white reaction rose in America, the appetite of the Garvey movement grew by what it fed on, and its power grew proportionately.

It was against this background that Garvey issued a call for an International Convention of the Negro Peoples of the World. Plans for the convention were carefully crafted, and the organizing committees spent months going over the details. All the while, week after week, Garvey stagemanaged the preparations, sending recruiting teams of singers and actresses and lecturers to Cuba, Jamaica, and Panama, dispatching Black Star ships to areas of maximum visibility.

The convention opened on Sunday, August 1, with three religious services at Liberty Hall, a low, zinc-topped structure at 114 West 138th Street. According to the *New York Times*, the "upper portion of Manhattan, from between Cathedral Heights and the Hudson River, was practically taken over by the delegates," who reportedly came from almost every state in the Union and twenty-five countries on four continents. There was only a handful of delegates from the black civil rights establishment, but William Monroe Trotter of Boston was there. So also was William C. Matthews, a leading Massachusetts Republican who was later elected UNIA general counsel.

Before the afternoon service, the delegates and UNIA members staged a silent march through Harlem. During the parade, large handbills were distributed announcing a "monster" rally at Madison Square Garden and proposing the election of "a President of Africa, a leader for the Negro people of America and a leader for the Negro people of the world."

The rally was scheduled for the next day, which dawned clear and cool with temperatures in the sixties. By midday the sun beamed over Lenox Avenue and the temperature was in the seventies. This was a good sign, and thousands lined the streets, waiting for the big parade which was scheduled to precede the rally. There was, as usual, a brief period of anxious waiting and watching, and then the first units came into view. At a distance the marching men looked like soldiers. As they came closer the crowd discovered with a shudder of delight that they were, in fact, soldiers, members of Garvey's embryonic army, the African Legion. The Legionnaires were smartly dressed in dark blue uniforms. They were unarmed, but this was a mere detail, which the imagination corrected. They had been long and brilliantly trained by their commander, E. L. Gaines, a former U.S. Army captain; and they moved along Lenox Avenue with dash and precision, conscious of the impact they were making.

The Legionnaires were followed by a fifty-piece band, contingents of local UNIA branches and UNIA businesses, and two hundred Black Cross Nurses in white uniforms. Behind the nurses were contingents of children and women. Two marchers at the head of the Women's Auxiliary carried a sign:

GOD GIVE US REAL MEN

There were other signs, placards, and slogans:

AFRICA FOR THE AFRICANS

NEGROES FOUGHT IN EUROPE
AND CAN FIGHT IN AFRICA

The line of march, eyewitnesses said, extended for miles and consisted of Africans in ceremonial robes, African-American dignitaries in academic gowns, and members of the UNIA in purple, green, and gold or the traditional red, black, and green.

On and on they came, past Patsy's Fruit and Vegetable Market, A&P New Economy Stores and Sam's Market, and the crowds lining the sidewalk shouted approval. A participant, Captain Mulzac, said that at its peak the parade "started at 116th Street and Lenox Avenue, and stretched down to 100th Street, over to Seventh Avenue, and back up to 145th Street! As far as I am aware it was the greatest demonstration of colored solidarity in American history, before or since."

All this made a profound impression on Harlem and sent additional thousands scurrying to Madison Square Garden, which was filled long before the opening hour by more than twenty thousand blacks who spilled out into the surrounding streets. "For more than two hours," the *New York Times* reported, "the [crowd] was worked up to a high pitch of enthusiasm by a quartet, soloists, and a band." Three massed bands accompanied the audience in the singing of the UNIA anthem, "Ethopia, Thou Land of Our Fathers." Then the man of the hour, Marcus Garvey, stepped to the platform. He was attended by aides, who addressed him as "Your Majesty," and he was dressed in an academic cap and gown of purple, green, and gold. The crowd rose and cheered for fully five minutes.

When the tumult died down, Garvey announced that he had sent a telegram of greeting to Eamon De Valera, "president of the Irish Republic." The message said, in part: "Please accept sympathy of Negroes of the world for your cause. We believe Ireland should be free even as Africa shall be free for the Negroes of the world."

The audience endorsed these sentiments with another ovation and then quieted down as Garvey began his address.

"We are the descendants of a suffering people," Garvey began. "We are the descendants of a people determined to suffer no longer."

The audience burst into applause and Garvey continued:

"Fifty-five years ago the black man was set free from slavery on this continent. Now he declares that what is good for the white man of this age is good for the Negro. They, as a race, claim freedom, and claim the right to establish a democracy."

Having laid down this theme, he announced a new black agenda:

"We shall now organize the 400 million Negroes of the world into a vast organization to plant the banner of freedom on the great continent of Africa. We have no apologies to make, and will make none. We do not desire what has belonged to others, though others have always sought to deprive us of that which belonged to us.

"We new Negroes, we men who have returned from the war—we will dispute every inch of the way until we win.

"We will begin by framing a Bill of Rights of the Negro race with a Constitution to guide the life and destiny of the four hundred million. The Constitution of the United States means that every white American would shed his blood to defend that Constitution. The Constitution of the Negro race will mean that every Negro will shed his blood to defend his Constitution.

"If Europe is for the Europeans, then Africa shall be for the black peoples of the world. We say it, we mean it."

At the end of the speech, Garvey received another ovation, and the *New York Times* reporter said "twenty thousand Negroes made the big hall rock when they yelled for an Africa free from the Strait of Gibraltar to the Cape of Good Hope—an immense republic of Negroes, officered by Negroes, for the Negro."

The momentum of the opening session carried over to the daily sessions at Liberty Hall, where the convention heard special reports from delegates and committees and drafted the declaration of independence.

This document consisted of twelve grievances and fifty-four articles and was modeled, in some respects, on the U.S. Declaration of Independence. It demanded, among other things, equal political and civil rights and African liberation. It also laid the groundwork for a worldwide African government and made the UNIA the sovereign representative of the race.

The final act of the convention was the creation of an African government in exile. Some two dozen officers were elected and an African court and nobility were created. The voting was conducted under a complicated formula which allocated some two hundred votes to the two thousand official delegates on the basis of their national origin.

To no one's surprise, the most important post, provisional president of Africa, went to Marcus Garvey. But, surprisingly, Garvey was not elected unanimously. He was opposed by a Nigerian, Dr. D. D. Lewis, who argued, not unreasonably, that an African should be elected president of Africa. In the final tally, according to the *Afro-American*, Garvey received sixty-four votes, and Dr. Lewis received thirty-three. The rest were scattered among other candidates.

The important but honorary post of leader of the Negroes of the world went to Mayor Gabriel Johnson of Monrovia, Liberia. The Reverend James W. H. Eason, a Philadelphia minister, was elected leader of American Negroes. Press reports said Eason intended to occupy a "Black House" in Washington, and that President Garvey intended to move to Liberia by January, 1922.

Finally, on Tuesday, August 31, the historic convention ended with a parade through Harlem and a reception at the New Star Casino, where Provisional President Garvey, dressed in a flowing robe of crimson and green and surrounded by members of his court, received delegates and friends.

Thus, Marcus Garvey, President-General of the UNIA and Provisional President of Africa, in his moment of triumph. It would be an exaggeration, but not much of an exaggeration, to say that the path for him from this peak was all downhill. For appearances to the contrary notwithstanding, Garvey was dangerously overextended. The main problem was the Black Star Line. Garvey and his associates had bought three run-down ships at inflated prices and had spent a fortune in unsuccessful efforts to make them seaworthy. As a consequence, the Garvey empire was in serious financial shape, and the problems grew worse with every passing month. In December, 1921, a bare sixteen months after the days of triumph, the Black Star Line collapsed. The final balance sheet told a sad story. Garvey and his associates had sold 155,510 shares of stock to

40,000 blacks, and had collected some $800,000 dollars. The cash balance on January 5, 1922, was $31.22.

There is no evidence to indicate that Garvey profited personally from this debacle. In fact, the evidence indicates that he was a brilliant organizer and a bad businessman, who was betrayed by his associates and the scheming white men who sold the ships. This did not deter federal officials, who indicted Garvey and three of his associates for using the mail to defraud in connection with the financing of the Black Star Line.

While this drama unfolded in big black headlines, leaks were developing in other Garvey ships. There was internal dissension in the organization, and Garvey critics were pressing suits on several fronts. At this juncture, Garvey made an extraordinary blunder, traveling to Atlanta, Georgia, to confer with the leaders of the Ku Klux Klan. After the meeting Garvey was quoted as saying he agreed with the Klan's assertion that this was by right "a white man's country."

This, to put it mildly, was a misreading of the mind of Black America, and it provided powerful ammunition for Garvey critics. J. W. H. Eason, the former UNIA leader of American Negroes, publicly denounced Garvey and said that he was insensitive to the problems of American blacks. When, in January, 1923, Eason was assassinated on the streets of New Orleans, there was a storm of controversy and eight blacks wrote a letter to the attorney general demanding an immediate trial of Marcus Garvey on the mail fraud charge.

When the Garvey case came to trial, Garvey played into the hands of his accusers by acting as his own attorney. And although the evidence against him was flimsy, he was convicted of mail fraud and later spent more than two years in the federal penitentiary in Atlanta. In 1927 he was pardoned by President Calvin Coolidge and deported to his native Jamaica.

And so, "within ten years after reaching New York," James Weldon Johnson wrote, "Marcus Garvey had risen and fallen, been made a prisoner in the Atlanta Federal Penitentiary, and finally been deported to his native island. Within that brief period a black West Indian, here in the United States, in the twentieth century, had actually played an imperial role such as Eugene O'Neill never imagined in his *Emperor Jones*."

Garvey left a legacy of exploded hopes and mammoth accomplishments. He had collected more money from blacks, some $10 million in one three-year period, than any other black leader, before or since, and he had created the largest black American mass movement. Beyond all that, he had permanently altered the consciousness of blacks.

This was a substantial legacy, but it was not enough for Garvey, who continued his crusade for African liberation. From Jamaica and later from London, he tried to rally the faithful, but he never regained his former eminence, and he died in London on June 10, 1940, never having set foot on African soil. It was said, of course, that he was a failure and a misguided dreamer. But this was a misunderstanding of the dream and the dreamer. For whatever the limitations of his program and the trappings surrounding it, Garvey was, as W. E. B. DuBois noted, the forerunner of "a mighty coming thing." And when the mighty thing exploded, some twenty years after Garvey's death, in Africa and the Americas, Garvey's name was restored to its rightful place, high on the list of dreamers who worked in the wilderness to prepare the way for a Promised Land they were destined not to see.

This Train

The Day They Didn't March

PRESIDENT Roosevelt was furious. He wasn't, he said, going to be bullied or threatened—he wasn't going to govern with a gun at his head.

The President had before him a letter from Asa Philip Randolph, a brilliant labor leader who had been called "the most dangerous Negro in America." In the view of Franklin Delano Roosevelt, and in the view of others, Randolph was dancing on the edge of sedition. For in the midst of the feverish mobilization efforts preceding America's entry into World War II, he was threatening to march one hundred thousand blacks on Washington, D.C., if the President did not immediately issue an executive order banning discrimination in defense industries and the armed forces. No one had ever tried anything like this before in black America, and no one knew for sure whether one thousand or three hundred thousand blacks would march. But the threat was there, and the threat was real. For Washington, D.C., was a Southern town with a Deep South mentality, and an "invasion" of one hundred thousand blacks could lead to bloodshed and anarchy. The march was scheduled for July 1, 1941, less than three weeks away. Was Randolph bluffing or could he deliver? What did he really want? Could he be diverted by praise, threats, or cajolery? Roosevelt, who loved a good fight, considered these questions, not for the first time, and then told Aubrey Williams, director of the National Youth Administration:

"Go to New York and try to talk Randolph and [Walter] White out of this march." He paused and then added with emphasis:

"Get the missus and Fiorello and Anna and get it stopped."

This was, as Williams recognized, a diversionary gesture, but it was a *serious* diversionary gesture. For Roosevelt was calling up the biggest white liberal guns of his administration. The missus, of course, was his wife, Eleanor Roosevelt, who was a legendary figure in the black community. Fiorello LaGuardia, the colorful New York mayor and civilian

Asa Philip Randolph, leader of the March on Washington movement, rose to power in the labor demonstrations of the 1920s.

March on Washington idea was conceived by Randolph (left) and supported by union officials like Milton P. Webster.

defense director, was another highly regarded white liberal. So also were Williams and Anna Rosenberg of the War Manpower Board. If they couldn't talk Randolph and his ally Walter White out of the march, nobody could.

The meeting was held at the president's direction at the New York City Hall on June 13, but before considering the details and the outcome, it is necessary to pause for a moment to introduce the man who dominated this and all other meetings leading up to what was called the most important act of the federal government in the field of race relations since the Emancipation Proclamation.

The central figure of this meeting and of the dramatic confrontation that followed was Asa Philip Randolph, international president of the Brotherhood of Sleeping Car Porters. He was fifty-two years old in this year, tall, handsome, with courtly Old World manners and the polished diction of a Shakesperian actor. A native of Florida, he had migrated to New York in the pre-World War I years and had drifted into socialist politics after a year or two at City College. He had been jailed briefly in 1918 for opposing the war effort and had edited, with Chandler Owens, a radical magazine called the *Messenger*. He later became president of the Brotherhood of Sleeping Car Porters and masterminded the long campaign which led to company certification and recognition. By 1940 he

Eleanor Roosevelt and Mary McLeod Bethune played important roles in behind-the-scenes maneuvering that led to FEPC order.

had earned such an enviable reputation that he was the one pole around which divergent elements in the black community could always unite. Randolph's strength was his selflessness and his passionate commitment to "the Negro masses." It was his belief that a black leader should have no other master except the black masses. "I do not wish," he said, "to secure any job from the President of the United States or anybody else who can give political favors. I consider that a leader of the masses must be free to obey and follow the interests of the masses and the sacrifice that is required of such a leader is that he must deny himself the opportunity of taking any government job, whether it pays $1,000 or $10,000 a year."

Such a man, scrupulously honest and totally devoted to the interests of the people, was obviously dangerous. But what made his personal commitment a matter of national interest was the climate of the times and the unprecedented mood of militancy in black America. The total

220

mobilization required by the racist Nazi ideology had focused renewed attention on the racist American ideology and had unleashed explosive forces in the black community, where preachers, politicians, and pamphleteers announced that blacks were sick and tired of dying abroad for a freedom that had no reality at home. This mood was heightened and focused by discrimination in war plants and segregation in the armed forces.

The new mood was an interwoven fabric of desire and despair, and it forced black leadership to new and more exposed positions. There was virtually unanimous agreement, for example, on two goals, fair employment and integration of the armed forces. And there was a new willingness of the part of churches, fraternal organizations and protest groups to submerge petty organizational differences in united and coordinated flights of militancy. "Never before in the history of the Nation," the *Chicago Defender* reported, "have Negroes been so unified on an objective and so insistent upon [goals]."

All this made a powerful impact in official Washington, which was divided into two major camps. One group suggested that the federal government prosecute black editors for treason and sedition. Another group, led by Eleanor Roosevelt, called for a meaningful federal response to racial discrimination. Mrs. Roosevelt, who said she had never seen such an explosive restlessness in the black community, urged her husband to make a public statement. And it was at her suggestion that he received a delegation of three black leaders—Randolph, Walter White of the NAACP, and T. Arnold Hill of the Urban League—on September 27, 1940. Roosevelt, as usual, was charming, sympathetic, and noncommittal. He told the three men that he would consider their requests for armed forces integration and fair employment and would make a suitable public response.

Twelve days later, on October 9, 1940, Stephen Early, the White House press secretary, announced a few minor changes in the utilization of black manpower but emphasized that "the policy of the War Department is not to intermingle colored and white enlisted personnel in the same regimental organizations." Early went on to say that the War Department had drafted the "new" statement of policy "as a result of" a conference the president had "with Walter White and, I think, two other Negro leaders. . . ." The clear implication was that the black leaders had approved or even suggested the policy. This infuriated Randolph, White, and Hill and caused an uproar in the black community,

Walter White of NAACP (left) and New York Mayor Fiorello La Guardia were involved in March negotiations.

where the three men were denounced as "stooges" who had sold out. The White House later "clarified" the statement, but the damage had been done. More importantly, as it turned out, the White House had crystallized a widespread feeling that it was useless to continue traditional protest methods. George Schuyler, a widely read columnist and a militant of that day, bitterly attacked the traditional method of conferences and petitions. "The masses" he said, "are getting fed up on these frauds." What was needed was an organization that "would have worked out some technique of fighting other than sending letters and telegrams of protest."

As Schuyler felt, so felt others, including Asa Philip Randolph, who left Washington in December, 1940, some two months after the White House conference, for a union field trip through the South. As the train rolled across the Virginia countryside where his ancestors had worked as slaves, Randolph brooded over the failure of the politics of protest. His mind went back to his father, a poor AME minister, and to all the men and women who had suffered in silence while men conferred and talked. He told himself that there had to be another way, and he turned to his traveling companion, Milton Webster, vice-president of the union, and said:

"You know, Web, calling on the President and holding these conferences are not going to get us anywhere."

Webster nodded in agreement.

"We're going to have to do something about it," Randolph continued.

Webster said nothing.

"I think," Randolph said, "we ought to get ten thousand Negroes and march down Pennsylvania Avenue asking for jobs in defense plants and integration of the armed forces. It would shake up Washington."

Webster said yes, the idea was sound. "But where are you going to get ten thousand Negroes?"

"I think we can get them," Randolph said, and fell silent, possessed

222

now by the power of the idea and the sound he heard in his inner ear of thousands of feet tramping down Pennsylvania Avenue.

Looking back later, Webster said that "the first place where Brother Randolph and I talked March on Washington was in Savannah, Georgia. The head colored man in town opened up the meeting, introduced me, and ran off the platform to the last seat in the row. It scared everybody to death." And yet, beneath this fear, there was a strange fascination, which could be seen in the faces of doubters and skeptics who rejected the idea outright but returned for another look and circled the thing, warily, hooked in spite of themselves.

Sensing that he had hit on something deep and basic, Randolph hurried back to Harlem to the Brotherhood headquarters on the third floor of a building that housed beauty salons and dancing schools; and there, in the midst of the hurly-burly of black life, he began the long and agonizing task of translating ideas into people and action. Always practical, always tactically astute, he first secured the silence and/or approval of established black power brokers, including Walter White of the NAACP, Lester Granger of the Urban League, Mary McLeod Bethune of the National Association of Colored Women's Clubs, and J. Finley Wilson of the Elks. Some members of the inner circle of the Black Establishment were conservative and others had ties to the white power structure. Given these facts, it is, as author Herbert Garfinkel said, "a measure of the extreme desperation of the Negro leaders that the proposed march was agreed to, however reluctantly." There was another and more profound reason. "It was Randolph's immense prestige among all classes of Negroes," Lester Granger said, "that made this idea something more than a pretentious notion."

With his flanks, and his back, protected, Randolph organized a national structure and announced to the press that there would be a march on Washington. In this statement, issued on January 15, 1941, Randolph said that the march was the only practical method available for mobilizing the enormous latent power of the black masses.

Only "power," he said, "can effect the enforcement and adoption of a given policy, however meritorious it may be. The virtue and rightness of a cause are not alone the condition and cause of its progress and acceptance. Power and pressure are at the foundation of the march of social justice and reform. [But] power and pressure do not reside in the few. . . . Power is the active principle of only the organized masses, the masses united for a definite purpose." He went on to say that in the whole history of black America no one had ever organized and focused the power of the masses. The march would therefore be the first attempt to bring to bear the "real, actual, bona fide, definite and positive pressure of the Negro masses."

The response to this statement was muted. The white press ignored the proposed march, and the black press relegated the news to the inside pages. The *Chicago Defender* said editorially that the statement was "timely and should be acted upon with dispatch." But the *Defender* doubted that it was possible to get ten thousand Negroes to march anywhere, except to a fraternal outing. "It is not difficult to get fifty thousand or more black folk to march with the Elks, the Odd Fellows, the Knights of Pythias, the Shriners, or with the Ancient United Knights and Daughters of Africa. [But] to get ten thousand Negroes assembled in one spot, under one banner of justice, democracy and work as their slogan, would be the miracle of the century. However, miracles do happen. We fervently hope that this one will happen. . . ."

Undaunted by skeptics and critics, Randolph pressed forward, concentrating on grass-roots organizing in bars, barbers shops, and churches. Within a few weeks, the novel and daring idea caught on and there were local March on Washington (MOW) auxiliaries in Chicago, Philadelphia, Newark, Atlanta, Richmond, Baltimore, Kansas City, Milwaukee, and Jacksonville. Membership in the auxiliaries and the national organization was confined to blacks. This was, in part, a tactical ploy to prevent a takeover by white radicals. But it also reflected Randolph's belief that there were some things black people "must do alone."

On May 1, 1941, Randolph issued a formal Call, urging ten thousand blacks to prepare for a mass march on Washington, D.C. on July 1.

> Dear fellow Negro-Americans, be not dismayed in these terrible times. You possess power, great power. Our problem is to hitch it up for action on the broadest, daring, and most gigantic scale.
>
> In this period of power politics, nothing counts but pressure, more pressure, and still more pressure through the tactic and strategy of broad, organized, aggressive mass action behind the vital and important issues of the Negro. . . .
>
> An all-out thundering march on Washington, ending in a

monster and huge demonstration at Lincoln's Monument will shake up white America.

It will shake up official Washington. . . . It will gain respect for the Negro people. . . . It will create a new sense of self-respect among Negroes. . . . MASS POWER CAN CAUSE PRESIDENT ROOSEVELT TO ISSUE AN EXECUTIVE ORDER ABOLISH-ING DISCRIMINATION in all Government Departments, Army, Navy, Air Corps and National Defense Jobs.

It is no derogation of the goals of the movement to say that this was, in part, a shrewd and coolly calculated move in a naked war of nerves between Asa Philip Randolph and the president of the United States. For although the buses had been hired and trains chartered, there is some evidence to indicate that Randolph and his aides hoped that the threat of a march would make a march unnecessary. Thus, on one level anyway, the preparations for the march can be seen as political theater designed to impress and overawe the White House.

The president and some of his aides perceived this, and their first tactic was to ignore Randolph. When this became impossible, the White

First FEPC committee named by President Roosevelt included Earl B. Dickerson (second from left) and Milton P. Webster (third from right).

House fell back to a second line of defense and initiated a series of well-publicized gestures designed to take the steam out of the movement. On April 11, Sidney Hillman, co-director of the Office of Production Management, urged defense contractors to hire black workers. President Roosevelt followed this up with a personal letter, condemning discrimination against blacks and other minorities. But this personal appeal, which many blacks had demanded, came too late; for forces had been set in motion which would be satisfied with nothing less than a presidential executive order. Riding the wave of this new determination, Randolph increased the pressure by upping his estimate of the expected crowd. In mid-May, he said at least fifty thousand blacks were expected. On May 31, the banner headline on the front page of the New York *Amsterdam Star-News* said:

100,000 IN WASHINGTON MARCH

It was at this point that the White House initiated the series of moves that led to the New York City Hall meeting on Friday, June 13. At this meeting, Mrs. Roosevelt, Mayor LaGuardia and other white liberals asked Randolph to call off the march. "You know where I stand," Mrs. Roosevelt said, "but the attitude of the Washington police force, most of them Southerners, and the general feeling of Washington itself are such that I fear there may be trouble if the march occurs."

Randolph remembered later that Mrs. Roosevelt "reminded me of her sympathy for the cause of racial justice, and assured me she intended to continue pressuring the President to act. But the march was something else, she said: it just could not go on. Had I considered the problems? she asked. Where would all those thousands of people eat and sleep in Jim Crow Washington? I told her I myself did not see that as a serious problem. The demonstrators would simply march into the hotels and restaurants, and order food and shelter. But that was just the point, she said; that sort of thing could lead to violence. I replied that there would be no violence unless her husband ordered the police to crack black heads. I told her I was sorry, but the march would not be called off unless the President issued an executive order banning discrimination in the defense industry."

After the meeting Anna Rosenberg called the White House and told a presidential aide that Mrs. Roosevelt and Mayor LaGuardia urgently recommended a meeting of Randolph, White, the president, and his top aides. "Fiorello," she reported, "thinks this will stop the march and nothing else will, except the President's presence and direction." This message was relayed to the president, who told an aide on the same day: "I will see Stimson, Knox, Knudsen, Hillman, White and Randolph on Friday next—or, if I do not go away and feel well enough, I will see them on Wednesday or Thursday."

This was a significant breakthrough, and Aubrey Williams called Randolph and urged him to halt preparations for the march "pending a conference" with the president. Randolph refused. A short time later, Randolph received a telegram from Secretary of the Navy Frank Knox: "Think it highly important that you come to Washington for conference on your project."

On Wednesday, June 18, Randolph and White were ushered into the presence of President Roosevelt. The president sat at his desk, surrounded by the most powerful men and women of his administration, including Secretary of the Navy Knox, Secretary of War Henry Stimson, William S. Knudsen and Sidney Hillman, co-directors of the Office of Production Management, Mayor LaGuardia, and Anna Rosenberg.

"Hello, Phil," the president beamed, extending a hand and putting his guests at ease. Taking note of Randolph's polished language, the president asked, "Which class were you in at Harvard?"

Randolph recognized the gambit for what it was and replied pleasantly, "I never went to Harvard, Mr. President."

"I was sure you did," Roosevelt said. "Anyway, you and I share a kinship in our great interest in human and social justice."

"That's right, Mr. President."

Without preamble, the president then embarked on a favorite and usually successful strategem, a long and amiable filibuster, filled with anecdotes and amusing stories. But Randolph was neither amused nor flattered and he seized the first opportunity to break in.

"Mr. President, time is running out. You are busy. We want specifically to talk to you about the problem of jobs for Negroes in defense industries. Our people are being turned away at factory gates because they are colored. They can't live with this thing. What are you going to do about it?"

"Well, Phil," the President said, "what do you want me to do?"

"Mr. President, we want you to do something that will enable Negro workers to get work in these plants."

The president said he would do something. "I'll call up the heads of the various defense plants and have them see to it that Negroes are given the same opportunity to work in defense plants as any other citizen in the country."

"We want you to do more than that," Randolph said. "We want something concrete, something tangible, definite, positive, affirmative."

"What do you mean?"

"Mr. President, we want you to issue an executive order making it mandatory that Negroes be permitted to work in these plants."

"Well, Phil," Roosevelt said, "you know I can't do that. If I issue an executive order for you, then there'll be no end to other groups coming in here and asking me to issue executive orders for them, too. In any event, I couldn't do anything unless you called off this march of yours. Questions like this have sociological implications. They can't be gotten at with hammers and tongs. They can't be settled with marches."

Neither, Randolph said, in so many words, could they be settled with good intentions. The president looked at Randolph, measuring him.

"How many people do you plan to bring?"

"One hundred thousand, Mr. President."

The president turned to Walter White. Randolph was an unknown equation, but White was an old and trusted adversary.

"Walter," he asked, "how many people will *really* march?"

"One hundred thousand, Mr. President," White said, without blinking an eye.

The president was genuinely alarmed.

"You can't bring one hundred thousand Negroes to Washington," he said. "Somebody might get killed."

Randolph said nobody would get hurt, especially if the president accepted his invitation to speak to the crowd.

This was a light and deft counter-punch, but it did not amuse the President, who said that the march was a grave mistake that would give the impression that Negroes were seeking to exercise force and to compel the government to do certain things. He added that it was not his policy to rule, or to be ruled, with a gun at his head.

"Then, Mr. President," Randolph replied, "something will have to be done and done at once."

"Something will be done, but there must be no public pressure on the White House."

"Mr. President," Asa Philip Randolph said, his deep voice booming, "something must be done now!"

Something was done, almost immediately. At the suggestion of Mayor

LaGuardia, Randolph, White and the presidential aides adjourned to the Cabinet Room to seek a compromise solution. After two hours of wrangling, a committee of five persons was appointed to draw up an executive order for submission to the president. The task of reducing the agreement to legal language was given to a young government lawyer named Joseph L. Rauh, who turned out several drafts which were returned with the explanation that Randolph did not consider the language strong enough. This went on for several days before Rauh exploded: "Who the hell is this guy Randolph? What the hell has he got over the President of the United States?"

What Randolph had on the president was the threat of a march which he refused to cancel despite the feverish behind-the-scenes negotiations. Some of his friends told him that the battle had been won and that he should, as a tender of good faith, halt preparations for the march. Randolph rebuffed these overtures, saying that he had a pledge of honor with the Negro masses and that he could not go back to them without a signed executive order.

At it turned out, Randolph's strategy was eminently correct. For Roosevelt balked at the last moment and resisted pressure from his wife and his aides, who urged him to sign the order, which had been sitting on his desk for several days.

At this point, on June 23, Randolph tightened the screw by dramatically and publicly inviting Eleanor Roosevelt to speak to the marchers at the Lincoln Monument. What happened next has been described by Joseph Lash, Mrs. Roosevelt's biographer. According to Lash, Anna Rosenberg, spurred on by Mrs. Roosevelt, "bought a new hat, marched into the president's office, fished out the order, and cajoled him: 'Sign it, Mr. President—sign it.'" There is a memo from Roosevelt to Rudolph Forster, the executive clerk. "Fix up for me a [sic] sign and send to Attorney General for language. Quick."

Attorney General Robert H. Jackson returned the papers on Wednesday, June 25, and President Roosevelt signed and issued Executive Order 8802 on that day. The order, which was the first decisive act by the federal government on behalf of blacks since the Reconstruction period, prohibited discrimination in defense industries and established a wartime Fair Employment Commission. It did not contain punitive provisions, and it did not deal with segregation in the armed forces; but it was nonetheless a decisive point of focus which changed the climate of race relations and the vision of black leadership.

Randolph, carrying out his end of the deal, postponed the march and hailed the order as "the most significant government act since the Emancipation Proclamation." The young activists of the Youth Division of the March on Washington Committee condemned the postponement, but Randolph told them that "the Negro masses who want jobs now would have hurled curses upon the heads of the leaders of the Negro March-on-Washington Movement if they had sacrificed an immediate and practical opportunity to secure employment opportunities for Negro masses in defense industries in order to satisfy a handful of Negro youth who apparently were more interested in the drama and pyrotechnics of the march than in the basic and main issues of putting Negroes to work."

Randolph prevailed. There was no march on Tuesday, July 1, 1941. The buses did not roll, the special trains did not leave the stations, the sound of thousands of tramping feet was not heard on Pennsylvania Avenue. It was business as usual at the White House, and there was a stillness in the air when Asa Philip Randolph and a handful of supporters gathered at the Lincoln Monument to celebrate a victory that was won because one hundred thousand people didn't march.

Write My Name

D-Day at the Supreme Court

THIS day was going to be a day to remember. But nothing—neither the weather, nor the headlines, nor the stars of the preceding night —foretold the magnitude of the changes the coming hours would bring. Before nightfall on this Monday, the Pandora's box of race was going to be forced open and terrifying vistas were going to assault the eyes of men and women. And in the wake of this event, some men were going to predict the imminent collapse of the Republic while other men, viewing the same set of facts, were going to say that their eyes had seen "the glory of the coming of the Lord."

This day, in short, was going to change everything, or almost everything, in the field of race relations. But—astoundingly—there was not one word of warning from the soothsayers or the headlines, which spoke of the old and therefore reassuring crises symbolized by the Mau Mau uprising in Africa, the Dien Bien Phu struggle in Vietnam, and the Army-McCarthy hearings in Washington, D.C.

"Brown decision" received name from petitioners Linda Brown and her father, Oliver Brown. Principals in school cases were Attorney John W. Davis, Solicitor General J. Lee Rankin, Thurgood Marshall of the NAACP, pictured at left, p. 237.

This day was Monday, May 17, 1954. On this day, as on other days before and since, tens of thousands of good burghers left their lily-white compounds in the Maryland and Virginia suburbs and rode into the increasingly black city of Washington to conduct the business of the U.S. government. It was a pleasant but cloudy day in Washington, with temperatures in the seventies; and phalanxes of tourists, armed with cameras, were mobilizing for assaults on the Lincoln and Washington monuments. The tourists, the monuments, the motorcades from Virginia and Maryland: all this was ordinary and reassuring. In fact, everything conspired on this day to suggest that this was just another ordinary Monday in the best of all possible worlds. The blacks were quarantined in their legally appointed Jim Crow schools, the benign and reassuring (to some) Dwight David Eisenhower was in the White House, spring flowers were in bloom, and there was no reason to believe that things would not go on this way forever. There was, to be sure, one possible source of trouble—and that was the U.S. Supreme Court, which met every Monday to announce decisions. And, as a matter of fact, a Supreme Court decision on school segregation was long overdue. But the decision had been delayed and postponed so many times that it had slipped out of focus in the public's mind.

If the public had forgotten, the press and the politicians had not forgotten. For almost four months now, a handful of lawyers and reporters had gathered every Monday at the Supreme Court building in the hope that the decision would come on that day. But the Mondays of January and February and March and April passed without event. And it seemed at first that Monday, May 17, would go by in the same fashion. In fact, reporters were told before the Court convened that it "looks like a quiet day."

This was an illusion. But this did not become apparent until late in the session, which started promptly at twelve noon. Every seat in the high-ceilinged, marble-columned courtroom was filled long before the opening gavel was sounded. And although there had been no advance public notice, several celebrities were on hand, including Attorney General Herbert Brownell, former Secretary of State Dean Acheson, and three of the top lawyers in the school segregation cases—George E. C. Hayes and James M. Nabrit of Washington, D.C., and Thurgood Marshall, chief counsel of the NAACP.

At twelve on the dot, the court marshal brought celebrities and non-celebrities to their feet with a whack of his gavel and announced, "The Honorable, the Chief Justice and the Associate Justices of the Supreme Court of the United States!" With a flourish, nine black-robed men strode through openings in the red velvet curtains and moved to a long mahogany bench, which sat on a marble platform a foot or so above the floor. For the first time in several weeks, veteran reporters noted, all nine justices were in attendance. Associate Justice Robert Jackson was recovering from a heart attack, but he had checked out of the hospital that morning and dragged himself to court. What was the meaning of this? The justices gave no sign. They stood poker-faced behind their

NAACP executives, including Roy Wilkins, Thurgood Marshall and Walter White, celebrated May 17, 1954, victory in New York offices.

black leather swivel chairs while the marshal intoned the traditional chant:

"Oyez! Oyez! Oyez!!!

"All persons having business before the Honorable, the Supreme Court of the United States, are admonished to draw near and give their attention, for the Court is now sitting. God save the United States and this Honorable Court!"

The gavel sounded again. The justices and spectators took their seats. All eyes turned now to Chief Justice Earl Warren, who dominated the proceedings from his chair in the center of the high bench. Warren, big-shouldered, silver-haired, bespectacled, was sixty-two years old. On his immediate right sat the senior associate justice, Hugo Lafayette Black, an Alabamian and former member of the Ku Klux Klan who had become the court's most consistent defender of civil liberties. At Warren's left sat another senior justice and another Southerner, Stanley Reed, of Maysville, Kentucky. To the left and right of these men, in descending order of seniority, were Felix Frankfurter, a former Harvard Law School professor; Robert Jackson, the former chief counsel for the United States at the Nuremberg trials; Harold H. Burton, a former mayor of Cleveland, Ohio; Tom Clark, a former attorney general; and Sherman Minton, a former senator from Indiana.

The justices represented a broad spectrum of (white) American life. Three (Black, Clark, Reed) were from the South, two (Burton and Minton) were from the Midwest, two (Jackson and Frankfurter) were from the Northeast, and two (Warren and Douglass) were from the West. All, with the exception of Burton and Warren, were Democrats, and only two—Black and Douglass—had been conspicuous in the advocacy of equal rights for blacks.

It was in and through these men that America approached its date with destiny. The approach was singularly lacking in drama. The Court first disposed of routine business, including the admission of 118 lawyers to the Supreme Court bar. When at last that was done, Chief Justice Warren recognized Tom Clark, who announced and read the Court's opinion in a case dealing with alleged monopolistic practices in the sale of milk in Chicago. Justice Douglass followed with two routine cases involving negligence and the picketing of retail stores.

All this was unbearably boresome, and the tourists who had come to the Court in search of history and drama were fidgeting and cursing themselves for their foolhardiness. At this precise moment, at the low ebb of the proceedings, Earl Warren picked up a document on his desk and said: "I have for announcement the judgment and opinion of the Court in No. 1—*Oliver Brown et al.* v. *Board of Education of Topeka.*" It was 12:52 P.M., and a shiver ran through the room. At the same time, clerk Harold Wiley slipped a note into a pneumatic tube that whisked it to the ground floor press room, where bored reporters were lounging and sipping coffee. Banning E. Whittington, the Court's press officer, extracted the note, read it, and put on his suit coat. This was noted by a number of reporters, including Louis Lautier, of the Negro Newspaper Publishers Association. "I thought," Lautier said later, "he was going to say he was going to lunch." Instead Whittington said, as he ran out of the press room, "Reading of the segregation decisions is about to begin in the courtroom." The press room exploded, and the reporters scrambled for the courtroom with Whittington leading the way.

As these events unfolded, bells started ringing in press rooms all over the world. The first public alert came from Associated Press: "Chief Justice Warren today began reading the Supreme Court's decision in the public school segregation cases. The Court's ruling could not be determined immediately."

NAACP leaders from South, including Medgar Evers (right, background) attended post-Decision strategy meeting in Atlanta.

Warren read this, his first major opinion, in a clear and undramatic voice. He began by tracing the twisted paths that brought America and one hundred years of American history to the bar of justice. The paths that framed his words began in slavery. They branched out then, crossed and doubled back on one another before halting temporarily at the Supreme Court, which ruled in the infamous Dred Scott decision that black people had no rights in America that white people were bound to respect. The Civil War reversed that decision, and the Thirteenth and Fourteenth amendments opened up new paths of controversy which again led to the Supreme Court, which again ruled in favor of reaction and injustice. The Fourteenth Amendment said clearly that "no State shall make or enforce any law which shall abridge the privileges or immunities of citizens of the United States; nor shall any State deprive any person of life, liberty, or property, without due process of law; nor deny to any person within its jurisdiction the equal protection of the laws." The Supreme Court interpreted this language narrowly, ruling in the *Plessy* v. *Ferguson* case of 1896 that laws requiring segregation were a reasonable use of state police power.

In an eloquent dissent, Justice John Marshall Harlan, the son of a former slaveowner, said "the substance and spirit of the recent amendments of the Constitution have been sacrificed by a subtle and ingenious verbal criticism." He predicted that the *Plessy* decision "will, in time, prove to be quite as pernicious as the decision made by this tribunal in the Dred Scott case. . . . [for] . . . . in view of the Constitution, in the eye of the law, there is in this country no superior, dominant, ruling class of citizens. There is no caste here. Our Consitutiton is color-blind, and neither knows nor tolerates classes among citizens."

Justice Harlan could not have been more right, but he couldn't get anyone to listen to him. And when the Supreme Court got through with the Fourteenth Amendment, the black American, as I have said elsewhere,* had no rights white Americans were bound to respect, unless the black American in question had a large amount of money, a firm of superb lawyers, and an infinite amount of time.

The situation did not change materially until the thirties, when the late Charles Hamilton Houston, one of the great and neglected figures of black history, almost singlehandedly created a countervailing force of

---

*Confrontation: Black and White.

tough and well-trained black lawyers. As vice-dean of the Howard University Law School, Houston set himself the task of creating "a West Point of Black Leadership." And under his leadership, the Howard Law School became an instrument of precision and purpose, turning out scores of brilliant legal tacticians.

Of these tacticians, it was Thurgood Marshall who came to symbolize the thrust and the sweep of Houston's dream. In 1935, only two years after his graduation from Howard, Marshall scored the first substantial victory against legal segregation, forcing the University of Maryland to admit a black student to its law school. By this time Houston was chief counsel of the NAACP, and he invited his star pupil to join him as special counsel. The two men then opened a legal offensive based on the premise that suits seeking equalization of school facilities would make segregation so prohibitively expensive that the South would voluntarily abandon Jim Crow. This strategy substantially improved the quality of black schools but had only marginal effects on segregation. So, beginning in the forties, the NAACP legal staff, now led by Thurgood Marshall, decided to shift gears and attack segregation frontally. This decision was based, in part, on several Supreme Court decisions that undermined the *Plessy* v. *Ferguson* doctrine. These decisions (in the fields of transportation and higher education) indicated to Marshall and other black lawyers that the time had come to challenge legal segregation. In 1951 NAACP attorneys and attorneys representing a group of Washington, D.C., parents, began to attack segregation on the elementary and secondary school levels in four states (South Carolina, Delaware, Virginia, and Kansas) and Washington, D.C. When these cases reached the Supreme Court on appeal, they were combined and docketed under the name of the first petitioner listed on the Topeka, Kansas, brief—the Reverend Oliver Brown.

On two occasions—in December, 1952 and December, 1953—the cases were argued before the Supreme Court. John W. Davis, who was considered the dean of American constitutional lawyers, was chief legal spokesman for the pro-segregation side; and he contended that there was no legal warrant for an adverse decision against segregation. This view was contested by the black petitioners, who were represented by a disproportionately large number of graduates and teachers from the Howard University Law School. One of the more memorable moments in the legal debate was contributed by Thurgood Marshall, NAACP chief counsel. Marshall, speaking in rebuttal, said:

"I got the feeling on hearing the discussion yesterday that when you put a white child in a school with a whole lot of colored children, the child would fall apart or something. Everybody knows that is not true. Those same kids in Virginia and South Carolina—and I have seen them do it—they play in the streets together, they play on the farms together, they separate to go to school, they come out of school and play ball together. They have to be separated in school. . . . Why, of all the multitudinous groups of people in the country, [do] you have to single out the Negroes and give them this separate treatment?

"It can't be because of slavery in the past, because there are very few groups in this country that haven't had slavery some place back in the history of their groups. It can't be color, because there are Negroes as white as the drifted snow, with blue eyes, and they are just as segregated as the colored men.

"The only thing it can be is an inherent determination that the people who were formerly in slavery, regardless of anything else, shall be kept as near that stage as possible. And now is the time, we submit, that this Court should make clear that that is not what our constitution stands for."

The arguments cited by Marshall and other black lawyers were eloquent, pointed, and persuasive, but it appears from the evidence that other factors played an equal and perhaps greater role in shaping the final decision. There was, for example, the act of fate that changed the climate of the Court between the first and second hearings. The first hearing had been conducted by Chief Justice Fred M. Vinson, a cautious white Southerner deeply committed to "law and order" and the Southern Way of Life. The available evidence suggests that Vinson adopted the Southern view of the case but couldn't create a working majority. This led to a bitterly divided Court and a legal stalemate, which was broken shortly before the second hearing by the sudden death of Vinson, who suffered a heart attack in his Washington apartment. This naturally saddened his colleagues, but at least one justice was struck by the fact that Vinson's passing made it possible to reorganize the Court around new axes. And this justice—Felix Frankfurter—told one of his former law clerks, according to author Richard Kluger (*Simple Justice*), "This is the first indication I have ever had that there is a God."

Whatever the nature of the forces at work, President Dwight Eisenhower gave Governor Earl Warren of California a recess appointment as the fourteenth chief justice of the Supreme Court. Warren was a popular politician with an ambiguous record on civil rights and civil liberties, and it is almost certain that he received the appointment because Eisenhower believed he would be a colorless and conventional chief justice. When the segregation case signaled that he was going to be just the opposite, Dwight Eisenhower told a friend that the Warren appointment was "the biggest damned fool mistake I ever made."

Warren lost no time in putting his imprint on the Court. At the first conference of the justices after the December, 1953, hearing, the new chief justice said frankly that the time had come to end public school segregation. This was a portentous moment, for Warren's statement meant that as of that date—Saturday, December 12, 1953—there was a solid majority of at least five in favor of overturning the *Plessy* decision. But this was not enough for Warren, who believed that such an important decision required the backing of a unanimous decision. And so in January, February and March of 1954, Warren and other justices worked quietly behind the shuttered doors of the Court in an ultimately successful effort to convert the holdouts. The evidence is not conclusive, but it seems that Felix Frankfurter was hesitant at first on technical grounds and that Stanley Reed of Kentucky was the last holdout. And it is certainly significant that in this internal debate the justices cited their varying experiences with blacks as factors in their personal decisions. Justice Black, for example, announced at one of the early conferences that he would vote to end segregation. He told his colleagues that he was a Southern white man and that he didn't need lawyers or sociologists or historians to tell him what the purpose of segregation was. The purpose, he said, was to discriminate against blacks in the belief that they were inferior beings. Justice Frankfurter, on the other hand, is recorded as having said that he had "never had close living relations to Negroes but [had had] much to do with the problem—was asst. counsel to NAACP; also belong to Jewish minority. . . ." According to the cryptic surviving notes of Justice Burton, some members of the Court deferred to the white Southern Justices, who were deemed to have more experience in the matter. The same notes and other evidence indicate that the final decision was shaped by a general belief that it was necessary to make the transition as painless as possible for the white South.

Coordinating and orchestrating these views and sentiments, Chief Justice Warren managed to get a unanimous vote, probably in late March. He assigned himself the task of writing the opinion, which was completed and approved on May 15. By this time there was wild and generally inaccurate speculation about what was happening in the private chambers of the Court. Only ten days before the decision, one celebrated writer quoted informed sources who said the Court was split down the middle—four to four—and that Chief Justice Warren was being courted and cajoled by both sides.

There was also concern and speculation at the White House. According to Warren's posthumously published book, President Eisenhower made an indirect but unmistakable appeal to him on behalf of the Southern cause. This was unconscionable and possibly illegal, but it was too transparently clumsy and it came too late to affect the words Earl Warren read on May 17.

Warren read the words in a hushed courtroom. Whether by design or inadvertence, the opinion was written in a cliffhanger style, which teased but withheld any real information until the last paragraphs. The first part of the decision traced the paths that brought the cases to the Court. The second part explored alternative solutions to the problem the Court faced.

Could the Court base its decision on the intentions of the framers of the Fourteenth Amendment?

No, Warren answered, citing the thinness of the evidence and the difficulty of determining the intentions of politicians with different purposes and different interests.

Was it possible to decide the cases on the basis of the existence or non-existence of integrated schools at the time the Fourteenth Amendment was adopted?

No, Warren answered, citing the thinness of the evidence and the further fact that the concept of public education meant one thing in 1866 and another and different thing in 1954.

On what basis then could the Court reach a decision?

The only possible basis, Warren said, coming closer to the issue, was a consideration of "public education in the light of its full development" and a consideration of the effect of segregation on public education and the minds of the children exposed to public education.

"We come then," Warren said, "to the question presented: Does segregation of children in public schools solely on the basis of race, even though the physical facilities and other 'tangible' factors may be equal, deprive the children of the minority group of equal education opportunities. We believe that it does."

In support of this belief, Warren cited evidence which suggested that

the separation of black children "from others of similar age and qualifi-
cations solely because of their race generates a feeling of inferiority as
to their status in the community that may affect their hearts and minds
in a way unlikely ever to be undone." Summing up, he said:

"We conclude that in the field of public education the doctrine of
'separate but equal' has no place. Separate educational facilities are
inherently unequal. Therefore, we hold that the plaintiffs and others
similarly situated for whom the actions have been brought are, by reason
of the segregation complained of, deprived of the equal protection of the
laws guaranteed by the Fourteenth Amendment."

The words, clear, firm, unequivocal, resounded in the courtroom,
evoking frowns, smiles, tears. Thurgood Marshall leaned over and said
to an aide, "We hit the jackpot!"

Not quite. Up to this point, Warren had been firm and forthright.
But now he and the Court backed away from the chasm before them.
Instead of ordering immediate compliance, the Court delayed implementation and ordered reargument on the details of formulating decrees.
It was said then, and it would be said later, that this was a tactical mistake
and that the Court at that moment should have remembered not Black-
stone but Shakespeare, who said, in another connection, that "if it 'twere
done . . . then 'twere well it were done quickly."

There was additional language, and the reading of the decision in the
District of Columbia case, but none of this changed the meaning of the
day. It was over. After eighty-eight years of equivocation and compromise
and betrayal, the legal monster called Jim Crow had been sentenced to
death and the only substantial question remaining was how protracted
and painful the burial would be.

The reaction in the courtroom mirrored the reaction in America. The
enormity of the decision, and the possibilities it portended, struck some
dumb and pushed others to the edge of hysteria. The most common
reaction was a kind of dazed unbelief. Men and women, black and white,
most of them strangers to one another, shook hands and embraced, saying
over and over to themselves and to others, that it was impossible but that
it had happened and they had heard it with their own ears. Ethel Payne,
a reporter for the *Chicago Defender*, recorded her feelings as she emerged
from the courtroom. "I'm so excited," she said, "I [feel] like I'm drunk.
I'm turning around like one of those spinning tops."

By the end of the session, the news had been flashed to the farthest corners of the world. Several American newspapers replated and ran extras, and special news reports and bulletins interrupted the regular programming of radio and TV stations. Within an hour the Voice of America was beaming the news by shortwave to Eastern Europe. In Europe, in Asia, in Africa, in cities and towns and hamlets all over the world, men and women received the news according to their different expectations.

In South Carolina James Hinton, president of the state NAACP, closed his insurance office and hurried home "to get [black people] ready."

In Washington, D.C., Mary Church Terrell, the ninety-year-old civil rights leader, got out of her sick bed and said: "I thank God, I lived to see the day...."

In Farmville, Virginia, Barbara Trent, a sixteen-year-old student at the Robert B. Moton School, burst into tears when her teacher announced the decision. "We went on studying history," she said later, "but things weren't the same, and will never be the same again."

The response in the white South was curious. A handful of diehards, like Governor Herman Talmadge of Georgia and Senator James Eastland of Mississippi, issued statements of defiance; but the general reaction was curiously and surprisingly mild. "In some indeterminate measure," Alexander Bickel wrote, "the initial muted reaction to the Court's decision may have reflected simply shock. In some measure also, we witnessed the calm of incredulity. People could not bring themselves to believe that integration would really happen, and they entertained hopes of voluntary self-segregation by the Negro community."

For precisely opposite reasons, the response of the masses of blacks was not as explosively demonstrative as some had hoped or feared. At mid-afternoon, U Street, the heart of black Washington, was quiet and orderly. This disturbed a young NAACP worker who told a *New York Times* reporter that "there should be dancing in the streets."

The reaction in Clarendon County, South Carolina, was scarcely more demonstrative. With a wary skepticism born of centuries of betrayal, the farmers of Clarendon County circled around the edges of the thing, testing it and trying to determine its size and dimension.

John H. McCray, an NAACP official, was surprised by the sober purposefulness of the people in Clarendon County, who only wanted to know one thing: when would integration begin. "We had expected to find jubilance, plenty of easy talk and maybe a celebration or two," McCray said. "We didn't."

These examples of caution and even skepticism should not be taken to mean that the import of the decision was not immediately recognized. On the contrary, the decision was hailed by a wide variety of black voices as "a second Emancipation Proclamation" which was, in the words of the *Chicago Defender*, "more important to our democracy than the atom bomb or the hydrogen bomb."

The most widely quoted man of the day was the architect of the victory, NAACP Counsel Thurgood Marshall. The *New York Times* quoted Marshall as saying that there would be no organized resistance to the Supreme Court decision. Asked how long he thought it would take to end school segregation, Marshall said "up to five years." He went on to say, according to the *Times*, that segregation in all forms would be completely eliminated in America by the one hundreth anniversary of the Emancipation Proclamation in 1963. Not only Marshall but significant sectors of the white population said the struggle would soon be over. Earl Warren recalled later that it was suggested at the Supreme Court that the processes set in motion on this day would be completed by the centennial of the Fourteenth Amendment—1966.

It didn't turn out that way. The day of decision and passion—and innocence—was followed by a generation of litigation and Bad Faith, and the dream was deferred once again.

Thurgood Marshall had some premonition of this. He went that night to an NAACP victory party which never really got off the ground. The event weighing on the party was too big, it had too many corners and edges, it could not be contained or expiated by contrived merriment. For all these reasons and perhaps others, Marshall wandered morosely around the room while his aides made aimless and desultory attempts to generate some enthusiasm. What was he thinking at this moment? Was he thinking of Charles Hamilton Houston who had died in 1950 on the outskirts of the victory he had helped make possible? Was he thinking of Joseph DeLaine and the other nameless martyrs and victims who had helped make it possible? Or did he see on the other side of the victory the pain and blood and struggle that this day would bring? We don't know. But it is a matter of record that Thurgood Marshall stopped of a sudden and said: "You fools go ahead and have your fun, but we ain't begun to work yet."

Walk Together,
Children

The Beginning
of the Black Revolution

IT would grow in size and weight. It would become a legend and a myth. It would bring blood and glory. But there was no glory in it in the beginning. In the beginning, there was tiredness, one black woman, and a bus.

It began, if events of such magnitude can be said to have a beginning, with the woman. It began on the December day that this woman—Rosa Parks—left her job at the Fair Department Store near historic Court Square in Montgomery, Alabama. The square, on this day, was festooned with red and green Christmas lights, and there was a big banner over one of the stores, saying "Peace on Earth, Goodwill to Men."

Rosa Parks paid no attention to the lights or the banner. She had been working since early morning as a seamstress in the department store, raising and lowering hemlines, mumbling yes ma'am and no ma'am through a mouthful of pins; and she was, she realized suddenly, unutterably weary. There was a little pain across her neck and shoulders, and there were telltale signs of throbbing protests in her aching feet.

251

Rosa Parks stood for a moment and considered these signs. Then she moved through the throng to the curb and looked up the streets for a bus. It was a little after five on Thursday, December 1, 1955. The Black Revolution was about to begin. Rosa Parks didn't know it; nobody knew it. Life flowed on in Court Square as it had since time immemorial. The whites were overbearing, the blacks were deferential, the businesses, the restrooms, the restaurants were segregated. It had always been like this. It would always be like this. It was a law of life; it was a law of nature. Or so most White people thought on the day it all started coming apart and coming together. The sit-ins, the Freedom Rides, Birmingham, Selma, Black Power, Watts, clenched fists, the "Afro," the assassinations of Medgar Evers and Martin Luther King, Jr., the swirling smoke of burning buildings, and the sharp ugly sound of gunfire within blocks of the White House: it was all there, in embryo, in the idyllic scene on Court Square. But nobody noticed. Nobody paid any attention to Rosa Parks, a slim woman of forty-two, tidily and precisely dressed, with every strand of hair in place and rimless glasses perched on her handsome face.

If the Revolution was going to come, it was extremely unlikely that it was going to come in such a gentle and genteelly dressed package. As a matter of fact, nothing was further from Rosa Parks' mind on this day. Although she was surrounded by history and historical artifacts, although

Overflow crowd spilled into surrounding streets at mass meeting on first night of boycott.

slaves had been auctioned in this square and although it was at the Exchange Hotel across the street that "the man and the hour" came together in the beginning of the Confederacy, Rosa Parks was consumed at this moment not by history but by the tedium of survival in the Jim Crow South. She was tired, and every atom of her being was concentrated on the task of finding a seat on a bus. This was, everything considered, a small thing to ask. But it was a dangerously complicated task in old Montgomery. And to understand what happened next, and in the weeks and years that followed, one must first understand the logistics of Jim Crow travel.

E. D. Nixon, veteran protest leader, assumed leading role in first stage of movement.

In Montgomery, as in most Southern cities, most of the bus passengers were black. Despite this fact, the first four seats on all buses were reserved for white people and could not be used, under any circumstances, by blacks. (It was a common sight in those days to see black men and women standing in silence and silent fury over the four empty seats reserved for whites.) Behind these four seats was a middle section, or no-man's land, of two or three seats which blacks could use if there was no white demand. But "the rule was," Rosa Parks remembered later, "that if the front section filled up and one white person came to sit in the middle section," all blacks in the middle section "had to get up and stand in the back." There was more, and worse, including a rule that blacks had to enter the bus in front, pay their fare, get off the bus and re-enter by the back door. This was a needless provocation, and it caused no end of trouble and hard feeling. In the twelve months preceding this Christmas season, at least three black females, including a fifteen-year-old girl, had been arrested for refusing to give their seats to white men.

There was no need for Rosa Parks to rehearse all this. This was a history engraved in her bones and viscera. In fact, she had been evicted from a bus some twelve years before for refusing to obey the rule that

Montgomery leader, Dr. Martin Luther King, Jr., greeted protesters at pickup station.

required blacks to pay in the front and enter in the rear. But she wasn't looking for trouble on this Thursday. What she wanted, what she had to have at this moment, was a comfortable seat. She had had one of those days we all have from time to time, and a person with a keen eye would have seen that this was not the day, this was not the hour, to give this mild-mannered woman a hard time.

None of this was verbalized, none of this reached the stage of consciousness; but it was there, deep in Rosa Park's mind, as she approached the first Cleveland Avenue bus that came along. At the last moment, she noticed that this bus was crowded, and she let it go by; for she had decided in her mind that "when I got on the bus I wanted to be as comfortable as I could. . . ." She went across the street to the drug store and got some pills for her aching neck. When she returned, she noticed "another bus approaching, and . . . didn't see anybody standing up in the back. But by the time I [got] to the bus door, a number of people had gotten on ahead of me, and when I got on the Negro section in back

254

was well filled." There was one vacant seat in the fifth row—the first row in no-man's land—and she sank wearily into a seat next to a black man, who was sitting by the window. The bus pulled out of Court Square and stopped at the Empire Theater. Several whites got on and took the designated "white" seats. This left one white man standing, and the driver—J. F. Blake—looked in the rear view mirror and told the four blacks in the fifth row to get up so the white man could sit down. There must have been something in the air on this day; for at first no one moved. Blake noticed this with some surprise and raised his voice:

"Y'all better make it light on yourselves and let me have those seats."

At that point the man sitting next to Rosa Parks stood up, and she shifted her legs in the seat and let him pass. As she moved to the window, she noticed out of the corner of her eye that the two women across the aisle had also vacated their seats.

Now, as tension rose in the bus, driver Blake approached Rosa Parks and asked if she was going to move. No, she said, she wasn't. Blake said that if she didn't get up, he would have to call the police. "Go ahead and call them," Rosa Parks said.

Blake stormed to the front, pulled the ratchet and got off. Several passengers who didn't want to be inconvenienced or who didn't want to get involved followed him. The remaining passengers sat quietly, staring at the woman who was causing all the trouble. Before too much time passed, the driver returned with two policemen, who asked Rosa Parks if she had understood the driver's request. She said yes.

"Why didn't you get up?" one of the officers asked.

"I didn't think I should have to," she replied. Then there came from deep inside her a terrible and unanswerable question.

"Why do you push us around?"

There was no answer, in the police manual, or in any book, to that question, and the officer mumbled: "I don't know, but the law is the law, and you are under arrest."

There then occurred one of those little vignettes that sometimes change the course of history. The officers asked the driver if he wanted to swear out a warrant or if he wanted them to let Rosa Parks go with a warning. The driver said he wanted to swear out a warrant, and this decision and the convergence of a number of historical forces sealed the death warrant of the Jim Crow South.

The scene shifted now to the police station, where Rosa Parks was booked, fingerprinted, and jailed. She was permitted to make one phone

Martin Luther King, Jr., was surrounded by reporters on first integrated bus run.

call, and she used it to reach E. D. Nixon, a big-shouldered, big-framed Pullman Porter who had been the moving edge of the Montgomery protest movement for more than two decades. Nixon called the police station and asked what the charge was. The man on the other end of the line said "none of your goddamned business" and hung up. Nixon, who was fearless, and who was neither intimidated nor surprised by the ways of the white South, called a liberal white lawyer, Clifford Durr, and they went to the police station and bailed Rosa Parks out. By this time it had occurred to Nixon that Mrs. Parks's plight, though regrettable on a personal level, was a godsend to the movement. She was not the first black woman to suffer such indignities, but she was the first with such impeccable credentials. She had served with him for a number of years as a local NAACP official; and she was known, moreover, to be a woman of unimpeachable moral character. This meant, as Nixon explained to her, that she would make a perfect symbol and test case. After some discussion with her husband, Raymond, and her mother, Mrs. Leona McCauley, Mrs. Parks agreed, and Nixon hurried home to see what he could do with this gift the Jim Crow system had put into his hands.

It was, by this time, late on Thursday night, and word was spreading through the black community. Among the blacks most immediately concerned were members of the Women's Political Council. A few months earlier, on the arrest of fifteen-year-old Claudette Colvin, members of the council had suggested a bus boycott similar to the bus boycott staged in the summer of 1953 by the blacks of Baton Rouge, Louisiana. This suggestion never got off the ground, but the arrest of Rosa Parks revived the old ideas and crystallized sentiment among leading members of the council, including Jo Ann Robinson, a brilliant and fiery professor of English at Alabama State College.

At the same time, either in cooperation with the council or indepen-

256

dently—the subject has thorns and the recollection of participants are conflicting and contradictory and charged, even at this late date, with large amounts of passion—E. D. Nixon decided that a boycott could be organized around the symbolic presence of Rosa Parks. And he was on the telephone early the next morning, organizing a boycott committee. The first person he called, shortly after 5:00 A.M., was Ralph D. Abernathy, the young pastor of the First Baptist Church. The second call went to the Reverend H. H. Hubbard, president of the powerful Baptist Ministerial Alliance. Somewhere down the line—Nixon believes he was third—was the name of Martin Luther King, Jr., a young minister who had recently assumed the pastorate of the small but prestigious Dexter Baptist Church.

Within a short time after he received the call, King was deeply involved in the pre-boycott planning. In a series of calls between Abernathy and King and Nixon, a strategy was devised for securing the support of the Baptist Ministerial Alliance and the equally powerful conference of AME Zion ministers. Before the sun rose very high on Friday morning, a list of potential supporters had been drawn up and an emergency meeting had been scheduled for 3:00 P.M. at the Dexter Avenue Baptist Church. This meeting was attended by a wide spectrum of community leaders. (It is an interesting fact that the leading force of the movement

Surviving leaders, including Rosa Parks (second from right) celebrated twentieth anniversary of the boycott in 1975.

up to that time did not attend. E. D. Nixon, who suggested the meeting and helped to arrange it, left Montgomery for Chicago on a regular Pullman run that afternoon and did not return to the city until Sunday morning.)

As might have been expected, this meeting was far from harmonious. The presiding officer, the Reverend L. Roy Bennett, president of the Interdominational Ministerial Alliance, opened the meeting by saying that the die was cast and that the time for talking was over. This ruling was protested by several leaders, who wanted to discuss the origin and the implications of the situation. Before the procedural hassle was straightened out, several persons left the meeting, and latent discords were revealed. When the shouting died down, and the assembled ministers, labor leaders and professionals had ventilated their hopes and fears, the idea of the boycott was endorsed. There were also certain concrete assignments and recommendations. Practically all of the ministers agreed to endorse the boycott from their pulpits on Sunday morning. Certain ministers, such as the Reverend W. J. Powell, agreed to get in touch with the eighteen Negro taxicab companies and arrange for minimum ten-cent fares during the Monday rush hours.

It was apparent to some of these leaders that events, not for the first time, were outracing the decisions of the decision-makers. The arrest of Rosa Parks had crystallized and focused long-smoldering emotions, and several groups and individuals were acting independently. Even as the leaders debated, for example, boycott leaflets—authored by Jo Ann Robinson—were being distributed in the black community. The essential message of this leaflet was adopted by the leadership group, and some seven thousand copies, with the enthusiastic support of Martin Luther King, Jr., were hurriedly run off on the mimeograph machine of the Dexter Avenue Baptist Church.

The message of the leaflets was plain and uncompromising:

Don't ride the bus to work, to town, to school, or anyplace Monday, December 5. Another Negro woman has been arrested and put in jail because she refused to give up her bus seat.

Don't ride the buses to work, to town, to school, or anywhere on Monday. If you work, take a cab, or share a ride, or walk. Come to a mass meeting, Monday at 7:00 P.M., at the Holt Street Baptist Church for further instruction.

At this juncture fate dealt the boycott leaders a high card. An illiterate maid asked her white employer to tell her what the leaflets said. The employer, enraged by the machinations of the blacks, called the *Montgomery Advertiser*, which printed the leaflets on its front page, thereby giving the boycott supporters invaluable free publicity.

No one knew then how the black community would respond to this appeal. The optimistic hoped that 60 or 70 percent of the black bus riders would support the movement. The realistic—and the cynical—feared the worst. And, interestingly, members of both groups had prepared a fall-back position. It was generally agreed, according to several key participants, that if the boycott was reasonably successful, it would be continued. And if it failed, the plan was to explain that it had always been planned as a one-day affair and that another one-day boycott would be called if there was another insult on the buses.

It is clear now, but it was by no means clear then, that there was nothing to worry about. Between Friday afternoon and midnight on Sunday, there was a silent and profoundly effective plebiscite in the black community of Montgomery. A thousand grievances, a thousand remembered slights welled up from the depths of the people. And by dawn on the first day of the Black Revolution, Monday, December 5, 1955, the fate and future direction of the movement had been decided —by the people.

This became clear when the first bus moved on Monday morning. There were swarms of blacks, hunkered down in sweaters and overcoats, on almost every street corner; and long lines of walkers filled the streets. But most blacks waved the buses on, saying that they were not "gittin' on," as one man put it, "until Jim Crow gits off."

When the first of the big yellow buses pulled into Court Square at 5:30 A.M., there was a sign tacked to the wall of the bus shed. The sign, printed with shoe polish on a big white cardboard, said: "People don't ride the bus today. Don't ride it, for freedom."

A white reporter for the *Alabama Journal* watched the unfolding scene with amazement:

"Negroes," he wrote, "were on almost every corner in the downtown area, silent, waiting for rides or moving about to keep warm, but few got on the buses. Negro cabs were packed tight and it seemed as if they stopped to pick up more passengers at every corner. Some appeared as if they would burst open if another passenger got in. Scores of Negroes were walking, their lunches in brown paper sacks under their arms.

None spoke to white people. They exchanged little talk among themselves. It was an event almost solemn."

Traffic was extremely heavy. Many employers were up early, driving to the black community to get their maids and yardmen. The motorized corps of the police department was out in full force, and squads of motorcycles followed empty buses "to protect Negroes," it was said, who wanted to ride.

Few wanted to ride. A Montgomery city policeman at Court Square said at 7:00 A.M. that he had seen only two blacks getting off buses. At that precise moment, boycott leaders were scanning the horizon to see which way the wind was blowing. Martin Luther King, Jr., and his wife, Coretta, as I have written elsewhere,* waited impatiently for the first bus, which usually passed their house around 6 A.M. King was in the kitchen when his wife shouted: "Martin! Martin!" King ran to the living room and Coretta King pointed to the bus which was inexplicably, gloriously, empty. King could hardly believe his eyes, but caution checked his joy. One swallow didn't make a spring, and one empty bus didn't make a boycott. It would be better perhaps to wait for the second bus. But it, too, was empty, or almost empty; and so was the third and fourth.

Excited now, envisioning the beginning of a new day, King ran to his car and drove around the city, scanning the windows of empty buses. An inexpressible joy welled up within him, and he told himself that a "miracle" had happened. So it had. That morning, blacks walked, rode mules, and drove wagons. The boycott was almost totally effective and would remain so for days and weeks and months to come.

One-day social miracles are rare; two-day social miracles are almost inconceivable, even to preachers. And that morning, after Rosa Parks was convicted of violating the segregation ordinances, King and other members of the leadership group, including her attorney, Fred D. Gray, began to explore the possibilities of a structure that would draw the miracle out. Since a mass meeting had already been scheduled for the Holt Street Baptist Church at seven, the leadership group decided to hold a planning session at 3:00 P.M. in the Mount Zion AME Church. This meeting, in turn, was preceded by a number of formal and informal caucuses. Two of these meetings are worthy of notice.

The first was held immediately after the Parks trial by E. D. Nixon,

---

* *What Manner of Man.*

Abernathy, and the Reverend E. N. French, pastor of Hilliard Chapel AME Zion Church. The three men left the trial and walked to French's office, where they agreed on several ideas. First of all, and most important of all, they agreed that the boycott should continue. Secondly, they agreed that a new and permanent organization should be formed. There was some bandying about at this meeting of possible names. Nixon was partial to the "Negro Citizens Committee." Abernathy was opposed to this name; he wanted nothing in the title to remind anyone of the White Citizens Council. Abernathy thought for a while and then suggested the name ultimately adopted, the Montgomery Improvement Association.

At this meeting, or at an earlier one, another crucial matter was brought into the open. There was, almost everyone agreed, a desperate need for a strong personality to lead the organization. It is generally agreed that the position was offered first to Nixon, and it is generally agreed that Nixon declined, citing his frequent absences from the city. Nixon confirms these reports and he says now that his candidate at that point was Martin Luther King, Jr.

There was another meeting of the minds in another mini-caucus between Rufus Lewis, a civil rights activist and nightclub owner, and P. E. Conley, an insurance man. Lewis says that he decided after the Dexter meeting that the boycott was doomed without a calm and far-seeing spokesman. According to his recollection, he and Conley put their heads together and decided that the man needed was his pastor, Martin Luther King, Jr. And it is his firm recollection today that he and Conley decided on Monday to seize the floor at the afternoon meeting and nominate King "before anybody else could get something started."

It was with these and other plans and ideas that Lewis, Conley, Nixon, Abernathy and others approached the afternoon meeting at Mount Zion. The meeting was somewhat disorganized, but it was decided finally to continue the boycott and to form a permanent organization. A committee, headed by Abernathy, was named to draw up the resolutions for the night meeting, and the house was opened for nominations for president. Someone suggested that in view of the hazardous nature of the undertaking that it would be better not to reveal the names of the leaders. There was an explosion at this point. E. D. Nixon, his voice breaking and his eyes blazing, denounced "scared little boys who want to pretend that they are men." He went on to say that it was impossible to keep an undertaking of this sort secret and that the assembled leaders had to decide, then and there, whether "they were going to be men or boys." Looking back many years later, Nixon said this was the essence of his speech, but that he used some words on that day that cannot be printed in a family publication.

Nixon's message was repeated and endorsed in more traditional language by Martin Luther King, Jr., and late in the afternoon of Monday, December 5, 1955, the men—and women—of Montgomery, Alabama, crossed a great divide, deciding without vote and without too many misgivings to go public, whatever the cost, whatever the consequences.

The next order of business was the election of officers. When the house was opened for nominations, Rufus Lewis seized the floor and, to the surprise of many, nominated the Reverend Martin Luther King, Jr., for the presidency. King was only twenty-six, and he had been living in Montgomery for only a few months. But the nomination was carried without opposition, partly because he hadn't been in town long enough to create hard-core enemies, partly because there weren't that many candidates for a new position that was almost certainly going to lead to jail or worse.

Interestingly and significantly, Martin Luther King, Jr., didn't hesitate or waffle at this critical moment in his life. Some of his friends expected him to decline the honor, as he had declined the presidency of the local NAACP chapter. But King surprised them, as he perhaps surprised himself, by stepping to the front of the room and coolly and deliberately taking charge.

Before the meeting adjourned, there was an interesting and ironic development. Some of the leaders, smitten perhaps by the enormity of the step they had taken, urged that the whole matter be reconsidered. "Despite our satisfaction at the success of the protest so far," King wrote later, "we were still concerned. Would the evening meeting be well attended? Could we hope that the fortitude and enthusiasm of the Negro community would survive more than one such day hardship? Someone suggested that perhaps we should reconsider our decision to continue the protest. 'Would it not be better,' said the speaker, 'to call off the protest while it is still a success rather than let it go on a few more days and fizzle out? We have already proved our united strength to the white community. If we stop now we can get anything we want from the bus company, simply because they will have the feeling that we can do it again. But if we continue, and most of the people return to the buses tomorrow or the next day, the white people will laugh at us, and we will end up getting nothing.' This argument was so convincing that we almost resolved to end the protest. But we finally agreed to let the mass meeting —which was only about an hour off—be our guide."

In the end, then, as in the beginning, the people decided. Even as the leaders debated, long lines of men and women—maids, porters, teachers, students, laborers—were gathering before the doors of the Holt Street Baptist Church. By 7:00 P.M., the church was packed and two or three thousand persons were standing silently in the surrounding streets, listening to the hymns and introductory statements on loudspeakers.

The meeting opened with "Onward Christian Soldiers." There was a prayer, interrupted, Joe Azbell of the *Montgomery Advisor* reported, "a hundred times" by "yeas" and "uh'uhs" and "that's right." The frenzy of the audience mounted as speaker after speaker came to the podium. And there was an explosion and a standing ovation for the heroine of the hour—Rosa Parks.

The two high points were provided by Ralph Abernathy and Martin Luther King, Jr. Abernathy read the resolutions which called for a continuation of the boycott until three demands were met: 1) courteous treatment of black passengers, 2) employment of black drivers on predominantly black runs, 3) seating on a first-come, first-serve basis with blacks filling the bus from the rear and whites from the front, and no reserved seats for whites or blacks. These resolutions were hardly revolutionary, but they constituted a new point of departure, and they were thunderously approved by the audience.

Martin Luther King, Jr., the new and virtually unknown leader of the new movement, provided the second high point. He had had no time to prepare a speech, and so he spoke that night with the voice of the people and the wisdom of the heart. He didn't quote Gandhi that night, but he did quote Jesus and, remarkably, Booker T. Washington. "Our method," he said, "will be that of persuasion, not coercion. We will only say to the people, 'Let your conscience be your guide.'" He went on then to mention the transforming power of love, saying: "Love must be our regulating ideal. Once again we must hear the words of Jesus echoing across the centuries: 'Love your enemies, bless them that curse you, and pray for them that despitefully use you.' If we fail to do this our protest will end up as a meaningless drama on the stage of history, and its memory will be shrouded with the ugly garments of shame. In spite of the mistreatment that we have confronted we must not become bitter, and end up hating our white brothers. As Booker T. Washington said, 'Let no man pull you so low as to make you hate him.'" Then, after the applause died down, King built to a climatic crescendo that would later become his oratorical signature. "If you will protest courageously, and yet with dignity and Christian love, when the history books are written in future generations, the historians will have to pause and say, 'There lived a great people—a black people—who injected new meaning and dignity into the veins of civilization.' This is our challenge and our overwhelming responsibility."

On this high note of challenge and inspiration, the meeting ended, and men and women went out into the night with tears in their eyes, steel in their hearts, and a sure sense that this day was the beginning of a new chapter in the history of black and white Americans.

*All God's
Children*

The Five-and-Dime Bastille

THE F. W. Woolworth store on South Elm Street in Greensboro, North Carolina, was an unlikely place for great events. In its standardized fixtures and its standardized wares, the Greensboro store was a computerized link in a chain-store operation that was designed to eliminate the unpredictable and the dramatic. In corporate head-quarters in faraway New York, executives with slide rules and mathe-matical formulae had anticipated almost every problem and forms had been provided for almost every contingency. This was the way the Amer-ican corporate structure worked: forms, wares, units, customers were interchangeable. And the Woolworth store in Greensboro (and other Southern cities) followed the same routine as the Woolworth stores in New York City and San Francisco. There was, of course, one difference. North Carolina was in the South, and the store in Greensboro bowed in certain areas to Southern customs. What this meant as a practical matter

Sit-in movement was started by four North Carolina A and T freshmen, Ezell Blair, Jr., Joseph McNeil, David Richmond, Franklin McClain.

was that blacks could shop in the store but couldn't be served at the lunch counter. This was inefficient and contrary to good business practices, but the corporate managers in New York City said their hands were tied. The law, they said, was the law, and if American businesses wanted to operate in the South, they had to follow Southern customs.

This was the situation on Monday, February 1, 1960, and it explains, in part, why this glittering emporium of small and colorful bargains became the Bastille of the Black Revolution. This much is clear in retrospect, but it was scarcely possible on this day to seriously contemplate the possibility of an American Bastille. There were, to be sure, disturbing rumbles in the news. In Algeria on this Monday right-wing colons ended their short-lived rebellion. In Paris President Charles DeGaulle asked the French National Assembly for extraordinary power to deal with the threat of civil war. In Brussels a young African named Patrice Lumumba was sparring with Belgian officials over the details of a plan guaranteeing an independent Belgian Congo.

This was the shape of the news on February 1. There was nothing definite in all this, but there was a vague feeling in the air that things

270

were slipping away from their moorings and that a new world was a-borning. All this was lived through in blindness and dim gropings. America just then was in the grips of the Age of Eisenhower Normalcy. The campuses were quiet—students were staging panty raids and swallowing goldfish—and there were few voices of dissent. The big news in Washington was the return of Dwight David Eisenhower after a weekend of golf at the El Dorado Country Club in Palm Springs.

The racial front was quiet. If we can believe headline writers, there were no racial crises in sight or on the horizon. After the stirring events of Montgomery and Little Rock, things had quieted down; and there was hope, as they said in Greensboro and other places, that the South could now settle down to a quiet period of solving its problems without the help of outside agitators.

In this setting of surface calm and ominous underground rumblings, the midafternoon scene in the Woolworth Store on South Elm Street was reassuring. Here, in a seemingly endless variety of boxes and bottles and scents, was the genius of the American Way of mass production and chain-store marketing. The counters were piled high with creams and deodorants and salves; and the aisles were thronged with customers who seemed to be hypnotized by the tempting array of bargains. Among the customers on this day were four young men who would soon be better known. They were obviously and definitely students. In fact, they seemed to advertise the fact, carrying notebooks and big textbooks like banners, presenting, for all the world to see, the scrubbed purposeful air of drones on their way to the library to cram for an urgent exam. One of the young men—Franklin C. McCain—was wearing an ROTC uniform. His companions—Ezell Blair, Jr., David Richmond, and Joseph McNeill—were neatly dressed in coats and ties.

No one gave the four students a second thought. Greensboro was a center of culture and education; it had grown accustomed to black students from the state school, North Carolina A and T, and the private college for women, Bennett. From time to time, there were problems with black students from the North, who sometimes "forgot" and transgressed against Southern customs.

Sympathy marches were staged by protesters in Northern cities.

But these were minor irritants, easily smoothed over and forgotten. No one in Greensboro, North Carolina, on February 1, 1960, seriously believed that black students were threats to the Southern Way of Life.

For these reasons then, and for others as well, including their neat appearance and respectful air, the four students blended into the Woolworth scenery. They went unnoticed to the notions counter, made small purchases, and asked politely—very politely—for receipts. They then walked in the general direction of the lunch counter, which was reserved for the exclusive use of white patrons and which bristled, at this hour, with activity. The four students stood for a few moments in the no-man's land between the aisle and the seats at the L-shaped lunch counter. Behind this counter white waitresses dashed back and forth, taking and barking orders. A black woman appeared, collected dirty dishes, and disappeared through a revolving door. The clock on the wall said 4:30. At that precise moment the four students took a deep breath and walked into history, taking seats at the counter and ordering four cups of coffee and cherry pie a la mode. It was a simple act, which was not, strictly speaking, comparable to the storming of the Bastille. But, allowing for differences in time and place, the act had a similar resonance. For by the simple act of walking across a few feet of open space and taking seats at a lunch counter, the four students laid seige to a whole structure of being and doing. And they did this deliberately and with conscious and militant forethought. What did they feel at this moment? Franklin C. McCain, looking back many years later, said he had a feeling of exhiliration. "I had a feeling of liberation," he said. "I had stopped doing what others had done for generations."

The implications of all this were not immediately apparent to the white waitress, who seemingly believed that the black students had made an honest mistake. She told them that blacks could not be served there. One of the students told her she was mistaken. They had just been served at the notions counter. Why couldn't they be served at the lunch counter?

The question was loaded. The waitress, perceiving this, retreated for reinforcements. Men came and wrestled with the question, but the answers did not satisfy the students. The discussion continued until the students closed the subject by announcing that they were not going to move until they were served. Without further comment, they opened books and began to study.

Unexpectedly at this point, there occurred one of those little scenes that are generations in the making. A black woman, a dishwasher, was summoned from the kitchen, and two visions, two worlds, two hopes, collided. It is extremely unlikely that this unnamed dishwasher ever accepted the implications of segregation. But she had grown up believing that it was impossible to change it. And she feared, as so many of her generation feared, that wild and impractical acts would only make the situation worse. She said so, in vigorous language, telling the students: "You're dumb. That's why we can't get anywhere today." One of the young men replied, softly, that he was sorry she felt that way. He added,

Thousands of students and adults thronged streets of South in protest demonstrations.

more in sorrow than anger, that the strategy of her generation hadn't worked, and that he was tired of waiting.

By now, a crowd had gathered. But, surprisingly, no one raised a hand against the students, who sat quietly, respectfully, their heads buried in books. While they studied or pretended to study, activity in the store ground to a halt. This was a new situation, and no one seemed to know how to deal with it. The store closed an hour later without serving the students, who kept their seats until the end.

The day ended thus, in stalemate, and with little or no notice in the outside world. There was no activity that night in the offices of the big civil rights organizations in Manhattan. The lights did not burn late in the offices of the Justice Department in Washington or in the homes of established civil rights leaders in Washington, Manhattan, and Atlanta. But that night in a room at Scott Hall on the campus of North Carolina A and T College, four young men made a decision that would change civil rights and America forever.

Who were these young men?

They were seeds, stalks, the first shoots of a bitter post-war history. With the exception of Franklin E. McCain, who was born in Washington, D.C., all were products of the South. Ezell Blair and David Richmond were natives of Greensboro. Joseph A. McNeill was from Wilmington, North Carolina. They had been born, all of them, in the turbulent years of World War II and had come to a sense of themselves in the clamor and clash surrounding the resistance to the Supreme Court decision of 1954. Blair, Richmond, and McNeill were eighteen. McNeill was seventeen. All were freshmen. All lived in Scott Hall. All had a new vision of black struggle and black destiny.

For five months, the four students had been holding what they called "Bull Sessions" in their dormitory rooms. Like other freshmen of that and all preceding and succeeding generations, they discussed philosophy, life, and girls. But somehow the talk always returned to "the problem"— the problem of being black and put-upon in a white racist society. The situation, they readily agreed, was intolerable. It was necessary, they agreed, for someone to do something. But who? Over and over again, endlessly, the students wrestled with that question. Finally, in January, 1960, the four young men decided that *they* would do something. But what and where? How could four college students with no organization or resources make a dent in a deeply entrenched system that had endured for decades? This was a question of theory; and the students, to their credit, transcended it by deciding to act, regardless of the consequences, in the faith that their act would energize larger circles of resistance. The strategy adopted was simple. They would take seats at a Jim Crow counter in a chain store and would refuse to move until served. What did they hope to accomplish by this? They hoped, first of all, to tie up business at the target lunch counter and to threaten the profit margin of the store. A chain store was selected because it was vunerable to counter demonstrations by black customers in the North.

This was the strategy, and on the night of February 1, the students decided to take it to higher levels by recruiting additional demonstrators. On the same night the students covered their flanks by conferring with George Simkins, Jr., the dentist who headed the Greensboro chapter of the NAACP. Dr. Simkins immediately contacted the leaders of the Congress of Racial Equality, which had a great deal of experience in direct-action campaigns. Both CORE and the NAACP rushed staffers to North Carolina, but neither played significant roles in the first demonstrations.

The next morning, the Greensboro Four returned to Woolworth with reinforcements. Marvin Sykes, a staff writer of the *Greensboro Record,* was there, and he filed the following story:

> A group of 20 Negro students from A&T College occupied luncheon counter seats, without being served, at the downtown F. W. Woolworth Co. store late this morning—starting what they declared would be a growing movement.
>
> Today's 20-man action followed appearance at 4:30 P.M. yesterday of four freshmen from Scott Hall at A&T who sat down and stayed, without service, until the store closed at 5:30 P.M.
>
> Student spokesmen said they are seeking luncheon counter service, and will increase their numbers daily until they get it.
>
> Today's group came in at 10:30 A.M. Each made a small purchase one counter over from the luncheon counter, then sat in groups of three or four as spaces became vacant.
>
> There was no disturbance and there appeared to be no conversation except among the groups. Some students pulled out books and appeared to be studying.
>
> The group today wrote to the president of Woolworth asking "a firm stand to eliminate this discrimination," and signed the

letter as members of the Student Executive Committee for Justice. [Spokesman Ezell] Blair declared that Negro adults "have been complacent and fearful." He declared, "It is time for someone to wake up and change the situation . . . and we decided to start here."

On Wednesday, February 3, Blair and his colleagues increased the pressure, filling Woolworth's with seventy students, including black coeds from Bennett College and white coeds from North Carolina's College for Women and Guilford College. Most of the students brought books with them and studied at the counter. Some read Bibles.

By Wednesday night, the sit-ins were attracting national attention. A wire service story from UPI said:

> It was difficult at times to move freely through the aisles near the long counter which extends through half the store and along the back wall. Some white customers reportedly were served upstairs in a section reserved for the bookkeeping department and other service and kitchen facilities. About a dozen white customers were served at scattered point along the lunch counter.
>
> William H. Gamble, dean of men at A&T College, said he was investigating the demonstration, but pointed out the college had no authority to restrict students' activities of this nature off-campus.
>
> "As long as they don't cut classes or foul up in some way, I don't see that it's any of the college's business," another faculty member said.
>
> The students said they were working in shifts, one in the morning and one in the afternoon, to avoid taking cuts. At least 20 coeds participated in the sitdown Wednesday. . . .

There was trouble the next day, according to another UPI report. "A group of pushing, shoving white teen-agers and young men . . . appeared on the scene for the first time and blocked aisles at times and occupied one section of the counter. Three teen-agers were removed by plain-clothes officers after they started yelling and swearing. The demonstration —in its third day—spread. Some of the 150 North Carolina A&T students moved to the S. H. Kress & Co. store down the street to launch a similar sitdown. . . ."

The struggle continued uninterruptedly until Saturday when the lunch counters were closed and negotiations were opened that led, four months later, to a student victory. By this time, however, the movement had spread to chain stores in other Southern cities and states. On February 8, sit-ins started in Durham and Winston Salem. On February 11, sit-ins started in Virginia. By the end of March, sit-ins had been staged in practically every Southern state, and more than one thousand college and high school students had been arrested for "trespassing" and "disorderly conduct."

The movement, based on the passive resistance techniques of Mahatma Gandhi, raced across the South with the fury of a forest fire. Chain stores, department stores, beaches, libraries, supermarkets and movies felt the heat of sit-ins, read-ins, swim-ins. The code of conduct drawn up by the Nashville Student movement characterized the entire movement:

> Don't strike back or curse if abused.
> Don't laugh out.
> Don't hold conversations with floor workers.
> Don't block entrances to the store and aisles.
> Show yourself courteous and friendly at all times.
> Sit straight and always face the counter.
> Remember love and nonviolence.
> May God bless each of you.

The South countered with traditional weapons—violence, mass arrests, and expulsions. But the effectiveness of these weapons was blunted by a split in the white South. Some merchants, with one eye on the cash register and the reactions of supporting adult customers, refused to press charges. Some public officials issued ambiguous statements, which called for law-and-order but left large loopholes, which the students brilliantly exploited.

Faces told the story of this remarkable student movement.

In a Chattanooga dime store, the face of a black boy trapped by a gang of swaggering white toughs was captured by a camera. Fear, pride, and anger struggled for dominance in that young face. Pride won and the black boy stood his ground to see what the hour would demand of him.

In Nashville, it was the face of a coed. She stared with Budda-like passivity at the shining coffee urn facing the counter. A white man crept up behind her and pushed a lighted cigarette into her hair. She brushed it away and turned. Her face—brown, open, round—smiled.

From Richmond came the images of two faces. A young man and a

young woman were being escorted to jail by two grim-faced policemen.
The face of the young man was calm, purposeful. A smile flickered at
the corner of his mouth. The girl held her head high. Her face betrayed
no emotion—only the eyes burned.

From Montgomery, from Houston, from New Orleans and Greensboro
and Atlanta and Jackson, from cities and hamlets all over the South came
similar faces. Disturbed by the passion in these faces, Carl Blair, president of the Montgomery (Ala.) Chamber of Commerce said: "There's a
Revolution of the Negro youth in this nation."

The Revolution released waves of dammed-up energy that flowed to
every section of the country. In Harlem, in Chicago, in Watts, black adults
manned picket lines at chain store outlets. And on college campuses,
students—black and white—shucked off "beat" and "cool" poses and
assumed the militant face that would characterize them for the rest of
the sixties. By the thousands now, students trooped from the cloisters and
set up picket lines. At Princeton University, students favoring the sit-ins
and students opposing them came to blows. At the University of Wisconsin, the sit-in movement split the campus into two vocal groups. The
implications of all this were shrewdly assessed in a statement by Melvin
B. Freedman, coordinator of the Mellon Foundation Research Program
at Vassar: "We can now find any number of prominent people quite
ready to say that the situation of the Negro in the South is not right.
There is the possibility that now that it has been demonstrated that there
is something there, people might be more disposed to get a rise out of
college students. This is the first time that Vassar girls have picketed in
twenty years."

There were some surprising voices in the new chorus of affirmation.
A Southern governor, LeRoy Collins of Florida, went on a statewide
television hook-up to tell citizens that it was "unfair and morally wrong"
for a business to serve blacks at one counter and bar them at another.
And President Eisenhower, who had maintained an air of benevolent
neutrality on the race question, came close to committing himself.

In a great upswelling of moral indignation, church groups, politicians,
and public figures climbed on the sit-in bandwagon. Wake Forest College
students moved from support of the sit-in students to an attack on their
trustees for barring black students. The Board of Social and Economic
Relations of the Methodist Church took note of its own exposed position
in a statement praising the protesters. "We confess with sorrow," the
statement said, "that as a denomination we have failed to live up to our

own pronouncements. In no section of our land have we carried out the teachings of our Lord with respect to race relations."

This statement and others of similar import reflected the national soul-searching set off by the sit-ins. In the wake of this development, new organizations, notably the Student Nonviolent Coordinating Committee (SNCC), emerged. This, in turn, pushed traditional black leadership to new plateaus of militancy. The grand outcome was that black affairs in America turned, as if on a hinge, and the stage was set for the confrontations of the sixties.

What did the four students who started the movement think about all this?

They were pleased, of course, and they continued to struggle. But as the years wore on, and as the focus of attention shifted from Greensboro to Birmingham to Watts, the four young warriors of Greensboro slipped once again into the background of a history they had illuminated and transformed by providing the most dramatic example in modern times of the power of individuals to shape and change history.

Good News

The Day They Marched

IT was the beginning of something and the ending of something.

It came 100 years and 240 days after the signing of the Emancipation Proclamation.

It came like a force of nature.

Like a whirlwind, like a storm, like a flood, it overwhelmed by its massiveness and finality.

A quarter-million people were in it, and of it; and millions more watched on TV and huddled around radios.

There had never been anything quite like it.

A TV spectacular, a Sunday School picnic, a political convention, an impressive demonstration of black unity, "a visible exhibition of interracial brotherhood," an almost unprecedented exhibition of resolve, a new concept of lobbying, a living petition, a show of strength, an outburst, a call to the national conscience: the mammoth March on Washington was everything they said it was, and more; and it moved men and women as they had never been moved before.

Some 250,000 attended March. Blind man (below) was among marchers.

It threatened, at points, to become a meaningless gesture, an extravaganza, an outing, a prayer said to the wind. But the people, the old ladies and the young boys, the students and the dreamers, the young girls in bright babushkas and the old men in shiny blue suits: the people—they redeemed it, and made it something to remember.

They came, these people, from points all over America, and several overseas; they assembled in Washington on the grassy slopes of the Washington Monument and walked about a mile to the Lincoln Monument, where they said with their bodies that black people had been waiting for 100 years and 240 days and that they were still not free and that 100 years and 241 days were too long to wait. There, in balmy 84-degree weather, in the shadow of Lincoln and the presence of God, they recalled (in Archibald MacLeish's phrase) "the holy dream we were to be"—recalled the dream and made it flesh and blood and bone in their black and white togetherness.

This, then, was the March: a long and uncomfortable trip on trains and buses and planes, a short walk down Constitution and Independence avenues, words said in the sun and, beneath it all, a quiet anger, a fierce hope and the wind and the fire of a dream.

Dreams brought the demonstrators to this particular place at this particular time—dreams and drastic demands within them. We are accustomed now to the dreams of the young, but there is a certain poetry in the fact that this march was the product of the dreams of a New Negro who was born in 1889. For

Marchers of all ages and descriptions participated.

Asa Philip Randolph, seventy-four, president of the Brotherhood of Sleeping Car Porters and vice-president of the AFL-CIO, the March was the culmination of a half-century of agitation. He had come uphill all the way, this old man; he had won the first FEPC order from President Roosevelt in 1941 by threatening a March on Washington, and he had been threatening marches ever since. In January, 1963, he suggested a march to dramatize the plight of unemployed Negroes, but nobody was listening and nobody seemed to care. Then came Birmingham; then came the thunder of blacks in the streets; then came the Summer of Discontent; and men remembered the Old Man and what he had done in 1941 and what he wanted to do in 1963. In the end, the five major black organizations—NAACP, SCLC, "SNICK," CORE and Urban League—closed ranks behind Randolph and his dream. A Jew, Catholic, a Protestant, and a labor leader completed the cast of leaders. They named Randolph director; and the Old Man went back to his Harlem office, and the years fell from him. He chose as his deputy director Bayard Rustin, a brilliant mover and shaker in the Freedom Movement, and another veteran of the March on Washington movement of 1941. Before Randolph and Rustin lay a formidable task: moving two hundred thousand or more people into Washington and out in one day, feeding, organizing

and, to be blunt, restraining them for twenty-four hours. That this was done, and with such aplomb, tells much about the quality of black leadership.

Through the late summer, as the fires of discontent burned in the streets, Randolph and his aides prodded, pushed, and organized. As they worked, ripples of fear spread across the nation. Washington, D.C., already more than one-half black, was hysterical; the general feeling, the *Washington Daily News* said, was that the Vandals were coming again to sack Rome. Powerful politicians and big men in labor and business urged the leaders to abandon the March; it was unwise, they said, imprudent, unnecessary, and perhaps illegal. The press took up the cry, saying with increasing stridence that the March was social dynamite and that violence was almost unavoidable. Despite the furor or perhaps because of it, preparations continued. In a yellow building in Harlem and in another yellow building in Washington, M-O-W men wrestled with unprecedented logistical problems: over fifteen hundred organizations

March coordinator, Bayard Rustin, orchestrated protest from New York office.

Highlight of day was "I Have a Dream" speech of Martin Luther King, Jr.

were contacted, regional directors were named, organizational manuals were issued.

March leaders went to extraordinary lengths to insure a peaceful demonstration. As originally conceived by the more venturesome leaders, the March was to be a rasp across an exposed nerve. One student leader announced early in the summer that he and his wife and baby planned to pitch a tent on the White House lawn. Others spoke of sit-ins in the offices of James Eastland and other senators. The leaders vetoed these plans; they banned inciting signs and forbade picketing at the White House and on Capitol Hill. An internal police system was set up to isolate and exclude troublemakers. The March, according to the leaders, was for Freedom and Jobs. The immediate aim was to prod Congress on the pending civil rights bill.

As the big day drew near, excitement grew. In the beginning, it

March leaders met with President John F. Kennedy at end of day.

seemed that the March would be a flop. Newspapers reported a lack of interest; they said sponsors were having trouble filling chartered trains and buses. In this, as in other things about the March, the press was wrong. Toward the end of August, March headquarters was swamped with requests from organizations who wanted to get on the bandwagon. The feeling was growing—it was in the air—that this one was going to be big and, as always, men and organizations wanted to be with the winner.

Staff members were hard at work in New York, Martin Luther King, Jr., was in his Atlanta home, Asa Phillip Randolph was in his Harlem apartment when the wheels begun to turn. Weeks before the March, Jay Hardo, an eighty-two-year-old man, left Dayton, Ohio, on a silver bicycle with a big American eagle on the handlebars. A week or so later, Ledger Smith, an NAACP member, left Chicago on roller skates. Four days before the March, David Parker, a Los Angeles pants presser, got into a battered old Ford with five friends and started the three thousand-mile trip across the nation. Parker said he was going to Washington "because my people got troubles."

In the final week, the ghettos of America stirred. In thousands of homes, bags were being packed, lunches prepared, goodbyes said. In thousands of bars and barber shops, the thing was being discussed pro and con. No one knew at this point how many would be there, but the feeling was growing that everybody who could, ought to be there.

Monday came, August 26, and the feeling took shape and substance. They were leaving now from New Canaan, Connecticut, and Barre, Vermont; they were leaving now from towns in Oregon and cities in California, from Las Vegas, Nevada, and Seattle, Washington, from Durham and Greensboro, from West Memphis and Selma, from Dallas and St. Paul and Miami and Gary.

Monday night came and twenty-three people, including three whites, assembled at the Dunbar Community Center in Little Rock and got on a bus; farther South the scene was repeated in Mississippi and Louisiana. Already now, cars were on the way from the West Coast and the Gulf Coast. And twelve youths from the Brooklyn chapter of CORE were walking down the East Coast.

Monday night wore away and blacks and whites gathered at the General Baptist Convention, Inc. headquarters in Milwaukee. At 7:13 A.M., three buses pulled out with more than one hundred demonstrators. That same morning, Tuesday, August 27, four busloads left St. Louis and six left Birmingham.

Across the country, in Washington, D.C., the tempo picked up. The leaders arrived and set up command posts; the vanguard of the well-heeled arrived and established beachheads in the lobbies of the swank hotels. By Tuesday night, practically all of the ten leaders were domiciled in the Statler-Hilton, where they worked late, tightening up and refining the plans.

As they worked, trains and planes began to move. Two chartered trains left Chicago. Chartered trains left Pittsburgh and Detroit. Another Freedom Special was pushing up the East Coast from Jacksonville, making stops at Waycross, Georgia, Savannah, and Richmond.

All across the nation now people were moving, going in ones and twos and hundreds to a rendezvous with history. As the sun moved west, a chartered plane took off from Los Angeles's International Airport. A few hours later, another plane, with about thirty stage and screen celebrities, including Marlon Brando and Harry Belafonte, jetted into the air from Lockheed Airport.

It was past midnight now and New York was ablaze with lights. Tens of thousands were assembling at staging areas in bus depots, community houses, and churches. The first of four hundred and fifty chartered buses left the Armory on 143rd Street at 1:30 A.M. Wednesday. Thereafter cars and buses of all descriptions streamed through the Lincoln Tunnel.

The dawn hours in Harlem on August 28 were bright with people and colors and hopes. Thousands of bystanders gathered at CORE's staging area on 125th Street between Seventh and Eighth avenues and cheered the demonstrators on ("You tell 'em; tell 'em for me"). At Pennsylvania Station, where fourteen special trains left between 2 A.M. and 8 A.M., authorities reported the largest early-morning crowd since the end of World War II.

Wheels turned, engines throbbed, and the great mass moved towards Washington in a massive orchestration of sound and movement and emotion. As they came, on buses and trains and in cars, they sang Spirituals, prayed, and talked. In the air over Nevada, a woman from California tried to explain to her white seatmate the meaning of Negroness. "You can never know what it's like to be a Negro. No matter how hard you try, you can't imagine going into a hamburger shop with your children and being told, 'We don't serve niggers here.' " On the ground, in Wisconsin, Fletcher Gee was saying: "I'm going to illustrate my willingness to be what I am. I'm going to illustrate my desire to be what I believe I should be."

At about the same time, Melva Franklin, a New York nurse's aide, was saying, in Pennsylvania Station, that she was "doing this for my grandmother, grandfather, and everyone else. This is the day my grandmother wanted to see." Far away, in a train rushing across Indiana, a woman was saying that she was "doing this for my grandchildren."

And in trains hurtling across Indiana, buses speeding through Delaware, planes high above Ohio, men and women were singing: "Good news, Freedom's coming."

On they came, on wheels of every description, and Washington waited, tight with tension. The day, Wednesday, August 28, 1963, dawned clear and slightly cool, with the streets deserted and a large number of white inhabitants in self-imposed exile in Virginia and Maryland enclaves. The government and private businesses, fearing violence or traffic tie-ups or both, had urged employees to take the day off. Bars and whiskey stores had been closed. Washington, in the early morning, looked like a city under siege. Burly MPs, black and white, directed traffic and scurried about the city in jeeps and command cars.

The crowd gathered slowly. At 7 A.M., there were only one thousand people at the Washington Monument. There was fear in some quarters and hope in others that the expected crowd wouldn't come.

But the crowd continued to increase, slowly at first and then with a rush. At 9:30 A.M., there were forty thousand people around the tall white pencil of the Washington Monument; an hour later, there were fifty thousand and police reported that the Baltimore-Washington expressway was packed solidly with cars and buses moving "bumper to bumper." By 11 A.M., there were at least ninety thousand people on the grassy slopes of the monument and the Ellipse behind the White House. When the parade began, there were close to two hundred thousand demonstrators.

There had never been such a crowd.

There were society women in new hats and old women in Sunday go-to-church black; there were bright young men from the top level of the agencies, looking important and hurried, and lost; there were pretty girls and plain ones, priests, preachers and rabbis, union members, seminarians, housewives, and teachers.

One remembers most the faces and the feet. There were feet of every imaginable description, some of them bare, some of them stylishly shod; the feet of old women who had stood long over white folks' stoves and the feet of old men who had stood long in mines and factories; feet used to the outdoors, flat, square, strong feet that ached easily and were favored gently as the people walked. These feet contrasted strongly with the feet of the young, feet fresh from college campuses and offices, feet modishly shod, free, it seemed, from the bunions and the calluses and the memories of the old. Of whatever description and however shod, the feet moved in protest and affirmation. And, above them, the faces shone with boundless pride and determination. There were the faces of the old, graven with hope and faith; the faces of Northern blacks, glad at last to be on the firing line; and, above all, the faces of the Southern young, terrible with anger, terrible with determination, terrible with pride.

The crowd was gay and sad, happy and angry. White correspondents went away and wrote long articles on "the remarkable sweetness" of the crowd, proving once again that they did not understand blacks or themselves. They had expected a wild mob and what they saw were students, organization men, and old women who could have been anybody's aunt. And so they were astonished, not realizing that things are seldom all one thing or another, that men can smile and cry inside, that they can bleed and sing to staunch the wound.

There was about this crowd the wonderful two-tongued ambivalence of the blues. It was neither all one thing nor all another. Many moods competed, but two dominated: a mood of quiet anger and a mood of buoyant exuberance. There was also a feeling of power and a certain surprise, as though the people had discovered suddenly who they were and what they had.

They had come from different places, in different ways, for different reasons. But once there, they were welded into a whole and living thing. The magic of the crowd began to work on them and they moved, pulled along by the force of an idea.

The people stood for a long time in the assembly area, listening to speeches and songs from stage and screen celebrities. Then, spontaneously, they began to move. Little knots stepped into Constitution Avenue and began to march. The trickle became a flood and, at 11:20 A.M., ten minutes ahead of schedule, the March began, with the followers leading. The marchers moved into two great waves, shoulder to shoulder, black people and white people, Jews and Gentiles, Old Negroes and New Negroes, organization men and radicals, Hebrews from Brooklyn, sharecroppers from Mississippi, Puritans from New England. On they came, a riot of sound and color, signs bobbing above the sea of their heads, Spirituals coming from the well of their throats; on they came, feet pounding on the hot pavement of history; on they came, wave after wave beating against the sandy beach of American indifference.

At the Lincoln Monument, the marchers regrouped on both sides of the reflecting pool and deployed under the giant elms and oaks. They stretched almost a mile to the east and stood in scattered groups in a great semicircle around the steps of the monument, where the speakers and honored guests were seated.

For almost three hours, the multitude listened to speakers, who demanded immediate passage of a civil rights bill and immediate implementation of the basic guarantees of the Declaration of Independence and the Thirteenth, Fourteenth, and Fifteenth amendments.

Out of the blurred montage of words and symbols seven clear pictures emerge: a picture of Asa Philip Randolph, the Father of the March, saying that this was the beginning and not the ending and that "wave after wave" would come back to Washington if immediate changes were not made in American life; of Eugene Carson Blake, head of the Presbyterian Church, indicting American Christians and saying repeatedly, "We come—late, *late* we come"; of Rabbi Joachim Prinz recalling the downfall of Germany and saying that the basic problem, then and now, was not evil but silence; of Mahalia Jackson rolling one hundred years of wrong into one lucid phrase; of John Lewis calling for a real, "a serious revolution"; of Martin Luther King, Jr., etching the blueprints of a dream; of Benjamin E. Mays speaking frankly to God in an eloquent benediction: "Here we are, God, one hundred and eighty million people ... *please*, God, in this moment of crisis, give the United States wisdom ... guide her, keep her, save her and help the weary travelers to overcome.... Here we are, God, *please*...."

Let us consider Mahalia Jackson, Martin King, and John Lewis: they are the keys to that day.

There is a nerve that lies beneath the smoothest of black exteriors, a nerve four hundred years old and throbbing with hurt and indignation. Mahalia Jackson penetrated the facades and exposed the nerve to public view. She was singing "I Been 'Buked and I Been Scorned," embellishing it with great gasps and whoops and hollers, and then, suddenly, it happened.

I'm gonna tell my Lord,
When I get home.
I'm gonna tell my Lord,
When I get home.
Just how *long* you've
Been treating me wrong.

A spasm ran through the crowd.

The button-down men in front and the old women in the back came to their feet, screaming and shouting. They had not known that this thing was in them and that they wanted it touched. From different places, in different ways, with different dreams, they had come and now, hearing this sung, they were one.

John Lewis, twenty-three, the new chairman of the Student Non-violent Coordinating Committee, came on, working in the big leagues for the first time. He had come armed with a prepared speech, which said that politicians, all politicians, were low and despicable people—and that none of them meant blacks any good. ("Where is *our* party?") He had wanted to tell them that blacks were still being whipped for trying to vote, and that old men and women were still in jail. He had wanted to say that if the March was only a gesture that it was obscene: that he and his kind, the children who made the revolution, had nothing but contempt for old men who dealt in gestures. He had wanted to say things about marching through Dixie like Sherman—he had wanted to say, oh, so many things but a white archbishop objected and the leaders persuaded him to tone the speech down.

He came on now, scowling, and he said pretty much what he intended to say—only in nicer language. And when he finished the older Negro leaders rushed to pump his hand, and most of the white liberals sat silent.

A second man, now: Martin Luther King, Jr., coming to the lectern late in the afternoon, when the shadows were long on the grass. He read for a time from a prepared speech; and then he began to improvise, speaking of a dream big enough to include all men and all children, speaking of the day when little black boys and little black girls would join hands with little white boys and little white girls as brothers and sisters.

"I have a dream," he said, over and over, and each elaboration evoked hystical cheers.

I say to you today, my friends, that in spite of the difficulties and frustrations of the moment I still have a dream. It is a dream deeply rooted in the American dream.

I have a dream that one day this nation will rise up and live out the true meaning of its creed: "We hold these truths to be self-evident; that all men are created equal."

I have a dream that one day on the red hills of Georgia the sons of former slaves and the sons of former slaveowners will be able to sit down together at the table of brotherhood.

I have a dream that one day every valley shall be exalted, every hill and mountain shall be made low, the rough places will be made plain, and the crooked places will be made straight, and the glory of the Lord shall be revealed, and all flesh shall see it together.

This is our hope. This is the faith with which I return to the South. With this faith we will be able to hew out of the mountain of despair a stone of hope. . . . With this faith we will be able to work together, to pray together, to struggle together, to go to jail together, to stand up for freedom together, knowing that we will be free one day.

This will be the day when all of God's children will be able to sing with new meaning "My country 'tis of thee, sweet land of liberty, of thee I sing. Land where my fathers died, land of the pilgrim's pride, from every mountainside, let freedom ring."

And if America is to be a great nation this must become true. So let freedom ring from the prodigious hilltops of New Hampshire. Let freedom ring from the mighty mountains of New York. Let freedom ring from the heightening Alleghenies of Pennsylvania!

Let freedom ring from the snowcapped Rockies of Colorado! Let freedom ring from the curvacious peaks of California!

But not only that; let freedom ring from Stone Mountain of Georgia!

Let freedom ring from every hill and mole hill of Mississippi. From every mountainside, let freedom ring.

When we let freedom ring, when we let it ring from every village and every hamlet, from every state and every city, we will be able to speed up that day when all of God's children, black men and white men, Jews and Gentiles, Protestants and Catholics, will be able to join hands and sing in the words of that old Negro spiritual, "Free at last! Free at last! Thank God almighty, we are free at last!

It was not so much the words, eloquent as they were, as the manner of saying them. The rhythms and the intonation and the halts and the breaks: these called back all the old men and women who had this dream and died, dishonored; called back rickety black churches on dirt roads and the men and women who sat in them, called them back and found them not wanting, nor their hoping in vain. The rhythms and the intonation called back all the struggle and all the pain and all the agony, and held forth the possibility of triumph; they called back Emmett Till and Medgar Evers and all the others; called back ropes and chains and bombs and screams in the night; called back one-room walk-up flats and roaches and rats, called them back and said they would soon be over.

When King finished, grown men and women wept unashamedly.

The speechmaking over, the songs sung, the prayers said, the people got back on the buses and trains and planes and went in the night to the places from whence they had come, marveling at the strange thing that had moved inside them. No one could say, really, how many votes they had changed in Congress. Almost everyone agreed, however, that the March impressed millions of whites in America and Europe.

More important, however, was the impact of the March on the participants. If the March changed no votes in Congress or no hearts in America, it did, at least, change the marchers themselves. Those who thought, in the beginning, that it was too respectable, and those who thought it was too radical; the young people who didn't want to wait another minute, and the old ones who had waited for eighty-one and eighty-two and ninety-four years; the smooth operators from New York and Chicago and the fieldhands from Mississippi; the church women from Atlanta and the gay crowd from Harlem: for a moment in time they were one.

They would disagree later; there would be disappointments, bombings, outrages; there would be backsliders and it would be necessary perhaps to do it all over again; but for one moment, for one unforgettable moment, the militants and the moderates, the timid liberals and the fire-eating activists, the old church women and the barmaids: for one electrifying moment they were one.

Oh, the river of Jordan is deep and wide,
    One more river to cross.
I don't know how to get on the other side,
    One more river to cross.
Oh, you got Jesus, hold him fast,
    One more river to cross.
Oh, better love was never told,
    One more river to cross.
'Tis stronger than an iron band,
    One more river to cross.
'Tis sweeter than the honey comb,
    One more river to cross.
Oh, the good old chariot passin' by,
    One more river to cross. . . .

              —Spiritual

Selected Bibliography

Aptheker, Herbert. *American Negro Slave Revolts*. New York, 1943.

———. *Nat Turner's Slave Rebellion*. New York, 1966.

——— (ed.). *A Documentary History of the Negro People in the United States*, 4 vols. New York, 1951–1974.

——— (ed.). *The Correspondence of W. E. B. DuBois*, Vol. I. Amherst, 1973.

Barber, J. Max. "What is the Niagara Movement," *Voice of the Negro*, September, 1905.

———. "The Niagara Movement at Harpers Ferry," *ibid.*, September, 1906.

Bardolph, Richard. *The Negro Vanguard*. New York, 1959.

Bennett, Lerone, Jr. *Before the Mayflower: A History of the Negro in America, 1619–1964*. Chicago, 1964.

———. *The Negro Mood*. Chicago, 1964.

———. *What Manner of Man: A Biography of Martin Luther King, Jr*. Chicago, 1964.

———. *Confrontation: Black and White*. Chicago, 1965.

———. *Black Power USA: The Human Side of Reconstruction, 1867–1877*. Chicago, 1967.

———. *Pioneers in Protest*. Chicago, 1968.

———. *The Challenge of Blackness.* Chicago, 1968.

———. *The Shaping of Black America.* Chicago, 1975.

———. "The Ghost of Marcus Garvey," *Ebony*, March, 1960.

———. "The Revolt of Negro Youth," *ibid.*, May, 1960.

———. "What Sit-Downs Mean to America," *ibid.*, June, 1960.

Berman, Daniel M. *It Is So Ordered.* New York, 1966.

Bishop, Jim. *The Days of Martin Luther King, Jr.* New York, 1971.

Bontemps, Arna, and Conroy, Jack. *They Seek a City.* New York, 1945.

Brackett, Jeffrey R. *The Negro in Maryland.* Freeport, 1969.

Bradford, Sarah H. *Harriet, the Moses of Her People.* Auburn, 1897.

Brawley, Benjamin. *A Social History of the American Negro.* New York, 1921.

Brazeal, Brailsford R. *The Brotherhood of Sleeping Car Porters.* New York, 1946.

Broderick, Francis L. *W. E. B. DuBois, Negro Leader in a Time of Crisis.* Stanford, 1959.

Brodie, Fawn M. *Thaddeus Stevens, Scourge of the South.* New York, 1959.

Brown, William Wells. *The Negro in the American Rebellion.* Boston, 1867.

Bunche, Ralph J. "A Brief and Tentative Analysis of Negro Leadership." Unpublished manuscript prepared for Carnegie-Myrdal Study, 1940.

———. "The Programs, Ideologies, Tactics, and Achievements of Negro Betterment and Interracial Organizations." *Ibid.*

Butler, Benjamin F. *Butler's Book.* Boston, 1892.

Clarke, John Henrik (ed.). *William Styron's Nat Turner: Ten Black Writers Respond.* Boston, 1968.

——— (ed.). *Marcus Garvey and the Vision of Africa.* New York, 1974.

Cornish, Dudley Taylor. *Negro Troops in the Union Army, 1861–65.* New York, 1956.

Cromwell, John W. *The Negro in American History.* Washington, 1914.

———. "The Aftermath of Nat Turner's Insurrection," *Journal of Negro History*, April, 1920.

Cronon, Edmund D. *Black Moses: The Story of Marcus Garvey.* Madison, 1955.

Daniels, John. *In Freedom's Birthplace.* Boston, 1914.

Delaney, Martin R. *The Condition, Elevation, Emigration, and Destiny of the Colored People of the United States.* New York, 1852.

Douglass, Frederick. *Narrative of the Life of Frederick Douglass.* Boston, 1845.

———. *My Bondage and My Freedom.* New York, 1855.

———. *The Life and Times of Frederick Douglass.* Hartford, 1881.

Douglass, William. *Annals of the First African Church.* Philadelphia, 1862.

Drewry, William S. *Slave Insurrections in Virginia (1830–1865).* Ph.D. dissertation, Johns Hopkins University. Washington, 1900.

DuBois, W. E. B. *The Philadelphia Negro.* Philadelphia, 1899.

———. *The Souls of Black Folk.* Chicago, 1903.

———. *Black Reconstruction.* New York, 1935.

———. *Dusk of Dawn.* New York, 1940.

———. *The Autobiography of W. E. B. DuBois.* New York, 1968.

——— (ed.). *The Negro Church*. Atlanta, 1903.

———. "The Niagara Movement," *Voice of the Negro*, September, 1905.

———. "The Growth of the Niagara Movement," *ibid.*, January, 1906.

Dufty, William. "A. Philip Randolph," *New York Post*, December 28, 1959–January 3, 1960.

Dyer, Frederick H. *A Compendium of the War of Rebellion*. Des Moines, 1908.

Ethridge, Mark III. "The Greensboro Four," *The South Today*, April, 1973.

Farr, Finis. *Black Champion: The Life and Times of Jack Johnson*. New York, 1964.

Fax, Elton C. *Garvey: The Story of a Pioneer Black Nationalist*. New York, 1972.

Ferris, William H. *The African Abroad*. New Haven, 1913.

Fleischer, Nathaniel S. *Black Dynamite: The Story of the Negro in the Prize Ring from 1782 to 1938*. New York, 1938.

Fleetwood, Christian A. *The Negro as a Soldier*. Washington, 1895.

Fox, Stephen R. *The Guardian of Boston: William Monroe Trotter*. New York, 1970.

Franklin, John Hope. *From Slavery to Freedom*. New York, 1947.

Gara, Larry. *The Liberty Line: The Legend of the Underground Railroad*. Lexington, 1961.

Garfinkel, Herbert. *When Negroes March*. Glencoe, 1959.

Garvey, Amy Jacques. *Philosophy and Opinions of Marcus Garvey*. New York, 1923.

———. *Garvey and Garveyism*. Kingston, 1963.

Gilmore, Al-Tony. *Bad Nigger! The National Impact of Jack Johnson*. Port Washington, 1975.

Gray, Thomas R. (ed.). *The Confessions of Nat Turner*. Baltimore, 1831.

Greene, Lorenzo J. *The Negro in Colonial New England*. New York, 1942.

Harlan, Louis R. *Booker T. Washington: The Making of a Black Leader, 1865–1901*. New York, 1972.

Hawkins, Hugh. *Booker T. Washington and his Critics*. Lexington, 1962.

Higginson, Thomas Wentworth. *Travellers and Outlaws*. Boston, 1889.

Holland, Frederick M. *Frederick Douglass*. New York, 1895.

Howison, Robert R. *A History of Virginia*. Philadelphia, 1846.

Humphreys, A. A. *The Virginia Campaign of 1864 and 1865*. New York, 1883.

Johnson, Allen, and Malone, Dumas (eds.). *Dictionary of American Biography*, 22 vols. New York, 1928–1936.

Johnson, Jack. *Jack Johnson is a Dandy*. New York, 1969.

Johnson, James Weldon. *Black Manhattan*. New York, 1930.

———. *Along This Way*. New York, 1933.

Johnson, Robert U., and Buel, Clarence C. (eds.). *Battles and Leaders of the Civil War*, 4 vols. New York, 1887–1888.

Kellogg, Charles Flint. *NAACP: A History of the National Association for the Advancement of Colored People, Vol. 1, 1909–1920*. Baltimore, 1967.

Kesselman, Louis C. *The Social Politics of FEPC*. Chapel Hill, 1948.

King, Martin Luther, Jr. *Stride Toward Freedom*. New York, 1958.

Kluger, Richard. *Simple Justice*. New York, 1975.

Lardner, John. *White Hopes and Other Tigers*. New York, 1951.

Lash, Joseph P. *Eleanor-Franklin*. New York, 1971.

Lee, Irvin H. *Negro Medal of Honor Men*. New York, 1967.

Lewis, Anthony, and the *New York Times*. *Portrait of a Decade: The Second American Revolution*. New York, 1964.

Logan, Rayford (ed.). *What the Negro Wants*. Chapel Hill, 1944.

———. *Howard University: The First Hundred Years, 1867–1877*. New York, 1968.

Loggins, Vernon. *The Negro Author*. New York, 1931.

Mays, Benjamin E. *Born to Rebel*. New York, 1971.

McKay, Claude. *Harlem: Negro Metropolis*. New York, 1940.

McPherson, James M. *The Negro's Civil War*. New York, 1965.

———. *The Struggle for Equality: Abolitionists and the Negro in the Civil War and Reconstruction*. Princeton, 1964.

Miller, Kelly. *Race Adjustment*. New York, 1908.

Miller, Loren. *The Petitioners: The Story of the Supreme Court of the United States and the Negro*. Cleveland, 1966.

Morrison, Allan. "A. Philip Randolph: Dean of Negro Leaders," *Ebony*, November, 1958.

Nell, William C. *The Colored Patriots of the American Revolution*. Boston, 1855.

Osofsky, Gilbert. *Harlem: The Making of a Ghetto, 1890–1930*. New York, 1966.

Ottley, Roi. *New World A-Coming*. Boston, 1943.

Payne, Daniel Alexander. *Recollections of Seventy Years*. Edited by Rev. C. S. Smith. Nashville, 1888.

———. *History of the African Methodist Episcopal Church*, 2 vols. Edited by Rev. C. S. Smith. Nashville, 1891.

Porter, Dorothy (ed.). *Early Negro Writing, 1760–1837*. Boston, 1971.

Puttkammer, Charles W., and Worthy, Ruth. "William Monroe Trotter, 1872–1934," *Journal of Negro History*, October, 1958.

Quarles, Benjamin. *Frederick Douglass*. Washington, 1948.

———. *Black Abolitionists*. New York, 1969.

Reddick, L. D. *Crusader Without Violence*. New York, 1959.

Ruchames, Louis. *Race, Jobs and Politics: The Story of FEPC*. New York, 1953.

Rudwick, Elliott M. *W. E. B. DuBois: Propagandist of the Negro Protest*. New York, 1969.

———. "The Niagara Movement," *Journal of Negro History*, July, 1957.

———. "DuBois versus Garvey: Race Propagandists at War," *Journal of Negro Education*, Fall, 1959.

———. "Race Leadership Struggle: Background of the Boston Riot of 1903," *Journal of Negro Education*, Winter, 1962.

Schor, Joel. *Henry Highland Garnet*. Westport, 1977.

Schulke, Flip (ed.). *Martin Luther King, Jr.: A Documentary, Montgomery to Memphis*. New York, 1976.

Siebert, Wilbur H. *The Underground Railway from Slavery to Freedom*. New York, 1898.

Simmons, William J. *Men of Mark*. Cleveland, 1887.

Slater, Jack. "1954 Revisited," *Ebony*, May, 1974.

Smith, S. D. *The Negro in Congress*. Chapel Hill, 1940.

South Carolina Constitutional Convention. *Proceedings of the Constitutional Convention of South Carolina held at Charleston, South Carolina, beginning January 14th and ending March 17th, 1868*. Charleston, 1868.

Spear, Allan H. *Black Chicago*. Chicago, 1967.

Steiner, Bernard C. *History of Slavery in Connecticut*. Baltimore, 1893.

Sterling, Dorothy. *Freedom Train: The Story of Harriet Tubman*. Garden City, 1954.

Steward, Austin. *Twenty-Two Years a Slave and Forty Years a Freeman*. Rochester, 1857.

Still, William. *The Underground Railroad*. Philadelphia, 1872.

Taylor, A. A. *The Negro in South Carolina During Reconstruction*. Washington, 1924.

Torrence, Ridgely. *The Story of John Hope*. New York, 1948.

Tragle, Henry Irving. *The Southampton Slave Revolt: A Compilation of Source Material*. Amherst, 1971.

Turner, Edward R. *The Negro in Pennsylvania*. Washington, 1911.

Ulmer, S. Sidney. "Earl Warren and the Brown Decision," *Journal of Politics*, August, 1971.

U.S. Bureau of the Census. *Negro Population in the United States, 1790–1915*. Washington, 1918.

U.S. Congress. *Congressional Globe*. Washington, 1865.

Vincent, Theodore G. *Black Power and the Garvey Movement*. New York, 1971.

Voice of the Negro. "The Significance of the Niagara Movement," September, 1905.

————. "What Is the Niagara Movement?" September, 1905.

War of the Rebellion, The: A Compilation of Official Records of the Union and Confederate Armies, 130 vols. Washington, 1880–1901.

Warner, Robert A. *New Haven Negroes*. New Haven, 1940.

Warren, Earl. *Memoirs of Earl Warren, Chief Justice*. New York, 1977.

Watson, J. B. "Recalling 1906," *Crisis*, April, 1934.

Weaver, John D. *Warren: The Man, the Court, the Era*. Boston, 1967.

Wesley, Charles. *Richard Allen, Apostle of Freedom*. Washington, 1935.

Williams, George W. *History of the Negro Race in America, 1619–1880*, 2 vols. New York, 1883.

————. *A History of the Negro Troops in the War of the Rebellion, 1861–1865*. New York, 1888.

Williamson, Joel. *After Slavery: The Negro in South Carolina During Reconstruction, 1861–1877*. Chapel Hill, 1965.

Woodson, Carter G. *The Negro in our History*. Washington, 1947.

———— (ed.). *The Mind of the Negro as Reflected in Letters Written During The Crisis, 1800–1860*. Washington, 1926.

Work, Monroe N. (ed.). *Negro Year Book, 1918–1919*. Tuskegee, 1919.

Wright, James M. *Free Negro in Maryland*. New York, 1921.

Writers Program, WPA. *The Negro in Virginia*. New York, 1940.

Alabama Journal, 1955, 1956.
Baltimore *Afro-American*, 1920, 1941, 1953, 1954, 1960.
Charlotte *Observer*, 1960.
Chicago Broadax, 1910.
Chicago Daily News, 1910.
Chicago Defender, 1908, 1910, 1941, 1954.
Chicago Tribune, 1908, 1910, 1941, 1954.
Colored American Magazine, 1901, 1902.
Crisis, 1920, 1927, 1934.
Ebony Magazine, 1954, 1960, 1974.
Freedom's Journal, 1927.
Greensboro *Record*, 1960.
Indianapolis *Freeman*, 1908, 1910.
Jet Magazine, 1954, 1955, 1960, 1963.
Montgomery Advertiser, 1955, 1956.
New York Age, 1905, 1920.
New York Amsterdam News, 1905, 1906, 1941, 1954.
New York Post, 1956, 1957, 1960.
New York Times, 1865, 1868, 1901, 1920, 1954, 1963.
New York Tribune, 1865, 1963.
New York World, 1920.
Newsweek, 1954, 1963.
Pittsburgh Courier, 1941, 1954.
Time, 1954, 1960, 1963.
Voice of the Negro, 1905, 1906, 1907.
Washington Bee, 1905, 1906, 1910.
Washington Post, 1954, 1963.

Index